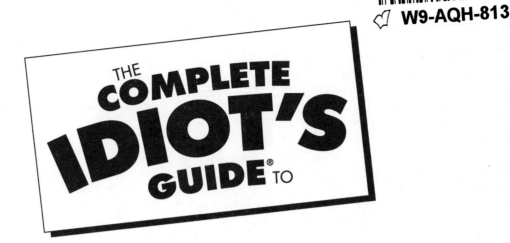

THE COMPLETE IDIOT'S GUIDE® TO

Organizing Your Life

Fifth Edition

by Georgene Lockwood

A member of Penguin Group (USA) Inc.

ALPHA BOOKS

Published by the Penguin Group

Penguin Group (USA) Inc., 375 Hudson Street, New York, New York 10014, USA

Penguin Group (Canada), 90 Eglinton Avenue East, Suite 700, Toronto, Ontario M4P 2Y3, Canada (a division of Pearson Penguin Canada Inc.)

Penguin Books Ltd., 80 Strand, London WC2R 0RL, England

Penguin Ireland, 25 St. Stephen's Green, Dublin 2, Ireland (a division of Penguin Books Ltd.)

Penguin Group (Australia), 250 Camberwell Road, Camberwell, Victoria 3124, Australia (a division of Pearson Australia Group Pty. Ltd.)

Penguin Books India Pvt. Ltd., 11 Community Centre, Panchsheel Park, New Delhi—110 017, India

Penguin Group (NZ), 67 Apollo Drive, Rosedale, North Shore, Auckland 1311, New Zealand (a division of Pearson New Zealand Ltd.)

Penguin Books (South Africa) (Pty.) Ltd., 24 Sturdee Avenue, Rosebank, Johannesburg 2196, South Africa

Penguin Books Ltd., Registered Offices: 80 Strand, London WC2R 0RL, England

International Standard Book Number: 978-1-59257-966-2
Library of Congress Catalog Card Number: 2009930700

12   11   10   8   7   6   5   4   3

Interpretation of the printing code: The rightmost number of the first series of numbers is the year of the book's printing; the rightmost number of the second series of numbers is the number of the book's printing. For example, a printing code of 10-1 shows that the first printing occurred in 2010.

Printed in the United States of America

Note: This publication contains the opinions and ideas of its author. It is intended to provide helpful and informative material on the subject matter covered. It is sold with the understanding that the author and publisher are not engaged in rendering professional services in the book. If the reader requires personal assistance or advice, a competent professional should be consulted.

The author and publisher specifically disclaim any responsibility for any liability, loss, or risk, personal or otherwise, which is incurred as a consequence, directly or indirectly, of the use and application of any of the contents of this book.

Most Alpha books are available at special quantity discounts for bulk purchases for sales promotions, premiums, fund-raising, or educational use. Special books, or book excerpts, can also be created to fit specific needs.

For details, write: Special Markets, Alpha Books, 375 Hudson Street, New York, NY 10014.

Publisher: *Marie Butler-Knight*
Editorial Director: *Mike Sanders*
Senior Managing Editor: *Billy Fields*
Executive Editor: *Randy Ladenheim-Gil*
Senior Development Editor: *Christy Wagner*
Senior Production Editor: *Megan Douglass*
Copy Editor: *Amy Borelli*

Cartoonist: *Steve Barr*
Cover Designer: *Rebecca Batchelor*
Book Designer: *Trina Wurst*
Indexer: *Heather McNeill*
Layout: *Brian Massey*
Proofreader: *Laura Caddell*

Contents at a Glance

Contents

Introduction

To have a vision for your life and take steps every day toward that vision is where true happiness lies. Ordering your life to support you in your vision is one of the most profound steps you can take. No matter how many times you've attempted to "get organized once and for all" and have perhaps fallen short of your desires, with some basic determination and this book by your side, you can start where you are and make it happen this time.

To paraphrase George Bernard Shaw, "Hell is to drift. Heaven is to steer." But why do we so often feel out of control? Perhaps it's because we know what we need to do, but we don't know *how* to do it. Consider this book a basic course in life navigation. You're about to become the captain of your own ship and learn how to plot your course through the day-to-day seas of life.

This is not a dictatorial, "do-it-my-way" kind of book. It's more like a Chinese food menu. You know, "Choose one from Column A, one from Column B." I've taken good ideas from wherever I could find them—self-improvement technologies, meditation, visualization, psychology, behavioral studies—whatever I've found that works, either for me personally or for people I know. You pick and choose what makes the most sense for you. Just know that the methods I've shared with you are basic, tried-and-true ones, but feel free to adapt them to suit your own style and personality.

Getting organized isn't something to do "someday"—it's essential to getting ahead and leading a joyful, productive life. The degree to which you need to change what you're doing now to enhance your daily existence and realize your dreams is something you have to find out for yourself. Let this book be your guide. I've structured it so you can first set your goals, tackle any immediate roadblocks, decide which areas are really urgent, and then turn to the section that most applies.

It's not all work and no play, either. There's lots of fun stuff throughout, and the chapters at the end of the book help you continue sailing your organized ship through smooth and choppy waters.

How This Book Is Organized

To make it easy for you to design your own organization plan, I've divided the book into seven parts:

Part 1, "What Do You Mean, 'Organized'?" looks at some past experiences or unrealistic ideals that might be getting in your way, and shows you how to figure out what's really important to make an immediate improvement and feel more in control.

You also explore some ways to get motivated, stick to your commitment to organize your life, and avoid some of the "booby traps" we all have a tendency to set for ourselves. You learn the Basic Laws of Stuff and the Basic Laws of Time, and how stuff and time work together to make your life either smooth or chaotic. And if "stuff" truly rules your life, I offer resources to get the help you need.

Part 2, "Stuff Simplified," gives you a simple system you can apply to any room, any task, and any kind of "stuff." You also learn the clear steps for handling all the mounds of paper that seem to come through the door and threaten to bury you.

Part 3, "Systems for Getting Stuff Done," moves into the action areas of your life and concentrates on the tasks that will speed you toward accomplishing the goals you set for yourself. You learn how to set up a central management area, and you get some step-by-step advice for devising personal systems for your major areas of activity.

Part 4, "Room by Room," examines each room in your house, one by one, and helps you "unstuff" each space and take it back for yourself and your family. You get to pay special attention to how you begin and end each day, with routines to help smooth out life's bumpy rides.

Part 5, "Money and All That Stuff," guides you through some simple strategies for budgeting and managing your money, examines systems for handling bills and taxes, and asks some basic questions about planning for the future. You'll find concrete ideas for keeping your finances healthy through good times and bad.

Part 6, "Getting People Involved," tackles the ways other people can unwittingly sabotage your organizational efforts and helps you get people on your side by encouraging understanding, exploring ways to communicate, and discussing when and how to hire other people to do the work for you.

Part 7, "Now That You're Organized, Keep It That Way!" helps you stay on track with a minimum of effort after you have your plan in place. You'll see how to adapt what you've learned to your particular lifestyle and how *not* to let the holidays or other special circumstances throw you off track.

At the end of the book, I've included some resources to take you still further in refining your organizational skills.

Extras

To give you additional food for thought—some shortcuts, tips, and resources to expand your knowledge of certain areas—I've scattered additional-info boxes throughout the chapters:

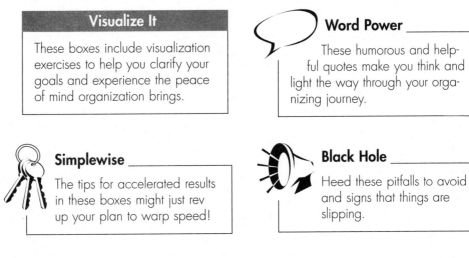

Visualize It

These boxes include visualization exercises to help you clarify your goals and experience the peace of mind organization brings.

Word Power

These humorous and helpful quotes make you think and light the way through your organizing journey.

Simplewise

The tips for accelerated results in these boxes might just rev up your plan to warp speed!

Black Hole

Heed these pitfalls to avoid and signs that things are slipping.

Trademarks

All terms mentioned in this book that are known to be or are suspected of being trademarks or service marks have been appropriately capitalized. Alpha Books and Penguin Group (USA) Inc. cannot attest to the accuracy of this information. Use of a term in this book should not be regarded as affecting the validity of any trademark or service mark.

Part 1

What Do You Mean, "Organized"?

Some people just seem to be born organized. But I believe most organized people are made, not born. As with other important areas in life, many of us never had anyone to teach us the skills needed to be organized, but with understanding and practice, these skills can be learned.

In Part 1, you learn about the beliefs and habits that could be holding you back in your efforts to take control of your time, your relationships, your career, and all the other things that make living worthwhile. You find out how to avoid the biggest trap that seeks to ensnare us all and the basic rules governing the material things we have and the things we want to do. If your relationship with stuff is truly out of control, there's plenty of help for you to turn to, and you also learn how to make your organization efforts compatible with what's really important to you.

Where Do I Begin?

In This Chapter

- How you got organization challenged in the first place
- How disorganized are you, really?
- The benefits of getting it all together
- How to set meaningful goals
- Effective resolutions—New Year's and otherwise

Before you dive in and start writing lists, tearing apart closets, and buying new storage containers, let's begin at the beginning. How did you get into this mess in the first place? Did it just happen, or can you find identifiable reasons why your life is so chaotic? Rearranging things on the surface isn't going to create the kind of deeper life changes I suspect you're striving for. You want this to be a whole new direction, not just another quick fix that doesn't last, don't you?

Growing Up Is Hard to Do

For some of us, me included, the roots of our disorderliness go way back. Our parents may not have understood why, but somehow we didn't think the way they did. My mother was either born organized or was trained to be organized. It was just how she was, and she believed it was the right way to be.

I identified more with Dad, who was industrious and curious and liked having lots of projects going at once. He was, in a word, *messy*. Needless to say, there was some tension in our house. To then have a creative-but-messy daughter, too, must have driven my mother nuts.

When a child doesn't fit the mold and get with the program that an adult finds second nature, this behavior can be seen as rebelliousness or laziness or, even worse, an inherent defect. But the "organization gene" isn't necessarily inherited. For some it's an acquired trait. Join the club!

The opposite scenario might just as well be true. Some of us were raised in chaos by one or both parents who didn't get the gene either. Chaos is all we've known. So how can we do something when we never learned how?

Our experiences from childhood that may contribute to our current state of affairs need to be addressed, but whatever the reasons we got to where we are now, they are only that—reasons. The good news is that organizing skills can be learned, and that's what this book is here to help you do! You can start right now to shed the constraints of old habits, old thinking, and old emotions and embrace the true freedom of creating a life of order and peace.

Throughout this book, I give you a series of visualizations in the Visualize It boxes. By replaying old "movies," we can see ourselves as we are and then redirect our visions to create what we want them to be. When you do these visualizations, pretend you're writing and directing a movie. Add as much detail as you possibly can. Notice any emotions that surface as your movie plays on the screen. Write down anything that comes to mind during your screening, or dictate your thoughts into a recorder. Write an essay or story, or draw what you see—whatever most helps you get in touch with your visualization experience. What you see and believe in your mind, you create in the material world. If you want to change what you're creating, one of the first steps is to "see" differently.

Visualize It

Close your eyes and imagine your childhood room. What does it look like? Do you share it with a sibling? How much privacy do you have? Are things scattered about, or is everything in its place? Who's responsible for taking care of it? How does being there make you feel? What do you remember your parents saying about it? Take your time and add lots of details. Pay attention to any fatalistic words like *always* and *never* that pop up, as these words can set the stage for your adult attitudes. Also be aware of verbal criticisms and supportive language. Write down any strong images or words that come up during this exercise. We'll refer to them later.

You Can't Have (or Do) Everything

Even as an adult, you may still be trying to gain your parents' approval. This can be especially difficult for women because housekeeping and making sure the family is well fed, clothed, and successful has traditionally been the woman's job. It's easy to get caught up in trying to be "as good as Mother" (or even better than Mom!), even though Mother might never have worked outside the home or had as many responsibilities or interests as you do today.

Recent studies show that although more women are in the workforce, and some even make more money than their male partners, most working women still do the lion's share of the housework and child care. Another study shows a trend that rather than duke it out over chores, *neither* partner is doing the work! I guess you can call that a truce of sorts, but in tough economic times, eating out and hiring a cleaning service may not be in the budget anymore.

Again, the important thing is simply to notice your feelings and experiences. Ask yourself some questions:

Of the chores that need to be done every day, every week, or every month (don't forget to include tasks such as bill paying, driving kids, making appointments, washing the car, and doing household repairs), how is the work distributed? You may want to make a list on one side of a piece of paper, divide the rest of the paper into columns, and check off which tasks you do and which ones your partner and your children do. Be honest and fair.

How many hours does each adult spend working outside the home or inside the home if there's a home-based business?

Do you feel household chores are evenly distributed? Are those feelings based on the facts? If you asked the other adults in the household how much of the workload they share, what would they say? How does that fit with your picture of how the work is distributed?

Ask other family members to make up a sheet of their own. How similar does it look to yours? Do this without judgment. You are doing some sleuthing to uncover the facts, and that includes others' perceptions and attitudes.

Note the answers and the emotions they bring up. Acknowledge them, learn from them, and move on. You'll have an opportunity to deal with this more in Chapters 8, 16, and 17.

Superwoman and Superman Are Myths

Not only does your upbringing affect your attitudes about being organized, but so do the media and the entertainment industry. TV personalities and the pages of many home and lifestyles magazines present as "normal" images that are impossible ways of living for most of us. Don't get me wrong; I subscribe to a few of those magazines. I even watch the TV shows on occasion. But do I really believe the lady on the screen edits her own magazine, does a weekly TV show, keeps several houses, irons her antique linens, shovels manure in her perfectly manicured garden, and single-handedly cooks up impromptu dinners for 50 from scratch? Nah.

Then there are those guys on PBS or The Learning Channel. They know how to fix *everything*. Their Craftsman tools are all in place, and their workshops look like no one ever works there. Of course, that's because after the show is over, someone else comes in, puts everything away, and cleans up for them!

And what about those magazines that suggest being a real man means you have to work out, always look great and wear the right jeans, rebuild motors on the weekend, play touch football with the guys, and to top it all off, cook gourmet meals? No sweat, right?

Beware of the unattainable ideals created by movies, TV shows, and advertising. Remember, these people are paid actors. A hairdresser follows them around, their hands never touch a dish or change motor oil, and their homes only exist as movie sets or showrooms. And the neat part is, they never really seem to work!

Advertising is about illusions, with sales the ultimate goal. In Advertising 101, students learn how to create a need for a new product. If you're *creating* one, that means there isn't one to start with, right? The advertising industry shows you squeaky-clean homes that you feel you must have to be good parents, model homemakers, and acceptable people. In addition to living in a perfect home or apartment, you should have white teeth, perfectly clean hair, sparkling clothes, and dry underarms.

Don't let yourself get caught in these marketing traps. See them for what they are: fantasies. Aim instead for a comfortable, orderly, clean, aesthetically pleasing place to live that works well to support your life goals and helps you get the important things—the ones you really care about—done.

> ### Word Power
>
> We are what we think. All that we are arises with our thoughts. With our thoughts, we make our world.
>
> —Buddha

How Would You Change Your Life?

You picked up this book for a reason. You were looking for answers. Getting organized may be a lifelong struggle, or you may simply find yourself in a temporary slump due to a life-changing event, an illness, or even a bout of clinical depression. Maybe your existence is so out of control you're truly desperate for a way out of the chaos because the consequences if you don't are immediate and dire.

Whatever the degree or the cause, something is going on and only you can know where you are in the organization continuum. You are looking for simple, common-sense ways to make your life run more smoothly, and you're ready to begin to make that happen. You're ready for more than a temporary cosmetic solution. You're willing to change old, deeply ingrained behaviors and adopt new, more productive habits.

> ### Visualize It
>
> Take a minute to visualize your ideal environment. Close your eyes and walk through your house one room at a time in your mind. Imagine each space clean and orderly. Imagine yourself greeting the morning with all your clothes ready to wear. See yourself eating a relaxed, nutritious breakfast at an inviting table. Next, visualize yourself at your job and see your office as a space that's a pleasure to work in. Daydream about what you would like to do with your leisure time. Experience the pride, confidence, serenity, enjoyment, and overall sense of well-being that living in this fantasy place gives you. Now say out loud, "I want this for my life!"

So what do you really want to change? Actually, the better question to ask is, what do you *want* in your life? I'm not talking about what your parents wanted for you, or what your spouse wants, or what you think you should want, or what the media tells you to want. What do you *really* want?

Make a list of the top five things that immediately pop up when you honestly ask yourself what you really want, arrange them in order of priority with what you want most at the top, and post them in a prominent place.

Here's what my own Five Things list looks like today:

1. Create regular time for spirit and personal growth.

2. Spend quality time with the people I love.

3. Make time and space to be creative every day.

4. Pay more attention to my health.

5. Start downsizing.

Some years ago my list would have looked a lot different. At the top was "Get out of debt and gain control of my finances." Yours might be as basic as "Have one quiet uncluttered place in the house where I can go to relax."

Review your Five Things at least once a day, starting now. As you begin to create your plan for getting organized, keep in mind what's truly important to you and be sure the systems you set up support your true desires. If you become aware of something you want more than the five initial wants you listed, by all means revise the list, but be sure it meets the *strong desire* quotient.

Setting Your Personal Organization Goals

Okay, you've been honest with yourself about what your life is like. You've thought about what really matters to you and how you'd like things to be. Now let's decide on some concrete areas to work on. Let's begin to create your own personal organization plan, broken down into more detail and using your Five Things as a guide; put them in the order of importance that most makes sense to you. When you know what matters most in your life, you can use this book to help you accomplish your goals. You don't need to read it from cover to cover at first. But even if you do, be sure to come back to this first chapter and narrow down those areas you know you need to get a grip on. Concentrating on these right away will have a significant impact on your life.

Black Hole

Using your spouse or your significant other as your buddy in setting your goals could have some pitfalls. Your partner may be one of the challenges you'll be dealing with later (see Part 6). But if he or she is the supportive, nurturing, team-player type, by all means, enlist your partner's help!

So how are you going to stay on track through this process? Consider drafting a written contract with yourself. Your Self Contract needs to be specific and have a time associated with it. It could say something like this:

I agree to spend a total of one hour a day [or start with 15 minutes if that's all you think you can do] for 1 week creating and following through on my plan to organize my life. At the end of a week, I will treat myself to a _____ [movie, pedicure, hour sitting in my hammock reading a book—you choose!].

Sign and date your contract. Renew it in a week, and extend the time period accordingly.

Share your contract with a buddy. Having a partner in crime can drive your likelihood of success up another big notch. Be sure you pick someone who'll be "in your face" about what you say you want. Do the same for your partner. Putting a due date on your contract makes your results measurable and real. Tell your buddy to get on your case when the date is drawing near. Meet regularly with your buddy in person or by phone to review your progress and celebrate when you meet a deadline. Have the same commitment to the other person's goals that you have for your own.

Wish-Full Thinking

You've identified your Five Things, the top five things you want most in your life right now. Now get out that pad and pencil again. We're going to do some broad-based goal-setting. Make a separate sheet for these seven major areas of your life:

- People (you get help with this in Chapter 8)
- Work (Chapter 9)
- Food (Chapter 11)
- Clothing (Chapter 12)
- Home (Chapters 10 through 13)
- Money (Chapters 14 and 15)
- Fun (throughout the whole book!)

On each sheet, make a random list under the main topic of how you'd like that area to be—your goals in that area. Don't hold yourself back or censor yourself. No matter how irrelevant or unachievable your wishes and desires may seem, write them down. Include your "if onlys"—the things you'd like to have or do if you had more time, money, or skill. By including everything, you'll get even clearer about what you really want.

For example, under Food, your goals might be to eat more healthful foods and perhaps lose some weight. How can being organized help you meet these goals? By having the proper foods on hand, by actually planning your meals to stay within certain nutritional guidelines, and by having the right equipment for preparing those foods handy, your chances soar. If your goal is to become a gourmet cook and start your own catering business, however, your kitchen and your meal planning would look completely different.

On the sheet for Money, your goal might be to get out of debt, or you may want to start planning for retirement—or both. Write down everything that comes to mind. If you're debt-free and already have a retirement plan in place, your financial goals might involve having more fun with your money, funding a future project you've always wanted to do, or helping others.

For Home, your goal may be as simple as being able to have company over for the first time in months (or is it years?) without being ashamed of the mess. Your organization plan will reflect your goals for each area.

The point is, if organizing your life is going to be lasting and meaningful, you don't just get organized—you *organize with a purpose*. It's up to you to discover what that purpose is.

Narrowing Your List

Continue writing your wish list for each category until you've completed all seven. Now on each sheet, circle the one wish that, if it were fulfilled, would have the most significant impact on your life right now. Put a number 1 next to it. To add a little perspective, think about what would make the most difference in your life if you only had a year to live. I'm not getting morbid here; I'm just trying to inject a little urgency into this exercise. Funny how such a thought cuts through the chaff and gets to the kernel of wheat in a hurry!

As you read this book, use these sheets as a reminder when you begin to list specific tasks taken from each chapter that will help you achieve your goals. You can save the back of each sheet for that if you like. These are the actions you can take to help you reach the goals you just decided are most important to you. In this way, wishes are transformed into goals, and goals into tasks; ultimately, all this is magically turned into results.

Going back to one of our earlier examples, let's suppose under Food, you listed as your primary goal "to lose 20 pounds and eat more healthful foods." When you turn to Chapter 11, you're going to be looking for the tips and projects that will help you organize your kitchen and adapt them to cooking healthier meals that will work with your new eating plan.

If you put "perform better in my job" or "set up my office so I can find things" on the worksheet, you'll want to pay special attention to Chapter 6 on handling paper and Chapter 9 on work systems. I know you'll find at least three simple things you can do immediately to get headed in the right direction.

Setting Priorities

Now number your sheets in order of priority, with number 1 being the most significant for you right now. If you believe the most important immediate area to work on is relationships, the People sheet will have a number 1 on it. If your doctor told you to lose 50 pounds or you're likely to have a heart attack, Food might take number 1. You get the idea.

How and what you organize first depends largely on your priorities. If you decide that weight loss is a top-of-the-list priority, your kitchen and food systems need special attention, as does your activity level. If your career is in high gear and you want to focus on furthering your education and getting ahead, but you've got the health thing pretty much in hand, other areas jump to the top of the list.

Next, on each sheet circle two more wishes (goals) with a very high priority. That should give you three circled wishes on each sheet. Decide, in order of importance, which should be number 2 and which takes the number 3 spot. If you're having problems with goal-setting and decide you need to do some extra work, consider reading one of the books I've recommended in Appendix A associated with this chapter.

You'll have an even more finely honed set of goals and priorities to work with. *The Magic Lamp: Goal Setting for People Who Hate Setting Goals* covers all aspects of goal-setting, including the things that get in the way. *The 7 Habits of Highly Effective People* focuses heavily on developing a mission statement. *Wishcraft: How to Get What You Really Want* and *I Could Do Anything If I Only Knew What It Was: How to Discover What You Really Want and How to Get It* gives you additional exercises to help you pinpoint your goals.

Black Hole

If you don't have a calendar/planner or a central planning place, you'll make the task of organizing much more difficult than it has to be. We deal with this in more detail in Chapter 7. For now, get a notebook just for your organizing plans and put it someplace where you'll be able to refer to it often.

Finally, place the individual lists of three goals for each category on one sheet you can put in your daily calendar book or on the wall near the desk or table you use to manage your daily affairs.

Commit or Fail

Let's examine your motivations for a minute. Has something happened, like maybe you blew an important appointment because you forgot or couldn't find the materials you were supposed to bring? Or did you just spend 2 hours looking for a wrench you know you have and finally ended up driving to the hardware store so you could buy a duplicate to complete the job?

> **Word Power**
>
> On the other side of the challenge there is a great reward.
>
> Keep going.
>
> When you've made the effort and cannot yet see the result, keep going. The very next step could be the one that brings you across the finish line.
>
> —Ralph Marston

An aggravating event can sure be the beginnings of getting motivated. But what if you use this trigger incident to propel you forward? How did you feel when that happened? If you traced the incident back to an organizational glitch, what would it be? Did you forget the appointment because you don't have a working system for keeping track? Do you have a routine for laying out what you'll need each day ahead of time, so you're prepared? Is the clutter in your workshop or garage so bad you don't know what you have? If you look at these incidents in their broader context, the motivation can be even greater and longer lasting.

As you go through this process of checking in with yourself, setting goals, and creating a plan around them, keep in the back of your mind which area seems to crop up most often as a bugaboo or seems to suck the most energy out of you. When I first started my journey toward taking back my life from the gremlins of disorder, our finances kept cropping up over and over again. I had money in the checking account but couldn't seem to pay our bills on time. I'd misplace important papers in the stacks and piles that accumulated in my home office. When tax time rolled around, it was a nightmare.

I can't tell you what a difference it made when I set up a filing system, got my banking put to rights, and set up a system for paying bills. As you do the preparation work in these first few chapters, try to zero in on what's going to make the biggest impact, and put that at the top of the charts.

This is going to take some work on your part, but it need not be overwhelming. You know the old question and answer: "How do you eat an elephant? One bite at a time." Well, that's what you're going to do—eat an elephant! I'm going to help you, of course, but I need you to pick up the knife and fork. Sure, you can just slap on some quick fixes, and they'll probably make a difference, at least for a while. But think of what a difference it'll make if you work on the big picture and set up organization systems that keep on working for you.

The Master Plan: Keep It Flexible

This isn't going to be like the fad diet many of us have experienced—something you go on for a week until you get tired of counting calories or denying yourself the foods you really enjoy until gradually the diet goes by the wayside. Why don't these diets work? They're too rigid. Expectations are too high. They make you feel deprived and stifled. They focus on the symptoms, not on making deeper lifestyle changes.

Experts agree that the best way to lose weight is to change your lifestyle to support healthful eating and make time for regular exercise. You need information to make that change. Which foods? How to cook? Which exercise? How to stay motivated? That know-how—some of it general, some of it specific to you (what foods you like and which exercise you most enjoy, for example)—let you create a plan that will help you achieve a more healthful lifestyle.

It's no different with getting organized. You need to do the following:

- Gather general information about how to organize the areas where you need it most.

- Collect information about your specific likes, dislikes, strengths, and weaknesses.

- Identify goals that really matter to you and back them up with a Self Contract.

- Set up a concrete plan.

- Break up the plan into simple tasks.

- Schedule tasks, and work toward your goals a little each day.

- Develop ways to check progress and reward yourself for achievements.

Take your time with Part 1 of this book. The mental preparation we're going to do together will set you up for greater success when you begin to take action later on. It's important to do this brain work upfront, before you start tearing apart your closets or canceling all your magazine subscriptions. You've already made a good start in the goal-setting area. And there's an added bonus: the techniques you learn here to get your life in order can be transferred to any other area of your life you'd like to change. Figure out what you really want, make a commitment to get it, get the information you need to achieve your goal, and work at it a little each and every day.

Be willing to adapt your plan as you begin to implement it. Think of your life as continually under construction, and be open to changing things as you go along. It's been said that life is the greatest do-it-yourself project you'll ever undertake. Acquiring the tools and skills you need will make you a better craftsman.

You Deserve a Break Today

Another fundamental concept for changing behavior is providing rewards when you do what you set out to do. Probably the greatest reward for getting your life organized is having more time to spend doing the things you most enjoy. Why not make a list of these things, and when you achieve one of your goals, reward yourself with some time spent doing one of them? I enjoy certain crafts and playing several musical instruments. When I've done something that was especially difficult or took special discipline, I reward myself with some time in front of the piano or a couple of hours of beading.

Be good to yourself. Changing your old ways won't be easy. We all resist change. It makes us uncomfortable. It can even be downright scary. Reward yourself as often as possible, even if it's just to look in the mirror to say "Well done!" Create small rewards for small things and bigger rewards for bigger things, and don't forget to include some rewards just because you love yourself.

Simplewise _____

I want you to have a life you love. I'd like to see you take your dreams seriously and be able to achieve them. You deserve to wake up every morning excited about the day and what it will bring, knowing that you are prepared and clear about the prize you're going after. You deserve to be a *winner*. When you want what I want for you, you'll certainly get a jump-start!

Rewards for getting organized are inherent. There's the good feeling you get when you can finally walk into your walk-in closet again. The feeling of a burden being lifted when you're out from under all those books and magazines and you can finally face the daily junk mail undaunted can be exhilarating. There's the simple pleasure of spending an afternoon lazing in a hammock with a glass of lemonade in your hand, knowing that the house isn't going to fall down around your ears. You're prepared and up-to-date at work, so when you choose to do something fun, you feel completely guiltless, and everything you need for your downtime will be right there where you put it.

Some rewards are even greater than you may realize. When you're in control of your belongings and your time, it's easier to create a bigger vision and work toward it. You have the luxury of contemplating the grander, more philosophical—even spiritual— things in life. So now is probably a good time for you to ask, "What's my vision of the future?"

Remember the age-old interview questions: "Where do you want to be tomorrow? Next year? In 5 years?" Ask yourself now. Give serious thought to these familiar questions. Then move on to two even heavier questions: "What do I want on my grave-stone? What do I want said in my eulogy?" Whoa! Cosmic, you say? Well, maybe. But answering these questions thoughtfully and honestly should set the stage for you to get the most out of this book and start thinking with the bigger picture in mind— what getting organized can actually mean for your future and the meaning of life.

Putting the *Resolve* in This Year's Resolutions

Each time we replace last year's calendar with a new one, we hear all about resolutions to be made (and probably broken) for the coming year. Usually these involve something we need to give up or deny ourselves, or they highlight bad habits we need to break. More often than not, these are the same resolutions we made the year before.

But from now on, you can look the New Year square in the eye filled with excitement and expectancy. You'll view it as a time for congratulating yourself on your achievements and for setting new goals that are meaningful, realistic, and fueled by your innermost desires. You'll learn to expect that the coming year will mean you'll have more of the things you wish for in your life and you'll be doing more of the things you love to do. Now that's a Happy New Year!

The Least You Need to Know

- Your upbringing has shaped your organization skills and habits.

- Setting standards too high actually interferes with lasting change.

- To ensure true success, set goals based on what you really want, not what others want for you.

- Being fair to yourself and rewarding yourself often will keep you motivated.

It's All About *Stuff* and *Time*

In This Chapter

- Taking inventory of your stuff and where it came from
- Examining how you buy stuff
- Making better decisions about the stuff that comes into your life
- Learning about time and how stuff affects it

As you begin to devise your plan to get organized, you need to consider two essential elements: *stuff* and *time*. Simple, right? Well, yes and no. Being honest about how these two elements really operate in your life can be a challenge. If you're willing to take a little time upfront to examine your personal habits and beliefs, however, you can make some powerful discoveries that lead to far-reaching changes.

Stuff includes all the physical things you own; things you spend time accumulating, maintaining, and disposing of; things you think about, worry about, and protect. Stuff also includes what you want or need to accomplish each day. There's always lots of "stuff to do," as well as the physical stuff you share your space with.

Time is how you measure your life—the minutes, hours, days, weeks, and years. Everyone has the same amount of time in every single day— no more, no less. The difference is how people choose to use their time.

One of the most compelling reasons to get organized is to free up more time to do the things you want to do. No more time lost looking for things, fixing or replacing things that got broken or damaged because they were stored poorly, or going out and buying duplicates because you can't find the originals. By learning about the dynamics of time and how to manage it, you can get the must-do things out of the way quickly so you can get right to the fun things.

How Did You Get All This Stuff?

Before we get into the nitty-gritty of organizing your life, we need to start at the beginning—the sources of all the stuff in your life. *Stuff* comes into your life in four ways:

You take it. When you leave your parents' house as a young person to go out on your own, you inevitably take some stuff with you. Maybe a small box of books, a few pieces of furniture perhaps, your old test papers and book reports, a scrapbook, and maybe a handful of extra kitchen utensils your mom doesn't use anymore. You know—a little stuff to get you started.

As you go through your daily life, you take more stuff and bring it home. All those free items (note the magic word—*free*) that agencies, companies, and organizations offer you just for being such a nice person—and a potential customer. Sometimes you pick up stuff in the supermarket from a smiling lady at the door, from a prominently placed brochure rack, or maybe you send for it in the mail or online (that includes all those downloads and printouts). Still, this is stuff you decide to bring into your life in one way or another. And, hey, it's *free!*

> **Word Power**
>
> Actually, this is just a place for my stuff. That's all I want, that's all you need in life, is a little place for your stuff. You know? I can see it on your table. Everybody's got a little place for their stuff. This is my stuff, that's your stuff. That'll be his stuff over there. That's all you need in life is a little place for your stuff.
> —George Carlin

It's given to you. People give you stuff. There's an overstuffed chair from Aunt Margaret, Grandma's framed pictures of the Statue of Liberty, and Cousin Charlie's used golf clubs (hey, you might take up golf someday). It's hard to say no, and besides, this stuff is also *free!*

Then there are the gifts you receive for all occasions. It starts with gifts for graduation, then housewarming gifts for your first apartment. There are birthday presents, maybe wedding gifts, gifts for anniversaries, and Christmas or other year-end holidays. Maybe the gift isn't really your taste, or you have absolutely no use for it, but gee, it's a gift! It's the thought that counts. And it was *free!* So it ends up in the attic, a storage closet, the basement, the breezeway, the junk drawer, or any other place you tuck away things you never use.

You inherit it. Relatives and family friends die. It's inevitable. Somehow their stuff finds its way into your stuff. You can't throw away Grandpa's pipe collection, even though you don't smoke. You can't pitch Mother's hand-crocheted doilies, even though you wouldn't be caught dead using doilies. They were *Mom's!* And by golly, they're *free!* So you integrate these possessions into your own or store them, keeping them safe to pass on to the next willing victim because they have sentimental value.

You buy it. Ah, now here's where it gets serious. When you're given things or inherit them, when someone offers you something for nothing, your desire to please and your love for the giver or the departed are strong motivators to keep stuff. But that doesn't explain why you buy so much useless stuff for *yourself—on purpose!* And if you do it at a wholesale club, you can multiply that inexplicable purchase by a dozen or more!

Why We Buy

How conscious were you when you made your last purchase? How did you decide to buy that item? Had you seen it on TV or in a magazine? Did you notice your neighbor with it and decide you *had* to have it, too? Let's look at some of the influences on our buying habits.

Total spending on advertising and marketing in the United States reached more than $400 billion in 2008, according to Outsell, Inc., an information industry consultant. The traditional advertising outlets of print, TV, radio, and movie revenues were surpassed by online spending for the first time. Online advertising is not just on your computer anymore, either. More and more advertising reaches you through your mobile phone and other interactive media. New terms like *advergaming* and *webisodes* have sprung up to describe new alternative media advertising and marketing avenues.

So that's approximately $1,500 a year to motivate one individual person via every method possible to buy particular products or services, change your attitudes, and influence your decisions. And that one person is *you.*

Black Hole

Don't let today's images of "the good life" in ads, TV programs, and movies pass you by without examining them. Are the images skewed toward a luxurious, stuff-filled lifestyle? Notice what's being presented, and compare it with your own values and beliefs about what "living the good life" really is.

Our kids are targets as well. According to the National Institute on Media and the Family, in elementary, middle, and high schools, direct advertising to students may be seen on book covers, "educational" posters in hallways, school lunch menus, school buses, teaching materials, special in-school TV channels, commercial search engines, student newspapers, school and other websites, athletic fields, scoreboards, gyms, libraries, playgrounds, classrooms, school events, soft-drink machines, fund-raisers, and products used and sold at school. Messages beseeching kids to buy or ask their parents to buy are everywhere.

School administrators, looking for ways to fund programs in cash-strapped schools and during tough economic times, say they cannot afford to turn away company advertisements and corporate sponsorships.

Is it any surprise that you sometimes wonder how that stuff got in your shopping cart in the first place? Why your cabinets and closets are crammed with stuff you never use? "Where did that come from?" you ask. "What was I *thinking?*" But instead of admitting you made a shopping mistake, you keep all that stuff, convincing yourself you can't possibly get rid of it because it's still perfectly good stuff! Sound familiar?

How to Control the Gotta-Have-It Habit

The first step to controlling the stuff you accumulate is to be aware of how, when, and why you decided to get it in the first place. In your notebook, keep a running list of the number of times you go shopping next week. Include on it the amount of time spent, what you bought (you can use general categories, but be careful to include everything), and what time of day you went. Notice whether you went alone or with your spouse or a friend, how you felt when you were shopping, whether you went because you had something specific to buy, and whether you stuck to your original purpose or came out with additional items or something else entirely.

Next take a leisurely walk through your house, look at all your stuff, and ask yourself where it came from. Focus on the stuff that takes up the most room first. If you bought it yourself, try to remember how you came to the decision to buy it. How often do you use it? What purpose does it really serve in your life? What impact would result if it were lost or stolen? Does it have a definite home in your living space, or is it just hanging around? A classic example is the exercise bike or treadmill that's currently being used as a clothes hanger.

Notice that I'm not saying you should cover your ears every time you hear a commercial, nor am I asking you to unplug your computer and TV and put them in the attic. I'm not suggesting you skip reading your morning paper or tune out your favorite talk-radio host. All I want you to do is to become more conscious of the hidden persuaders around you and take more conscious control of your buying decisions and your own thoughts. This is the first important step in organizing your life.

Be more critical of the *way* you view or listen to the mass media, too. The next time you see an advertisement, here are some important questions to ask to help you become a consumer critic:

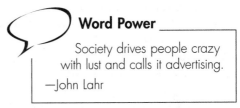

Word Power

Society drives people crazy with lust and calls it advertising.

—John Lahr

- ◆ What claims does the ad make, both obvious and subtle?

- ◆ Are the claims substantiated?

- ◆ What methods are being used to influence your thinking? Pricing gimmicks? Sex appeal? Vivid images? Demonstration? Staged testimonials? Peer pressure? Supposedly scientific studies? Guilt? Fear?

- ◆ What is the ad's key point? Is it directly related to the product?

- ◆ How much do you really know about the product from the ad?

- ◆ Do you already own an item that performs the same function as well or better?

- ◆ If this stuff is so great, how come you got along without it until now?

Make this a game you play with your spouse or kids when you go shopping or consume media and entertainment. This way, you'll help teach others critical thinking while you hone your own skills—and have fun doing it.

Buy! Buy! Buy!

The irrational accumulation of things we don't use, don't need, and eventually don't want is what I call the Acquisition Trap, and we all fall victim to it now and again. The Acquisition Trap is a system of assumptions, beliefs, and ideas about the nature of material things and what they can do for us. This system, which often works on us unconsciously, influences many aspects of our lives: where we live, how we work, and who or what we associate with our purchases. The Acquisition Trap seduces us into believing that owning something will make us sexy, or successful, or smart, and that a particular object or possession represents love, happiness, self-esteem, joy, or knowledge.

Simplewise

If you'd like to learn more about living with less and avoiding the Acquisition Trap, the Simple Living Network website, www.slnet.com, offers a free e-mail newsletter and lots of great resources to create a less acquisitive lifestyle.

Owning a library of beautifully bound books won't make you an educated person. Reading them will. Wearing a certain scent won't make you irresistible to the opposite sex. Your overall appearance and personality is what attracts others. Toting a $500 briefcase won't make you successful in business. Experience, determination, and creativity will.

Be aware of the Acquisition Trap and decide whether you might be caught in it. This isn't about beating yourself up or feeling guilty—it's just about paying attention to your habits, which can ultimately lead you to living a freer, more organized life.

Less Stuff, More Time

As you begin to apply the ideas in this book, you'll make new decisions about what stuff you have and what stuff you want to devote your time to acquire and maintain. You'll be paring down, examining your work habits, gaining control of your finances, and arranging your life so you can have more fun and spend more quality time with the people you love. You'll begin to free yourself to focus on the people and activities that actually give meaning to your life. You'll voluntarily eliminate the excess and concentrate on the good stuff. You may want to go even further and fully embrace a simpler way of life. You'll purge what doesn't work for you and organize the rest.

To help you stay on track, I've devised the following Basic Laws of Stuff. Refer to them every time you get the urge to collect more stuff. I hope they'll remind you why you really don't want to!

The Basic Laws of Stuff

Law 1: Stuff breeds. The more you have, the more you need. Well, okay, if you leave two objects in a dark corner, they don't actually reproduce, but sometimes it sure seems that way. Let's suppose you buy a new computer system. This basic system consists of a keyboard, a mouse, the CPU, and a monitor. Oh, and of course there are all those manuals and cables. And let's not forget a printer. Oh, and extra printer cartridges. You should probably have an external hard drive to back up your files. Of course you'll need new software and maybe an Internet router so you can go wireless. Plus there are various gadgets and cleaning solutions to keep your computer in tip-top shape. And so on, and so on.

Lots of things operate like this. Consider the food processor and all the special attachments, racks, and caddies that go with it, not to mention cookbooks, DVDs, and whatever else you need to get the most out of your appliance.

Maybe you're thinking about starting a collection of some kind. All those collector plates need hangers, or holders, or shelves. Those baseball cards need albums or boxes to keep them in. The cute little porcelain figurines need a display case or even a piece of furniture. Even the stuff used to store other stuff, such as Tupperware, just begs for something to hold all those lids when you're not using them!

Law 2: The useless stuff crowds out the good stuff. The more you have that's useless, obsolete, broken, or just plain junk, the harder it is to find (and find places for) the stuff you really value and use often. Finding the good stuff takes twice as much time and raises your blood pressure in the process. The more you have in your life that's extraneous and without purpose, the less time and energy you have for the *good* stuff.

Law 3: Dust loves stuff. Bugs love stuff. Rodents love stuff. Moisture loves stuff. When you store something unused for long periods of time, odds are that when you finally need it (if you ever do), it'll be useless or damaged anyway.

Law 4: Stuff loves to stay where it lands. It takes time and energy to put things away. That's why the coat or sweater that's flung over the chair tends to stay there forever. Inertia is working against you. If you don't put it away, right away, it takes more energy the longer it stays there.

Law 5: Stuff expands to fill the space available. The bigger the house and the more storage space it has, the more stuff tends to accumulate.

Simplewise

You can make the corollary to Law 4 work for you. The easier you make it to put stuff away, the more likely you will. Refer to later chapters for tips on how to coordinate storage space with your daily habits.

Law 6: Over time, stuff becomes invisible. Ever notice how after you put something on a bulletin board or the fridge, in a few days you can no longer see it? Things fade into the background through familiarity. I call this the Disappearing Stuff Phenomenon. After that scrap of paper hangs in plain view for a while, it can be completely visible, but you still won't see it.

Law 7: Stuff costs you money more than once. Don't fool yourself that the only cost of an object is its purchase price. First you pay to buy the item. Then you have to get it home. This may involve driving your car, taking public transportation, or incurring shipping charges. Next you have to store it, which may mean buying a container or a shelf to put it on. If it's valuable, you may need a security system, not to mention paying additional insurance premiums. If you move to another house (which will probably be bigger, because you need more storage), you need to pay to move it.

And if all this isn't enough, your stuff continues to cost even beyond the grave, when you saddle your family with the unpleasant task of getting rid of it after you die. Think about the real cost of stuff next time you rush out to grab that "bargain."

Law 8: Stuff has a powerful effect on your state of mind. Clutter can be oppressive and depressing. If the possessions we depend on every day are in need of repair, that can add to our feelings of depression and failure. Stuff can weigh us down. We feel burdened by it and what we have to do to get and keep it.

Law 9: Stuff takes on value only when it is used. Unused stuff is just junk or clutter. How often you use it gives it increased value. Less use, less value. Stuff that may seem not to have any utilitarian value can add beauty to your life, and therefore is being "used" by your senses and your soul. These aesthetic additions to your environment should be chosen with great care, to give you enjoyment every time you look at them. If you don't love it or use it, lose it!

Law 10: Stuff doesn't make you happy; you do. I think this law speaks for itself. You know the drill: money can't buy happiness. Well, it's the same with stuff. Both are just tools to help you achieve your own happiness.

Try spending an entire week without bringing any more stuff into your life. Call a moratorium on shopping, and use what you already have as much as possible. During this time, review the Basic Laws of Stuff and see whether you don't become more aware of how stuff gets into your life.

Visualize It
This visualization helps you understand how strongly stuff affects your mental state: picture yourself in a room—for example, your office or garage—where everything is uncluttered, well positioned, and clearly labeled. Take a moment to notice the positive associations evoked by this smoothly functioning and spacious setting. Now imagine the stuff in the room beginning to expand, as paper spills out of the drawers and files onto the floor, labels get switched, and boxes begin to crowd out the elbowroom. What are your emotions now?

The Basic Laws of Time

The other half of the organization equation is time. In a way, I discussed time indirectly when I talked about how having less stuff can give you more time to do the things you love most. But time has its own properties and dynamics. And stuff struggles with time in our lives, requiring us to make constant day-to-day choices that influence how the former affects the latter. Experts tell us how to "manage" our time, but it helps to know a little bit more about its very nature. We couldn't very well have the Basic Laws of Stuff without giving equal attention to the Basic Laws of Time, now could we?

Law 1: Time can be neither created nor destroyed. Phrases such as *making time, buying time,* or *saving time* actually reflect the misconception that time is a thing. Time is a concept humankind has created to measure and give proportion to the cycle of birth and death. Of course, we need this concept to make sense of our existence, but every now and then, it's worthwhile to remind yourself that your ideas about time are just that: *ideas.* It's up to you to make use of the time each of us has in a way that's meaningful and leaves you feeling satisfied and rewarded. You are in complete control of your time, even if you think you're not.

Law 2: Nobody gets more time in a day than you do. Ever notice how some people seem to get tons of stuff done in a day or week? You'd swear they had 36-hour days instead of the meager 24 the rest of us get. But remember, we all have the same period between sunrises. It's just that some people know the secrets for using their time to the fullest. Soon you'll know them, too.

Law 3: Time isn't money, it's your life. It's fashionable to talk about time as it relates to the bottom line. I prefer to think of time as a collection of moments, filled with possibilities and beyond price. Certainly we need to know whether our efforts to earn a living are producing an adequate wage for time spent, but along with a growing bank account, there should be deposits of love and joy in the bank book of life.

Law 4: The value of time is created by opportunity and choice. What makes one moment more fulfilling than the next? I'd like to suggest that the opportunities we find or create and the choices we make are what give our time value and pleasure. Even missed opportunities and bad choices can be valuable if we allow ourselves to learn the lessons they can teach us.

Law 5: When time is lost, it can never be reclaimed. When you find yourself wasting time watching TV or engaging in idle gossip, remind yourself that these moments are gone forever and can never be retrieved. Imagine how you might want them back if you suddenly find out you have a short time left on the planet. Don't squander your most precious asset.

Word Power

Planning is bringing the future into the present so you can do something about it now.
—Alan Lakein

Law 6: Time invested in planning, preparing, and organizing is vital to making the most of your time. You may rebel at the idea of regularly scheduled planning sessions and careful preparation for both mundane and important events. In the beginning, it may seem that getting organized would take up too much of your time. But by the time you finish this book, you'll understand why time spent planning, preparing, and organizing more than repays itself in the long run.

Law 7: You can always begin where you are. The first step to managing your time and moving toward your goals is to start. You know, "just do it!" Take stock of what tools and skills you have, make a plan, and take action. When you begin the process, you'll figure out what else you need along the way. Recriminations and excuses are a waste of time.

Law 8: Identifying your personal time wasters leads to mastery. Who knows where the time goes? You do! If you can't seem to remember, keep an activity log for a week and you'll clearly see the black holes that suck up your valuable time. Write down all the things you do and for how long, even the mundane things, and then total the categories up for each day. After you've identified the nonproductive uses of your time, write them up as a list and post it where you can see it each day. Be honest. How much time do you spend watching TV? On the phone? Chatting with your neighbor? Reading through junk mail? Surfing the web? Knowing your time weaknesses helps you avoid them.

Law 9: Time seems to expand when you set limits. The more you make conscious decisions about where, how, and with whom you want to spend your time and energy, the more of these commodities you'll seem to have. Setting limits means saying no to some things and yes to others. Bowing out of activities that don't support your goals and dreams frees time for what really counts. Taking people up on offers of help or paying someone else to do certain tasks are ways of saying yes to more time for yourself.

Law 10: The secret is to enjoy the passage of time. If you're doing more now and enjoying it less, something's definitely wrong. Just being busy doesn't mean you're productive or happy. Do the work to identify your goals, create systems to achieve them, and allow yourself the time to enjoy the rewards. Time will be your friend, not a high-pressure enemy.

Organization is not an end in itself. You can't do it once and for all. It's an ongoing process, especially if you're an active person with lots of interests, goals, and people in your life. Sure, if all you want to do is get up in the morning, eat, read the paper, eat, watch TV, eat, stare into space, and go to bed, it's probably pretty easy to be organized.

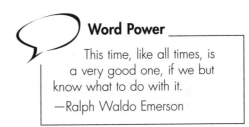

Word Power

This time, like all times, is a very good one, if we but know what to do with it.

—Ralph Waldo Emerson

But if you're running a business, managing a household, pursuing hobbies, doing things with friends, serving in community organizations, taking classes, or whatever else you do, there's a lot more to being organized than throwing out the newspaper each day, washing the dishes, and turning off the tube. In fact, you picked up this book in the first place because you have a busy life. You want to get more out of it and be in control of your time and space. With your sincere willingness, some soul searching, and the information contained in this book, you can transform your life from merely okay to *awesome!*

The Least You Need to Know

- Unstuffing begins with understanding how things get into your life in the first place.

- The media and advertising have a powerful influence on your buying decisions.

- The basic principles of *stuff* and *time* operate in everybody's life.

- Getting control of your stuff and your time is the beginning of gaining control of your life.

Chapter 3

Excuses! Excuses!

In This Chapter

- How to break old habits and form new ones
- Common excuses and how to stop making them
- Breaking the grip of procrastination
- Finding the time to get organized
- The cost of organization

If getting organized is so great, why doesn't everybody do it? Well, nobody said it was going to be a snap. In fact, for people who weren't born with the "order gene" or didn't learn organization and time-management skills at an early age, it can be downright difficult! There's effort involved, and sometimes the greatest effort goes into overcoming the obstacles we put in our own way.

There are four main reasons people fail to get organized:

1. They have limiting ideas and beliefs about what they can do and what "stuff" really is.

2. They procrastinate.

3. They believe they don't have the time to get organized.

4. They think the tools for getting organized will cost too much.

Recognize your reasons in any of these? Well, in this chapter, we take a closer look at each reason and show that beginning to get organized this very minute is not only possible, but essential to achieving your goals. We also analyze the many messages we play in our heads for why we don't or can't get organized and expose them for what they are—excuses preventing us from getting what we really want in life.

How Habits Help or Hinder

A habit is what develops when you repeat an action often enough that it becomes the customary way you do something. It's business as usual in the behavior department. If a habit doesn't seem to benefit us, we talk about "breaking it," much as we talk about taming a wild horse. Habits are hard to break, and the longer you've had them (the more times you've repeated and reinforced them), the more difficult they can be to change.

Black Hole

Ideas, assumptions, and habits of thinking that served you in an earlier life situation may no longer be in your best interest now. Holding on to old patterns can block your efforts to make important changes. Be aware and let go!

The good news, though, is that you already know how to break old habits. Really, you do! Because you got these habits through repetition, the way to change them is through the same process—repetition. And if you can break habits, you can also make them. Pick a new behavior, repeat it every day for 3 or 4 weeks, and you own it.

Habits can be behaviors that just happen or ones you create consciously. You can create the habits you want to have.

When you're trying to make a major change in your destructive habits, another area to look at is your beliefs. We all have automatic reactions to things, and many times we've acquired these reactions, these ways of thinking, *without* thinking—even if they may not be suitable for our present lives and goals. It's time to examine some of those beliefs and see whether they might be getting in the way of getting your act together.

Excuses for Stuff

If you're wondering how you ended up with all this useless stuff in your life, read on. The following excuses could be some of what you tell yourself and other people that give you permission to live in a junkyard.

I Might Need It Someday

Maybe yes, maybe no. If you don't throw away the item, will you even be able to find it when you need it, and will it be in any useable condition by then? Chances are, if you haven't used it in the past 2 years, you won't need it in the next 2. On the off chance you do, you can probably get it again or, better yet, borrow it!

Besides, you're getting organized for the life you live today. If tomorrow brings different challenges, you can always revise your plan and arrange to have on hand the tools you need.

I'm Just Sentimental

Okay, be sentimental. I consider myself a sucker for things that remind me of the people I love or experiences I treasure. But I also recognize that "things" are not living or breathing like the people or events they represent. My mind's eye is a better keeper of my memories. So how about being selective? And how about taking those mementos and turning them into something you'll enjoy every day, like a collage or an album?

When it comes to memories, not all experiences and people are created equal. Pick the ones that are truly special and memorialize them. Ask yourself, "Is this really important to me, or am I just keeping it out of habit, fear of showing disrespect, or fear of loss?"

One way I satisfy my sweet tooth for the past without taking up a lot of space is by keeping a journal. Through my written descriptions of people and things, I can relive my experiences again and again. The composition books I use to record my memoirs take up far less space than boxes of out-of-focus photographs or shelves full of knick-knacks. Some people more artistic than I am add sketches to their journals and even poems or songs. An occasional photo to accompany the text might be an added way to enhance your personal chronicle. You can reread your journals as part of your annual New Year's ritual and remind yourself you've created something that has meaning, not just accumulated more stuff. If it's just gathering dust in the attic, what does that say about how much it *really* means to you?

More Is Better

The habit of stocking up can come from a variety of sources. It can be a way of feeling more secure—prepared for hard times. People who survive a major economic crisis, whether personal or on a larger scale such as a depression or a war, can overdo it in

Black Hole _____

When you're considering buying in bulk, keep in mind the difference between irrational hoarding and wise preparation. Keep on hand whatever you really need in case of a natural disaster or other emergencies, but beware of turning your home into a warehouse.

times of plenty to make up for what they lacked in times of scarcity. And wholesale clubs, discount stores, and thrift stores make it easier and cheaper to add to the stockpile.

We need to apply a little good sense here. How many people are in your family, and how fast will they consume the goods you're amassing? Will you be able to store them in the meantime, and will they still be fresh or useable when you get around to needing them? Do you have room to store them so you can easily see what you have, so that you won't end up buying still more?

So be realistic. It's not a bad idea to store some essentials in case of a natural disaster or difficult times, or to stock up to avoid having to run out to the market constantly. But be sure you have a system for rotating older items with fresh ones, and give some serious thought to what you really need.

I'm Saving It for My Kids

This one is closely related to the sentimental excuse. If you believe you're filling your attic and basement with things to pass on to your progeny, ask yourself, "Is this something they'd really want?" If you already have adult children or grandchildren, you can ask this question with specific personalities in mind. In fact, why not ask them directly? If you're saving things for children who are yet to be, you might want to honestly ask whether the average child of the new millennium will care about this stuff. Remember, tastes and fashions change.

Simplewise _____

Try to limit your collections to things you can display or store easily, and trade up to get rid of the lesser examples you have and acquiring better ones as you go along. That's a good rule for decluttering on many fronts. If a new one comes in, an old one goes out!

If you're pretty sure it's something any generation would love, why not pass it on now? Your children or grandchildren might enjoy using these family heirlooms, and you can experience the sense of connection and history that seeing them cared for in the here and now can bring.

One caution: if it's something you're truly ready to give away, do just that—give it away. No strings, no conditions. If the recipients hate it, they should be free to refuse it or pass it on. And promise them you won't be heartbroken if they break it.

It's Really Old

Ah, we've finally hit upon my own personal clutter trap. I love history, and I'm especially attracted to things from the nineteenth century. Victorian antiques could easily be my nemesis. But just because it's 150 years old doesn't mean it's worth having. (I have to keep telling myself this.)

Unless you're actually in the business of buying and selling antiques, even valuable old junk is still junk if all it does is clutter up your house.

It's Still Perfectly Good

It's only perfectly good if it's good to you now. Even if something's in tip-top shape, if you never use it, it's just a perfectly good piece of junk. Pass it on to someone who really needs it, or sell it at a garage sale, and make room for the things that are truly "perfectly good" because they have usefulness and meaning for *your* life now. Just get rid of it and enjoy the breathing room.

It Was a Bargain

Need we go back and review the lure of advertising discussed in Chapter 2? Remember, sales are gimmicks to get you into the store. Many times stores run a sale to get rid of something that's going to be discontinued soon or that a manufacturer has too many of. (Could it be it's not selling well for a reason?) Unless the item is something you use regularly, or you made a careful decision to acquire it, a sale really isn't a bargain.

Consider this when you're clipping all those coupons, too. It's the same principle.

What should get you into a store is the fact that you need something specific and are prepared to buy it. Just think of all the time you'll save when you give up reading and shopping those circulars!

They Call It a Time-Saver

Even if this isn't one of your bugaboos, I bet you know someone who can't resist the latest newfangled thingamajig. Some people are just gadget freaks. They love all sorts of who's-its and what's-its and can always think of an excuse to get them. Usually it's in the interest of making some task easier, saving money, or saving time.

Always build into the true cost of that gadget the time it takes to earn the money to buy it and to maintain the space you store it in. Also add the time it takes to find it, get it out, and use it, *plus* the time it takes to clean it after the task is done.

Black Hole _____

Keep a vigilant eye on the hidden time demands of so-called time-savers. For example, a food processor does a lot of things more quickly than preparing food by hand. But unless you're cooking in quantity, the time it takes to chop onions by hand will be a lot less than the time it takes to take out the processor, use it, clean it, and store it again. The simple tool is often the best tool.

I've found online reviews really helpful here. Often after checking other people's experiences with a new product, my desire to have it fades quickly. It can take you from the hype to the reality with a great big *thud*.

The Big Put-Off

Putting off until tomorrow what you need to do today is known as procrastination. We all do it now and then, but for some it can become a chronic condition. Sometimes knowing why we do something that has a negative effect on our goals and desires can be the beginning of changing how we behave.

Now that we've looked at some of your excuses for keeping or acquiring more stuff, let's dive into the reasons you have for just not "getting around to getting organized."

Some underlying causes of procrastination are …

- You're not really committed.
- There's something you don't want to face.
- You don't know how.
- You have some belief that's getting in your way.
- You're setting too high a standard.
- You're afraid you'll fail.
- You're trying to do too much at once.
- You haven't clearly defined your goals.

- ◆ Your energy level is low.

- ◆ You aren't convinced of the benefits.

The fact that you're reading this book and have gotten this far says to me you're at least somewhat committed to unstuffing your life and claiming the peace and order you've been craving. If you didn't do the exercises in Chapter 1, go back and do them now, especially if you skipped the goal-setting section. When you have a mission and you know why you're doing something and what the benefits will be when you accomplish it, your excitement will drive you forward.

If you're still dragging your heels, ask yourself what you're afraid of. Is it a possible conflict with your spouse? Are you afraid you might fail? Is it resistance to change? Let me ask you to put these concerns aside for now. We're going to deal with them in various ways throughout this book, and you'll have lots of small, specific steps you can take to help you confront your fears and accomplish your goals.

Examine your beliefs as well. Look for things you hear yourself saying often, such as "I can't," or "I always," or "If only," or "Once I have … then I can." Replace this language with "I am," "I want," or "I can and I will." Concentrate on what you have control over and the skills and resources you already possess. Focus on *acting*, rather than being acted upon and reacting to. Make a mindful decision every day to be pro-active and positive. Feed your mind daily on positive messages from books, online subscriptions, visualizations, and associations with positive people. You control what comes into your life.

Visualize It

When we don't have the benefits of a course of action clearly in mind, we will put it off. Visualization helps here. Picture yourself at work in a place where you can find everything in your files and never forget an appointment. See yourself dressing in the morning with a wardrobe that's well planned; easy to choose from; and always clean, pressed, and mended. See yourself preparing a meal in a sparkling, efficient kitchen where everything's within easy reach. Visualization is a powerful tool to help you break through stagnation and procrastination! Playing the same "movie" over and over, adding greater detail each time, makes it even more powerful.

If your energy level is low, everything becomes a chore. Are you in poor health, not getting enough sleep, partying too much, or experiencing temporary depression? If you answer yes to any of these, give yourself the physical and emotional attention you need first and then get to work. As Messies Anonymous founder Sandra Felton says, "messiness is a disease of self-neglect." Begin your journey toward getting organized by taking better care of yourself.

Pulverizing Procrastination

Now that you've had a conversation with yourself about some of the underlying causes of your procrastination, here are some tips for breaking through the bottleneck:

Tackle it head-on. Ask yourself, "What's the real reason I keep putting this off?" And answer, "I will not let this stop me any longer!"

Take one step. Do *something* right away to get you started. Action produces momentum. Get started. Organizing guru known as the FlyLady instructs her online followers to start with a shiny sink. Almost anything can act as a shiny sink, starting with making your bed every morning to clearing just one surface in an otherwise chaotic room, disposing of the junk and putting away what's left.

Do the hardest thing first. Or do the easiest thing first. (See which approach works better for you.)

Clear the decks. Set aside time, clear a work area, and assemble the tools you need to get started. Make an appointment with yourself, and write it in your calendar.

Break down your plan into tasks. Write down the three larger tasks that will make the greatest immediate difference, and divide each into its smaller parts or bites. (Remember what I said in Chapter 1 about how to eat an elephant?) See whether the task can be broken down in terms of time or physical space. Do five files, clean one cabinet, or set the kitchen timer and spend ten minutes on the task. If you don't have a kitchen timer (the kind that ticks!), get one! You'll be using it a lot on your Organizing Your Life journey.

Do something toward your goal every day. Even if it's a very small thing, do one.

Set deadlines for yourself. Reward yourself when you meet them.

Set a fixed time to take on a task every day or week, and stick to it. This helps form a habit, and it takes less energy over time to get it done. My mother and grandmother always did the laundry on Mondays. This was non-negotiable and automatic. It took away for the need to ever ask "When will I do the laundry?" It works!

If one way isn't working, try another. Adopt a whatever-it-takes attitude.

Don't let too much attention to detail or perfectionism get in the way. Visualize the end result, and be realistic about how you'll get there.

Enlist some help. Finding someone to share a task with can get you started and keep you going. Enlist your kids, your spouse, or a buddy. Set specific goals, check in with your partner in crime regularly, and enjoy a reward together when you follow through.

Do it now! Get in the habit of doing things right away. If you have something to put away, do it. Don't put it on the counter on the way to the garage or on the stairs to be put away later. Finish it. The sense of completing tasks on a regular basis will reinforce itself.

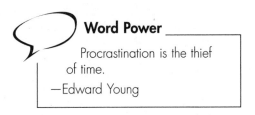

Word Power

Procrastination is the thief of time.

—Edward Young

Increase your rate of motion. Set a timer, put on some upbeat music, challenge yourself, and make the time go faster. Create momentum using whatever tricks work for you. Get wise to yourself.

When You Hit a Roadblock

If you keep putting off things in spite of all these efforts, maybe you *really* don't want to get organized. Shelve the idea until you're ready to commit some significant thought and energy to it.

If you're not ready to give up just yet, hire someone else to do it. Perhaps hiring a professional organizer will be the jump-start you need, and you'll be able to finish the job yourself and maintain the systems a professional organizer can help you create.

I Don't Have the Time to Get Organized!

Think you don't have the time to get organized? Actually, you don't have the time *not* to get organized. Just consider all the extra steps, the time wasted, the duplicated efforts, the frustration, the feelings of losing your grip, the missed appointments and important events, and the lost moments. Getting organized will fill your pockets with time to spare.

I Don't Have the Money to Get Organized!

Organization is a state of mind, not a thing. It doesn't have to cost a lot of money to get organized. In fact, you can't afford *not* to. Lots of low-cost or even recycled storage and organization solutions are available, and I point them out to you throughout this book. Wherever possible, I give you several alternatives, including budget-conscious ones, for the materials suggested.

However, spending a little extra money on the right tools and equipment can save you gobs of dough in the long run. Quality storage containers and tools quickly pay for themselves. Weigh the cost of something that helps you get and stay organized against the cost of chaos. I think you'll find it's worth it in the long run to spend money on a few quality items that do the job well and last a long time. Besides, after you read the chapters on organizing your finances later in this book, you'll have the money in your budget to do it right!

Stop Making Excuses and Go!

Let's face it. People who are always making excuses are a drag. Just think about the people in your life who do it and how you feel about them. They're not high on your list of folks to while away the hours with, right?

Don't be one of those people! Start today. Take your first step toward achieving what you truly desire. If you keep making excuses and procrastinating, you give up control. Why drift through life when you could be at the helm, steering in the direction *you* want to go? Concentrate on what you can change, and begin.

The Least You Need to Know

- Habits are made through repetition and can be changed the same way.

- By looking at your beliefs in light of your goals, you can spot obstacles to your progress.

- Procrastination has a variety of causes, and you can immediately take simple steps to combat it.

- You can't afford the time or the money it costs to stay disorganized.

Chapter **4**

When Stuff Rules Your Life

In This Chapter

◆ Determining if your relationship with stuff is seriously out of control

◆ Psychological disorders and medical conditions that may contribute to chronic disorganization and obsessive cluttering

◆ Getting help and support for recovery and growth

Most of us recognize ourselves in the first three chapters of this book. If you weren't struggling with clutter and disorganization, chances are you wouldn't have picked up this book in the first place. Even the most organized people have to do periodic tweaking, can find themselves getting behind, and may sometimes be prone to procrastination. But there's a line beyond which disorganization becomes a debilitating and possibly even dangerous disorder.

In this chapter, we discuss some serious personal issues. It's beyond the scope of this book to fully cover their complexities, so I give you some basic information along with resources to lead you to the real experts—mental health professionals, support groups, and some helpful books. If you're dealing with any of these serious issues, I encourage you to reach out and get the help you need. I hope reading this chapter will be an important first step.

Hoarder's Disorder: A Severe Case of the "Messies"

For some of us, the terms *messy* or *disorganized* just don't quite express it. The chaos in our lives is extreme and chronic. The debris and mess seriously hamper our ability to function day to day and may even have a negative impact on our ability to have a happy marriage, parent our children effectively, hold a job, and maintain healthy and satisfying friendships. The problem may be so extreme that our surroundings have actually become unsafe or unhealthy or both. When clutter can mean being evicted from your dwelling or risking losing your children or being fired from your job, it's time to take some drastic measures.

Black Hole

Ignoring the signs that a deeper problem is operating in your life can mean serious repercussions later down the road. People who recognize their needs and seek help are smart and courageous!

Extreme behavior with regard to clutter can come under a variety of names and categories. Variously labeled "clutter disorder" or "hoarder's disorder" or "hoarder's compulsive disorder," this is a new area being explored in psychology. Many therapists who were not trained or experienced in treating it only a few years ago are becoming increasingly aware of it as a recognized clinical disorder needing treatment.

Hoarder's disorder is usually considered an obsessive-compulsive disorder (OCD) by the medical community and can be caused or at least exacerbated by a chemical imbalance in the brain. Research into this behavior is ongoing, but it's recently been estimated that some 1 million Americans suffer from hoarder's disorder.

Extreme cluttering and disorganization may also be manifestations of other psychological problems or even neurological disorders. A recent study presented in the *American Journal of Psychiatry* suggests a strong neurological/biological component to the disease. Professionals can be located to provide treatment, and self-help groups, both local and online, offer the support and information needed to make great strides in conquering the problems of obsessive hoarding.

But what, exactly, is hoarder's disorder? Here's the definition provided by the Mayo Clinic staff at mayoclinic.com:

> Hoarding is the excessive collection of items, along with the inability to discard them. Hoarding often creates such cramped living conditions that homes may be filled to capacity, with only narrow pathways winding through stacks of clutter. Some people also collect animals, keeping dozens or hundreds of pets in unsanitary conditions.

Hoarding, also called compulsive hoarding and compulsive hoarding syndrome, can be a symptom of obsessive-compulsive disorder (OCD). But many people who hoard don't have other OCD-related symptoms, and researchers are working to better understand hoarding as a distinct mental health problem.

Sandra Felton, founder of Messies Anonymous, a recovery organization authorized by Alcoholics Anonymous to use its 12 Steps and 12 Traditions, and author of numerous books on chronic cluttering and disorganization, describes her life before she got help:

> I had big houses, little houses, no children, children, maids, no maids. But under all circumstances I was a messie. This was not only frustrating, but surprising, since I was quite capable in other areas of my life.

Mike Nelson, author of *Stop Clutter from Stealing Your Life: Discover Why You Clutter and How You Can Stop*, puts it this way:

> I had to admit that I was different from other people, that I was powerless over my compulsion, before I could seek help and begin to recover. My life today is hundreds of times better than it was before I faced my cluttering. Cluttering is a personality dysfunction. It has nothing to do with lack of self-control or being a bad person.

Simplewise _____

To better understand hoarder's compulsive disorder and possible treatment, the book *Buried in Treasures: Help for Compulsive Acquiring, Saving, and Hoarding* by David F. Tolin, Randy O. Frost, and Gail Steketee is a good starting point.

Are You a Compulsive Clutterer?

But how do you know whether you're in the "extreme" category? There are warning signs. Ask yourself the following questions. If you answer yes to several of them, this may be the time to come to grips with what's happening and seek professional help.

Yes	No	
❏	❏	Is the accumulation in your house a severe health concern or safety hazard? Consider piles of paper that could be a fire hazard or garbage that has encouraged an invasion by vermin and/or insects.
❏	❏	Are any exits or windows blocked by the accumulation of clutter or debris? Are any doors between rooms blocked by clutter?
❏	❏	Are hallways or stairways lined with stored items so only a small pathway remains between rooms?
❏	❏	Do you have a deep fear of people coming to the house and seeing the clutter and dirt? Do you pretend not to be home so you don't have to open the door? Would you be in danger of eviction if your landlord were to see the condition of your apartment?
❏	❏	Do you regularly lose sleep over lost papers, money, or other valuable items?
❏	❏	Do you sometimes have to clear a spot on your bed just to be able to sleep?
❏	❏	Do you have to eat somewhere other than the kitchen or dining room table because there's no room to put your plate?
❏	❏	Do you chronically miss appointments and important occasions, even though you have the best intentions of making them?
❏	❏	Has the safety of your children ever been compromised because of clutter or disrepair in your home?
❏	❏	Do you regularly pay late-payment fees or penalties not because you don't have money to pay the bills, but because you can't find them, can't remember to deposit checks, or are unable to keep track of your checkbook balance?
❏	❏	Do you avoid leaving the house or cancel appointments for lack of clean or mended clothes?
❏	❏	Do you drive a vehicle with expired insurance or registration, even though you have the money to pay these fees?
❏	❏	Is there so much stuff in your car no one else can ride with you?

Yes answers to these questions could be indicators that your disorganized habits go deeper than the average person's. If you're not sure, seek the help of a professional and be open about your behaviors and concerns. There's a lot we don't understand about severe and chronic disorganization and related disorders. Only recently, for example, have they been linked to attention deficit disorder (ADD), obsessive-compulsive disorders, and certain speech pathologies, such as stuttering.

In the most extreme cases, there may be stacks of newspapers from floor to ceiling, leaving only narrow passageways from room to room; clothes covering all the floors; broken furniture and appliances left blocking doors and windows; and boxes of saved paper, plastic bags, and jars throughout the kitchen, as well as food scraps and other waste; and cans filling basements and porches. Sufferers may be unable to leave their homes, handle their finances, or have meaningful relationships.

Word Power

Clutter is anything we don't need, want, or use that takes our time, energy, or space, and destroys our serenity. It can be outgrown clothes or obsolete paper. We may be selective in some areas, but not in others. Objects may be strewn about or wedged into drawers; neatly stacked or stowed in storage.

—from The Twelve Steps of Clutterers Anonymous

ADD and ADHD

Conditions that can manifest in extreme cluttering and disorganization are attention deficit disorder (ADD) and attention deficit/hyperactivity disorder (ADHD). People with ADD often have trouble setting priorities or planning what order to do a series of tasks or activities. They may start something but be unable to finish. Sometimes ADD sufferers find their mind so cluttered with competing thoughts and messages it can be hard to function. Mental clutter manifests itself in physical clutter and disorganization.

If you're not sure whether you or someone close to you might have ADD or ADHD, several self-tests or quizzes are available online to give you some clues. Just type "ADD self-test" into your favorite search engine, and select a couple of the results. If you suspect you have ADD or ADHD, seek medical testing and diagnosis as a next step.

Compulsive Shopping

Compulsive shopping or spending disorder can be another culprit in the fight against clutter and disorganization. In this instance, the accumulation of stuff is an offshoot of the problem. The main cause, however, is a compulsive need to buy things, even when they're not needed and they're not serving any purpose. Compulsive shopping disorder can cause financial ruin and destroy relationships, in addition to contributing to clutter and disorganization.

If you're not sure whether you might have a compulsive spending problem, ask yourself these questions:

Simplewise _____

To help with understanding and overcoming compulsive spending, April Benson's book *To Buy or Not to Buy: Why We Overshop and How to Stop* can help.

- Do you continue spending on credit, even though you're unable to pay off your current credit card debt?

- Are you facing bankruptcy or at least serious financial problems, yet are unable to curb your spending?

- Do you often have arguments with your partner, family members, or friends about your spending?

- Do you have a closet stuffed full of clothes you never wear, some with the price tags still on, yet find yourself shopping for more?

- When you're in a store, do you find you cannot leave without buying something?

- Do you spend inordinate amounts of time shopping or thinking about shopping?

- Do you shop to avoid pressure, to escape or fantasize, to increase your self-esteem, or to feel more secure?

- Do others regularly make comments about your excessive spending?

- Do you often spend money you don't have on things you don't need, or perhaps already have several of at home?

If you answered yes to any of these questions, you may be suffering from compulsive shopping disorder. If you're not sure, ask a professional to help with a diagnosis.

Other OCDs

Compulsive spending and hoarder's disorder are only two types of obsessive-compulsive disorders. Other OCDs manifest in behaviors that are the reverse of disorganization or out-of-control spending, such as compulsive neatness. Both extremes mean that stuff somehow rules your life and interferes with your enjoyment of regular activities and other people.

If you can't stand to see something out of place, if you have to constantly straighten and clean, or if it's difficult for you to relax without thinking about tidying up or cleaning, you may have OCD. Again, if you're uncertain, seek the help of a professional to get a more accurate diagnosis and devise a treatment strategy.

When Something Else Is Wrong

Other mental health issues and, possibly, medical conditions may interfere with an individual's ability to manage his or her life and stay organized. Some of these are depression, bipolar disorder, chronic fatigue syndrome, Epstein-Barr virus (EBV), and fibromyalgia. Any chronic disease or condition could be a contributor to extreme or chronic disorganization and cluttering.

If you're not sure what may be exerting its influence in your situation, a health-care professional, a professional therapist, counselor, psychologist, or psychiatrist can help you sort it out. If you suspect a particular culprit, by all means share your suspicions with your mental-health or medical professional. If you haven't had a thorough medical exam in some time, now would be a good time to make an appointment.

It's important that you identify the source of your problem and get help. You don't have to live with anxiety and chaos! You deserve better. If you or someone you love needs help, lead the way.

Help Is on the Way

All the disorders and conditions I've mentioned can be treated. Excellent help is available, and the resources in this chapter should help you at least get started on the road to a better future. There are varying degrees of distress, of course. But for some people the situation is grave, and drastic measures need to be taken. Don't wait to seek professional help if you feel this is the case. Do it now!

If you believe the situation is less severe, however, you can take steps to help yourself, armed with good information and the support of other people who suffer from the same problems. In fact, for some, the ongoing support of people with problems like the ones they face in addition to working with a mental-health professional is the best route to real recovery. I've provided some well-respected resources for you here to explore. There are many more, so if you don't find what you need right away, keep looking!

> **Word Power**
>
> Messiness is a disease of self neglect.
> —Sandra Felton

Finding the Help You Need

When attempting to locate any self-help group in your area, first check with the headquarters of the proper organization, and ask for a local contact person. If you're close enough, you may be able to join the group. Many online support groups also have places where you can post requests for local meeting locations. If you still can't find what you're looking for, you may want to think about starting your own.

Call the contact person at the national organization or the closest chapter and pick her brain. She'll probably have lots of ideas to share about how she got started and what to avoid in starting your own group. If you decide you want to do that, put up a notice on bulletin boards at local churches, libraries, post offices, Laundromats, health-food stores, and any other public place where you think you might find people who'd like to work with you on starting a group. (Ask permission first, of course!) Leave your name with local mental-health professionals as well. If you have a community self-help clearinghouse or hot line, let them know of your desire to form a group and ask them to refer people to you.

Put a notice in the public service announcement section of your local newspaper. Consider any newsletters of organizations that might reach people for your group. Contact professional organizers in your area and let them know what you're trying to do. A professional organizer often knows people like you who might benefit from such a group. To find one, contact the National Association of Professional Organizers at www.napo.net or by e-mailing napo@napo.net.

Even if you decide not to join a group, you may want to subscribe to an online newsletter or mailing list for support. One of the best ways is to simply go to Yahoo! Groups (www.groups.yahoo.com) or Google Groups (www.groups.google.com) and put in key words to find what you're looking for. Chances are you'll come up with many to choose from. Try subscribing to one or two and see if they suit you. If not, unsubscribe and find another to try. Look for groups that are well established and have a substantial following. Most likely they will be of the most benefit.

Now because I know you're buried in mounds of dirty laundry, piles of paper, and whatever else may have accumulated in your life and could use a hand with this, I've done some of the research for you. There's much more out there than what I've listed in the following sections, but this should be enough to point you in the right direction.

Simplewise _____

It's important to understand that the members of these groups are not medical or psychology professionals, but simply folks like you struggling with the same issues. They are not a substitute for professional advice or treatment, but they can be an additional resource on the road to recovery.

Hoarder's Disorder

Support groups are available for people with clutter disorders. These groups are 12-Step groups, similar to alcohol and drug recovery groups and based on the principles of Alcoholics Anonymous. They follow a defined structure and set of principles and have produced some dramatic life-changing results. They're free, and if there isn't one in your area, it's easy to start one of your own.

Here's where to find help:

> **Clutterers Anonymous (CLA)**
> PO Box 91413
> Los Angeles, CA 90009-1413
> www.clutterersanonymous.net
> This group has local meetings and literature to help with cluttering by working the 12-Step program. CLA also has a regular newsletter available by subscription.

> **Messies Anonymous (MA)**
> 5025 SW 114th Avenue
> Miami, FL 33165
> www.messies.com
> Founded in 1981 by confessed messie Sandra Felton, these groups use her books to guide in the recovery process. Her book applying the 12 Steps and Traditions is called *Hope for the Hopeless Messy: Steps for Restoring Sanity to Your Cluttered Life*. It describes in detail how to start a local MA group. Her site also offers

15 online support groups (including one for people who are involved with messies but are not one themselves), and she has created audio- and videotapes to teach skills and gives seminars nationally.

OCD

The Mayo Clinic defines OCD as "a type of anxiety disorder in which you have unreasonable thoughts and fears (obsessions) that lead you to engage in repetitive behaviors (compulsions). With obsessive-compulsive disorder, you may realize that your obsessions aren't reasonable, and you may try to ignore them or stop them. But that only increases your distress and anxiety. Ultimately, you feel driven to perform compulsive acts in an effort to ease your distress."

Currently there's some controversy in the field as to whether hoarding actually is OCD, but if you have other OCD symptoms, this might very well be a good place for you to explore your options for support and recovery.

Here's where to find help:

> **Obsessive-Compulsive Foundation**
> PO Box 961029
> Boston, MA 02196
> 617-973-5801
> www.ocfoundation.org

> **Obsessive-Compulsive Anonymous**
> PO Box 215
> New Hyde Park, NY 11040
> 516-739-0662
> www.obsessivecompulsiveanonymous.org

Compulsive Spending/Shopping Disorder

Compulsive spending and shopping are just finding their way into the language of mental-health professionals. Often it isn't a recognized problem until debts have piled up and then the focus becomes on handling debt, not necessarily on what caused it. Regardless of how you approach the problem, some of us are compelled to shop beyond what we need, can use, or have room to store.

One mental-health professional may be ahead of the curve on this one. His name is Terrence Shulman, and he's the founder of The Shulman Center and Shopaholics Anonymous, plus the author of several books on the subject.

Here's where to find help:

> **The Shulman Center**
> PO Box 250008
> Franklin, MI 48025
> 248-358-8508
> www.theshulmancenter.com

> **Shopaholics Anonymous**
> www.shopaholicsanonymous.org
> You can also start with handling the debt and at the same time be looking at how you got into the money hole. This classic 12-Step group has a solid history of helping people overcome overspending and debt.

> **Debtors Anonymous**
> General Service Office
> PO Box 920888
> Needham, MA 02492-0009
> 1-800-421-2383
> www.debtorsanonymous.org

General Emotional Disorders

Not sure what's going on? Maybe you need a more general place to start that will help you hone in on what really is the trouble.

Here's where to find help:

> **Emotions Anonymous International**
> PO Box 4245
> St. Paul, MN 55104-0245
> 651-647-9712
> www.emotionsanonymous.org

Attention Deficit Disorder

Whether you're an adult with ADD or the parent of an ADD child, ADD professionals and support groups are likely available in your area.

Here's where to find help:

> **Attention Deficit Disorder Association (ADDA)**
> PO Box 7557
> Wilmington, DE 19803-9997
> 1-800-939-1019
> www.add.org

Bipolar Disorder and Depression

Depression and/or bipolar disorder can often lead to chronic disorganization and an inability to deal with clutter. Sometimes the first step is contacting local support groups.

Here's where to find help:

> **Depression and Bipolar Support Alliance**
> 730 N. Franklin Street, Suite 501
> Chicago, IL 60654-7225
> 1-800-826-3632
> www.dbsalliance.org

Pendulum Resources
www.pendulum.org
This online portal can lead you to all sorts of resources, whether online, in print, or local. The site comes with the following legal disclaimer: "Pendulum Resources is maintained by consumers; therefore, information on this site is not to be construed as medical advice. Rather, it provides general information and support for previously diagnosed conditions. We do not provide specific medical advice. See your mental health or health care provider for diagnosis and for answers to specific medical questions."

Simplewise

Pendulum's disclaimer is true for many of the resources you'll find, but it doesn't make them any less valuable. Just be aware of the difference between people helping people and medical treatment.

Chronic Fatigue Syndrome/Myalgic Encephalomyelitis/Fibromyalgia/ Epstein-Barr Virus

Lack of energy and profound fatigue, even flulike symptoms, are hallmarks of chronic fatigue syndrome (CFS). Those with fibromyalgia can have an extreme sensitivity to pain. Myalgic encephalomyelitis is a neurological disease that also results in extreme fatigue, as well as muscle weakness, visual problems, and other symptoms. Epstein-Barr virus is a herpes-related virus that can last several months and is easily misdiagnosed. It's related to infectious mononucleosis, and some researchers believe it may be the cause of CFS. These conditions are often missed in routine medical exams and diagnosis.

Here's where to find help:

> **Mayo Clinic**
> mayoclinic.com
> For general symptoms and information, type the name of the disease you're seeking information for in the search box.

> **The International Association for Chronic Fatigue Syndrome/Myalgic Encephalomyelitis/Fibromyalgia**
> 27 N. Wacker Drive, Suite 416
> Chicago, IL 60606
> 847-258-7248
> Admin@aacfs.org
> www.iacfsme.org

If you don't see what you're looking for, open your favorite search engine and put in any of the terms I've mentioned in these sections. You'll find tons of information for each, including help understanding what these disorders are, clues to help you decide what might actually be going on in your own particular case, and resources for finding professional help and support groups in your hometown. If you don't have access to the Internet, check your local Yellow Pages, or call the nearest mental-health facility.

Word Power

It is hard to fight an enemy who has outposts in your own head.
—Sally Kempton

Want to Learn to *Fly?*

Perhaps you've read all through this chapter and just don't recognize yourself here. But still, you feel your level of disorganization is chronic and debilitating, and you need more help than this book can provide. I have one more suggestion for you!

I discovered the FlyLady a few years ago, and I can't help but sing her praises. Basing her system on the "Slob Sisters" system outlined in the *Sidetracked Home Executives* book series, Marla Cilley has improved on their ideas and created a support system ideal for those who need highly structured daily help getting their housework done and clearing their lives of clutter. Her book called *Sink Reflections* also outlines the FlyLady system, although just about everything you need can be found online.

To subscribe, go to the FlyLady website at www.flylady.net. While you're there, check out the archives and get started on your routines and periodic "27 Fling Boogies." Everyone can benefit from the FlyLady's wisdom, but her principles and detailed systems are especially helpful for those who have serious challenges and need regular daily reminders and support. Her fun attitude, focus on self-love, contests, games, and challenges will keep you going even when you think you've run out of steam.

Don't underestimate your own ability to do this. After you've identified a problem, you can begin to solve it. Many of these disorders can be overcome with hard work and persistence. I have nothing but admiration for people who face their challenges, be they physical or mental or both, and work on their own recovery. I hope in some small way I've helped you or someone you love find a path to recovery. May you gather the courage, energy, and self-love to triumph and be well!

The Least You Need to Know

- If disorganization and clutter interfere with a person's ability to function on a most basic level, there's likely a more serious disorder that needs to be addressed.

- Although each disorder or physical condition has its own particular symptoms, all can lead a person to live a highly disorganized life.

- Seeking professional help and joining a support group are effective ways to cope with emotional disorders and diseases that affect the ability to organize and manage one's life.

- There's no limit to what you can do with courage, persistence, and the right support to overcome chronic disorganization and cluttering. You can do it!

Part

Stuff Simplified

The chapters in Part 2 really get you into unstuffing mode. By reducing the amount of clutter that comes into your space, as well as getting rid of what's already there and in your way, all the rest of your efforts at organizing your life will go more smoothly.

First, you get all the basic steps for managing your stuff. Then we devote some extra time to the bane of our modern existence—paper!

Chapter 5

Utterly Uncluttered Space

In This Chapter

- Simple decluttering principles you can adopt right away
- Questions to ask yourself when unstuffing your stuff
- Doable steps for clearing out the clutter
- The real costs of having too much stuff in your life

You're impatient, I know. So why not get started right this minute? Get out of that chair! Don't even think about going for the remote! Stop whatever you're doing, and get the urge to purge!

In this chapter, I give you quick and easy steps to get you started unstuffing. These are basic principles you can begin using immediately to make the rest of your organization efforts fall into place. They can be used to unstuff a drawer, a cabinet, a closet, or a whole room. You can use them in 15-minute quickie purging sessions or spend a whole day doing a clean sweep of an area you just can't put up with anymore. You're in charge. These basic steps are your keys to creating new habits.

Getting Started

Pick one small area to begin. Don't try to do anything too big. It can overwhelm you and then you're back to square one. If you can, pick an area that supports your highest priorities. Key areas would be a corner of your bedroom (to ensure a peaceful night's sleep) or maybe a drawer or cabinet in the kitchen (the hub of the house), but you choose. Just pick a place to start and make it small and manageable.

A couple of suggestions I might make for the first few unstuffing sessions, though: if you pick a place that's out of sight like a drawer or cabinet, you don't get the reinforcing satisfaction of walking by and seeing your accomplishment. I also suggest you pick a project that's not likely to be undone by others in the household who aren't with the program yet. There's nothing more disheartening than to spend your time and enthusiasm on a job, only to have it back to clutter city in the blink of an eye. I suggest your desk, your vanity, or your bathroom area, or how about clearing off your bed so tonight you slip into a good night's sleep?

Decide not to allow yourself to get distracted. Don't answer the phone if it rings. Pick a time when you're not likely to be interrupted. (My best time is early in the morning before the rest of the household wakes up!)

As you note places where buying or adding some storage solutions would make a difference, jot them down in a notebook. (You might want to have one just for your organization exercises and ideas and for taking notes as you work through this book.) You may also notice some things that need repairs, maintenance, or some really heavy cleaning. Don't let yourself get sidetracked. Right now you're only unstuffing. Just jot down these areas in your notebook. You might list things like "Clean out light fixture" or "Look into stain on ceiling for possible leak" or "Fix loose drawer." Just list them in your notebook. For now we're just dealing with the stuff.

Simplewise _____

When you do your first timed sort, put anything you just can't make a decision about (but try hard to right away) or stuff that needs further sorting in the *Keep* box. Remember to set the timer for 15 or 20 minutes, and *go!* Don't spend too much time deliberating, but try to let go of as many things as you can right from the start. The idea is to create momentum and keep yourself going.

Don't worry about any priority order or deadlines for your to-do list right now either. This list will become your Master To-Do List (to be discussed further in Chapter 7), but for now, you don't need to think about what it's called. Just keep a running list of anything that needs to be done or that you'd like to do someday. Record any ideas that pop into your head while you're plowing through your stuff. If you're purging a drawer and you think having dividers or containers would help, write that down. If you're going through a bunch of papers and think you need a new file folder or set of files, make a note of it.

Next, find four boxes. Label them *Put Away/Return*, *Keep*, *Pass On*, and *Fix*, or use your own labels if you like (although I refer to these labels throughout the book). Have a big trash can nearby. If you have a recycling program in your area, you may want the recycling bin nearby for newspapers, magazines, plastics, glass, and other recyclables you plan to toss.

The *Put Away/Return* box is for stuff that doesn't belong where you found it. It may be other people's junk (or treasures) or simply items you know belong in another room or somewhere else. If you find books or videos that need to be returned or have borrowed stuff you need to give back to its rightful owner, put those things in this box as well.

The *Pass On* box is for stuff to hand down, give to charity, or sell at a garage sale—anything you don't need anymore that's too good to throw away.

The *Keep* box is for things you know you need or want. It's also for stuff you just can't figure out what to do with during this speed purge. Maybe you don't have a place for it right now. (Though you'll need to find one if you decide to keep it around.) Even worse, you may not know what it is (*mystery* stuff)! If at all possible, quickly ask yourself the questions in Step 2 (coming right up) and make a decision now to trash/recycle it, pass it on/return it, or put it away where it belongs. But if you're just not sure where it goes right now and it takes a lot of time to decide, you'll at least have a temporary place for it in the *Keep* box.

The *Fix* box should only be used for items you really believe are worth fixing. If it's been broken for 5 years and you've lived without it this long, don't bother. More about this category later.

Now armed with your organizing notebook and your boxes, and your trash and recycling bins, you're ready to begin working through the steps.

Step 1: Empty the Space

If it's a drawer, dump everything in a box or container. If it's a closet or cabinet you've targeted for your first organizing project, find a staging area where you can put the contents temporarily while you work your magic. This can be a countertop, a table that's been cleared off, or any surface that will let you spread things out, see what you have, and sort easily.

Now that you've cleared everything out of the space, give it a good cleaning.

Step 2: Use It or Lose It

You're going to repeat this step twice. It's actually the step where you sort through what you have to make decisions about—what to keep and what to let go. The first time we're going to make a game of it. We're going to play "Beat the Clock" and trash as much as we can in 15 minutes. Set your session to music if that gets you going. I recommend something upbeat and catchy. I like disco or Motown for unstuffing at my house!

If you don't have a kitchen timer that ticks away the seconds, I suggest you get one. The sound of the minutes ticking away is part of the game. Try to touch each item only once during this first quick sort. Pick up the first item and make a decision as quickly as possible. Remember, the clock is ticking!

Challenge yourself to cut the amount of stuff you have in the particular space you've chosen by a third or half. Impossible? Give it a try! As you handle each item (only once) ask yourself these questions:

When was the last time I used this? The key word here is *use*. If it's been more than a year, give serious thought to putting it in the trash or the Pass On box. If you're sure you've used it in the last year, go on to the next question. One great way I've heard this question phrased was by professional organizer Peter Walsh on the *Clean Sweep* television show. He asked the homeowner who was holding on to something he rarely used, "Is it a friend, an acquaintance, or a stranger?" Well, which is it?

How often do I use it? If you don't use it very often and it's in a location where regular daily activities occur, put it in the *Put Away/Return* box. You need to find a place other than your most precious everyday living space. But before you do that, ask yourself the next question.

Could I borrow, rent, or improvise with something else the few times I might need it? If the answer is yes, put it in the trash or Pass On box.

Black Hole _____

Don't throw out, give away, or sell anyone else's stuff without asking, as tempting as that may be when you're in the purging mood. How would you like it if someone did that to you? Put it in the Put Away/Return box and give it back to the owner to deal with. You might want to show him or her these questions!

Is it a duplicate? If it is, you probably bought another one because you were unhappy with the old one or you couldn't find it. If you know you have one that works better, keep the best one and toss or pass on the extra one. Put the one you want to keep in the Keep box or the Put Away/Return box if it belongs in another area.

Is it out-of-date? Examples are canned foods and medicines that are past the expiration date or clothing that'll never be back in style. Throw outdated canned items away or add the contents to the garden compost, and pass on outdated clothes. Dispose of medicines safely.

If I didn't have this anymore, what impact would it have on my life? This is a deeper question, but ultimately one you need to ask. Think worst-case scenario. Imagine the dog chewed it up or a flood carried it away or a burglar ran off with it. Is this item something you'd have to go right out and replace? This exercise will probably direct still more things into the trash, recycling bin, or Pass On box.

Do I value this item? If the answer is yes, put it in the Keep box. But the word *value* can be a loaded one. Perhaps a different way to put it might be "Do I *care* about this?" Yet another closely related question would be "Would I buy it again today?" If it's just gathering dust or thrown in a heap, how much could you *really* value it? What was once beautiful to you might no longer hold the same luster or excitement. If your tastes have changed or something better has caught your fancy, let it go!

Is this item in need of repair or damaged? Put it in the Fix box if it needs a minor repair to make it useable. But be honest about the cost of the repairs versus the cost of replacing the item. Set a time limit to get it done, and put that action on your Master To-Do List in your organization notebook.

Am I keeping this because I'd feel guilty if I tossed it or gave it away? People give you gifts because they want to please you. If you don't use or like something you've been gifted, pass it on to someone who will. It will make you feel good, which is the whole point of gift giving! Let go of that guilt!

How easily could I get another one if I needed it? If it's a hard-to-find item and likely to be used even once in a while, it might be worth keeping. But your arguments for keeping it should be compelling!

Black Hole

Strong emotions may come up for you during the unstuffing process. This is perfectly normal! Acknowledge them and give them expression (speak them out loud if that helps), but don't let them prevent you from moving forward. That's why 15-minute increments might be just the ticket for your initial efforts. This allows you to feel the emotions as they surface. Use your notebook to journal, or simply note these feelings.

One more idea for the Pass On box: how about sharing? Do you know someone who would use an item more than you do? Give it to that person so he or she can store it, with the condition that you can borrow it back when you need it. Consider this solution for stuff such as camping gear, bicycles, tools, and sports equipment.

Ding! The timer just went off. How did you do? Hopefully, the trash, the recycling bin, and Pass On box are pretty full. But now we're going to do a more detailed sort of the Keep box and go through the process again.

Set aside some more time when you can carefully consider each item and challenge yourself to reduce the stuff you have in the Keep box. Another 15 or 30 minutes is probably a good objective. Don't try to do too much in any one decluttering session. As you get in the groove, you may find you want to devote more time. You may turn into a marathoner soon, but for now, start small and see how it feels to you.

Think about the space you have available and what your goals are for that space. Think, too, about the function of that space and whether what you're keeping really serves that function. Indeed, decide whether it serves you in your life and the things you want for yourself. Go through the Keep items now and do a more detailed sort through anything that needed it during your 15-minute blitz purge. Whatever fell into the mystery category (what *is* this anyway?) during that first purge needs to be decided on during this second pass. Make a determination; if you can't make a determination, get rid of it. Take your time, but don't labor over this second sort too much. Just do it!

Now let's move on to Step 3.

Step 3: Get Rid of It—Now!

Anything you put in the trash, recycling bin, or Pass On box needs to go. Take the trash and recycling out of the house to go in the next pickup. Put those books that need to go back to the library and the videos that should be returned to the video store into the car now. Designate a tote bag for these items that you'll use from now on. Bag up the items earmarked for charity and put them in the car, too. Pack up Grandma's china and give it to your daughter-in-law, *now*. Pack up and ship or haul items that need to be returned as soon as you can.

The important thing is to get it out of your space *pronto*. And no tiptoeing back out to the car under cover of night to take things back, either!

Visualize It

Take a moment to visualize the power of 15 short minutes. Mentally walk through your day, picturing all the times when you could easily set aside 15 minutes for your organizing tasks: 15 minutes first thing in the morning, before you fly out the door; the length of a coffee break; a fraction of your lunch hour; half a TV show; the last thing you do before you go to bed. Make a list of the small units of time you could use to declutter that are well suited to your schedule.

Step 4: Group Like Things Together

At this point, all you should have is your Keep box and your Fix box. After you've done your purge of stuff you don't need or want, and you've returned, passed on, or trashed the rest, what you have left is stuff that's worthwhile to have in your space (or it will be after you've fixed it!).

The next step is to sort your stuff so it's easy to find, easy to use, and easy to put back where it belongs. One way to do this is to store like things together. You may need to set up additional boxes or containers here, depending on how much you have for your fine sort. If you're working on a part of your office, for example, you may want to have boxes, slots, or sorters labeled Supplies, File, Read, Manuals, or whatever categories make the most sense to you. Look for ways to group similar things in one place, and make their final resting place a logical one.

Keep office supplies in one cabinet, container, or drawer. Having them scattered all over means you have to look several places every time you want a paper clip. Do the same thing with cleaning supplies, canned or packaged goods in the kitchen, tools, craft items, paper, or whatever comes up for the space you're working in. Grouping like things together makes them easier to find, and you'll know what you have so you don't end up buying more when you already have a bunch.

The containers you're using in this sort may not end up being the ones you use for final storage in the end, but they'll help you do your sort. Shoeboxes, empty plastic food containers, jars, and trays will work for now.

Simplewise _____

Don't ignore those mobile clutter catchers such as purses, backpacks, and briefcases. A self-contained space like one of these is just perfect for a 15-minute purge. You probably won't need boxes, just piles, using the same categories previously listed. Keep only the essentials, and purge the rest. Eventually, this habit will become part of your weekly routine.

Ways to group might vary. There can be general categories, such as Gift Wrapping Supplies, but they may need to be further broken down into Gift Cards, Bows, and Paper. Be flexible, too, because the best way to group something might be to gather all the things for one task in one container or location. Putting all the things you need to polish your shoes into one container, for example, might be the best way to group like things in this particular instance.

While you're working through this step, note whether the categories you're coming up with fit the room and the function of the room. If you're doing the junk drawer in the kitchen, and you're finding lots of hardware or office supplies, sort them together, but then put them away where they will be living permanently when you're done.

Step 5: Consolidate and Compress

Consolidating is a natural outgrowth of Step 4. When you start grouping like things together, space seems to appear from nowhere. Putting things that were once scattered in several places into one compact container means they take up less space.

There's a cost associated with being spread out all over the place. The cost is in cluttered, unusable space and wasted time. One way to reclaim it is by consolidating what you have. You might find out you have unnecessary duplicates, including broken items you've replaced. If you've replaced the broken item already, put it in the Pass On box and give it to Goodwill Industries or a similar charity that repairs broken items and sells them. Your broken item will give work to someone who needs it and money to a worthwhile organization. If you haven't gotten a new one, chances are that because it's been broken all this time, you don't really need it anyway. If you need the item and it's broken, put it in the Fix box and either fix it or send it out to be repaired this week. But set a time limit, and put the task on your to-do list (and calendar). Otherwise, if you don't think you'll get to it, throw it out and add purchasing a new one to your list!

If you find lots of duplicates as you consolidate, keep the best ones and pass along the others. If it's something you keep in quantity, such as paper clips or rubber bands, be honest about how many you'll use in 6 months or a year, and share the rest. Unless you're planning to open an office-supply outlet, stocking up beyond a reasonable point is probably a poor use of your space.

Here are some other areas where you can consolidate and compress:

Consolidate clothes by getting rid of duplicate, outdated, ill-fitting, and unused items. If it needs mending, start a mending container and either do it yourself or send it out for repairs this week. We tackle your clothes closet in Chapter 12, but this will be a good start.

 Simplewise _____

You can also apply the consolidation principle to tasks. Look for shopping areas where you can get a lot done without driving all over creation. Piggyback activities such as shopping and exercise. I park my car downtown and walk to the post office, bookstore, food specialty shops, and the bank. Not only do I get a lot done in a short period of time, I also get some needed exercise.

Use existing containers that are just taking up space, such as jars, drawer units, bins, boxes, sectional boxes and chests, dividers, baskets, caddies, racks, and shelves. If you're not using them, lose them! Look for ways to downsize storage wherever you can. If you have a box with only a few things stored in it, perhaps a smaller container will do.

If you're unstuffing something like a closet, remove all the empty hangers and shoe-boxes. The idea of consolidating and compressing is to fit the same items into far less space.

Look for other areas where you can "fold" or compress time. Cook double batches of a favorite dish at one time and freeze one. You only have to clean the kitchen once, but you've prepared two meals.

Step 6: Go for Quality, Not Quantity

Another way to sort and pare down is to keep only the best. This may not seem like a way to reduce the junk in your life, but it very well can be. If you have a tool that works well every time, chances are you won't need another for a long time. You may not think you can afford it, but if you examine the true cost of buying inferior merchandise, you may find it's actually cheaper in the long run to buy the very best.

Let's take the vacuum cleaner, for example. If you buy an inexpensive one or one that's poorly designed and can't handle many jobs, you'll need several other devices to do the work you need to do. One appliance, carefully chosen for its power, utility, and features, should cover almost any job you might encounter. Where do you think all those half-working appliances in your basement or garage came from, anyway? They probably ended up there because you bought something else that did the job better (or need to). Why not do it right the first time?

While you're sorting, if you come across something you just know doesn't work right or you avoid using because it's of inferior quality, toss it and get something that does work.

The same applies to the things you surround yourself with for decorations or beauty. Choose the best of what you have. A few truly beautiful things prominently displayed in a place of honor will give you much more pleasure than a lot of so-so knickknacks scattered everywhere.

Step 7: Think Multipurpose

Why have six tools when one can do the job? Marketing experts work long and hard to make you want to buy new products, but there's a good chance you already have something in the house that'll do the job just as well. Look for appliances and tools that can handle many jobs, not just one. They take up less space, cost less in the long run (although they might be expensive to buy initially), and cut down your maintenance time.

Your Pass On box should be full of items that do a single task that can be done just as well by something else you have on hand for another job. I mean, do you really need a hot dog cooker when you already have a grill or a skillet? Do you need a margarita maker when you already have a blender?

Step 8: Alphabetize

I never realized the power of this simple step but, believe me, it will help you sail through your day in ways you didn't know were possible. As you work through whatever spaces you've decided to apply these steps to, and after you group things together and consolidate them in containers or on shelves, consider whether putting items in alphabetic order is an appropriate next step. It's not worthwhile for everything, and I'm not encouraging obsessive-compulsive behavior, but you might be surprised how much easier it is to find things and put them back where they belong when they're in alphabetic order.

Alphabetizing saves me time every single day. I can quickly find a spice when it's on the rack in alphabetic order. Books, videos, you name it—you'll save oodles of time, all the time, if you just use the old A-to-Z method.

Step 9: Label It

Labeling is another powerful tool that makes life easier for you every day. Label everything you can get your hands on. That way you don't have to look through the wrong drawer because it's labeled. You don't need to wonder what's in that box because the contents are on the label outside.

Simplewise

I highly recommend getting a labeling machine. I'm not a great advocate of gadgets, but this is one I wouldn't be without. Look for one that allows you flexibility in label size, and be sure the type styles are easily readable from a distance. You'll be more likely to label things and they'll be uniform and quick to spot.

Now that you've purged and sorted and you're ready to put things away, be sure you can retrieve them again easily—and are more likely to put them back in the same place—by grouping similar things together in labeled containers.

Step 10: Put It Away

When you can't find things that are useful or valuable to you, it's like not having them at all. Just like they say in the real estate market—it's all about location, location, location!

In this step, you work with your Put Away/Return and Keep boxes. If you have a lot of stuff in your Put Away/Return box, it means that stuff that belongs somewhere else is finding its way into the wrong space. Remember, putting stuff away is a habit. Start today. When you take something out, put it back where you found it. It takes more effort to put something down where it doesn't belong and put it away later than it does to put it in its rightful place immediately. It's a matter of momentum. It's worth the extra steps. When you're about to let something land just anyplace, ask yourself, "Where does this belong?" and put it there *now*. If it doesn't have a place, that may be part of the problem. When things don't have a home, they end up floating around in your space, adding to the clutter.

Now grab your Keep box. What's in that box should meet three criteria:

- ♦ You use it regularly.

- ♦ You like it (a lot).

- ♦ It has a place in the space.

Next put away your Keep items. If you don't have a place for it yet—a real home or address—you'll need to plan for that. But instead of thinking "Where can I store this?" I want you to think "Where do I use this?" Be sure the place you store the item makes it easy to get to with the least amount of motion. Assess the furniture, built-in storage, and possible storage solutions for the space where you use the item, and put any ideas, purchases, or changes on your list in your organizing notebook.

Black Hole _____

Beware of saving things for garage sales. They either end up accumulating in the garage or find their way back into the house again! If you really have enough for a garage sale, put the ad in the newspaper right away! But honestly, when clutter is a serious problem, I advise getting it out of your space immediately. Bag it up and send it off to charity. Get a receipt, and you can recoup a little at tax time. The exhilaration of having it gone is contagious. Don't give yourself a second chance to hang on to all that junk!

Now grab your Put Away/Return box and put the stuff in it where it belongs. Get it out of the space you're trying to organize right now.

As you're putting things away, we're going to revisit the real estate idea again. I like to call the storage areas closest to where you spend the most time and engage in most of your activities *prime real estate.* It has the most value, so put the things you use most often there. By moving something to where the task is done, you activate it. Be ruthless about this space! Protect it from stuff that doesn't belong there. Be sure the stuff that lives there is stuff you really need and use or truly love to have around.

Secondary storage is for stuff you use, but not every day. This might be a shelf that's not so easy to get to or the back of a closet. Or maybe it's a shelf in the basement or in the garage.

The *deep freeze* is for rarely used items such as seasonal items or tax records. This would be storage that's the most difficult to retrieve stuff from. Be careful of this one, though. It can become a clutter trap all too easily. Remember, the key word to keep uppermost in your mind is *use.* If you only think you *might* use it, don't store it at all. Part with it now. Don't get in the habit of putting stuff in the deep freeze "just in case." Then it's just clutter.

Now that you've got the three basic categories of space in your mind, the next step is to put your valuable, usable stuff in the right places. When looking for places for things, here are some important principles to remember:

Get stuff in the general area where it will be most useful. Simple, right? But in the course of everyday living, often things end up getting stored in the darnedest places! If you found golf balls in the kitchen junk drawer, put them with the golf clubs. If the hairbrush somehow ended up in the living room, be sure it finds its way back to the bathroom.

Whenever possible, put things in containers with like things. Choose containers that are uniform and covered. Units with drawers are generally better than those that stack because stacked boxes have to be moved if you're to get to the ones on the bottom. Be sure labels will stick to them or you can devise some other way of denoting what's inside.

Simplewise

Whenever you've got stuff in your hands, recite, "Don't put it down. Put it away!" Make it your mantra. *Away* means "in its place." If it doesn't have a home, make one for it.

Be sure the location and containers you choose will keep your valuable stuff safe from The Destroyers. Who or what are The Destroyers? If you're a clutterer, you know them intimately, I'm sure. They're the natural enemies of stuff such as dust and dirt, moisture, sunlight, and pests. Pests include insects and vermin, and even domestic animals can do damage. Something valuable stored poorly can become junk overnight.

You've done your first unstuffing session! Now don't you feel better?

So Now What?

Take a break, reward yourself (tea, anyone?), survey your handiwork, and schedule some time with yourself to start again!

Repeating these steps again and again, starting with the spaces that bug you the most or cause you the most pain, is the way to reach your goals. The more times you repeat the process, the better you'll get at it!

Keep going with your purging, sorting, and putting away until you finish a room. Use the room-by-room detailed approach outlined in Part 4 to refine the process. This is not a once-and-for-all thing. You'll probably find yourself unstuffing different areas (sometimes the same ones) several times a year using these steps, but it gets easier as these skills become a part of you and you get in the unstuffing habit. When you experience the uncluttered space you've reclaimed, you'll be more likely to keep stuff from accumulating. Don't let more clutter in the door. Shopping is not a hobby. With each purchase you think of making, ask yourself first, "Do I have a *use* for it?" Then ask, "Do I have a *place* for it?" Put it back on the store shelf unless or until you do.

Remember, junk has costs other than money. It robs you of time, energy, peace of mind, and perhaps, ultimately, happiness. It tears you down and chips away at your self-esteem.

Visualize It
Close your eyes for a few minutes and imagine the area you've just subjected to the 10 steps. Remember what it looked like when you started? See it the way it is now? Imagine yourself and your family using that area. Imagine opening that newly cleared-out drawer or cabinet and having what you need at your fingertips, exactly where you put it. Congratulate yourself for a job well done. Bask. Luxuriate. Now open your eyes and look at this utterly uncluttered space anew. Well done!

A house filled with clutter is hard to keep clean. It isn't welcoming. We don't want to invite people over because it just takes too much effort to make it vaguely presentable for company. Why would you want to live in a house that's not good enough for company? Aren't you and your family as important as your company?

If all this stuff doesn't add to your life and help you accomplish the things you believe to be most important, *lose it!* It didn't get this way overnight, so it's going to take time to clear it out, but you've just learned the process to make that happen. Now plan the next area to give the 10-step treatment. Pick a time and write it down on your calendar. You're off and running, so don't stop now!

The Least You Need to Know

- ◆ You can learn basic principles to apply to all areas of organization.

- ◆ By applying doable steps to any area, large or small, you can get a head-start on putting it in order.

- ◆ An essential part of successful unstuffing is identifying the items you simply don't use and getting them out of your space right away.

- ◆ Smart storage habits, consolidation, and grouping like things together can help you streamline your space.

Chapter 6

Mastering the Paper Monster

In This Chapter

- ◆ Controlling the mountains of paper in your life
- ◆ Filing paper so you can find it
- ◆ Cutting down on junk mail, spam, and unwanted phone calls
- ◆ Using your computer to reduce piles of paper

I admit it. Paper is my nemesis. My husband's, too. We both have an addiction to information, and we love books. But we've made great strides in controlling our paper passion, and you can, too.

Remember way back when we were told that the computer age would bring about a paperless society? With the advent of word processing, databases, electronic spreadsheets, and e-mail, we wouldn't need to put things down on paper anymore. We'd do everything on our computer screens.

Well, the so-called paperless society is suffering from a paper glut! According to the Environmental Protection Agency, more than 100 million trees and 28 billion gallons of water are used each year just to produce catalogs and direct-mail sales pitches. State and local governments spend hundreds of millions of dollars disposing of junk mail that doesn't find its way into the recycling bin. Almost half of it—44 percent—is thrown in the trash, without ever being opened.

Even more alarming to me was this statistic: each of us will spend approximately 8 months of our lives just dealing with junk mail! Now if that doesn't put it into perspective, I don't know what will. Add to that all the office paper, personal correspondence, newspapers, magazines, and books, and, well, you get the picture.

We all have bills, correspondence, receipts, bank statements, investment reports, insurance and tax papers, legal papers, reading material, instructions and warranties, business cards, reminders and invitations, keepsakes and photos, recipes, and … the list goes on and on. It's whether or not we confront the paper in our lives, sort it, systematize it, store it, or dispose of it that makes the difference between being on top of the paper pileup or buried by it. And whatever we do with it, we also need to build into our paper handling systems a way to protect our identity and privacy in an age of burgeoning crime in these areas.

In this chapter, you take another giant leap toward unstuffing your life by getting a grip on all the paper that comes your way, handle (sometimes again and again), and save (usually far too much for far too long). I give you 10 simple ideas, plus some ways to implement them, that will keep those stacks of paper from piling up in the first place. Let's get to work and end your struggles with paper (and its cousin, digital "paper").

Idea 1: Stop It!

One way to spend less time and energy handling paper is by reducing the amount that comes into your household in the first place. You can cut junk mail in a big way, for example, by stopping it at the source.

One of the fastest and easiest ways to remove your name and address from the many mailing lists that are bought and sold between direct marketing companies (who generate the junk mail in the first place) is to send your name and address on a postcard to the Direct Marketing Association (DMA):

> **Direct Marketing Association**
> Mail Preference Service
> PO Box 643
> Carmel, NY 10512-0643
> www.dmachoice.org

The easiest way by far is to do it online. Just register, and you can manage which credit card offers, catalogs, magazine offers, and other solicitations such as AARP or various charities, medical research organizations, and insurance companies you'll receive. Even if you decide to use the old-fashioned method, there's lots of good information and answers to commonly asked questions on the website.

If you notice a reduction in some mail but continue to receive other unsolicited mailings, that may mean a particular company doesn't participate in DMA's program. In this case, you have to contact the company directly. You can easily compose a form letter and simply make copies, filling in the name of the company as needed.

Not sure what to say? Just download the Stop Junk Mail Kit from www.stopjunkmail. org and use its five easy steps. You'll also download a form to use when corresponding with companies.

Simplewise

In addition to its Stop Junk Mail Kit, the Stop Junk Mail Association (www.stopjunkmail. org) also offers several sample letters and templates you can download to have your name and address deleted from individual list marketing companies and lots of helpful links.

The DMA service links you to the credit bureaus' online opt-out service. This should handle the problem for the most part.

The law requires that credit card companies refrain from disclosing a customer's personal information for marketing purposes if the customer requests. If you'd rather call or write, start with your credit card company's toll-free customer service number or write to them directly and ask them to keep your name and information private.

You can also attack the problem from another angle, by contacting credit bureaus if for some reason the online opt-out link doesn't work for you. Depending on which state you live in, these bureaus may be required by law to delete your name from their marketing mailing lists if you request it. There are three major credit bureaus you should contact—Equifax, Experian, and TransUnion—and all three can be reached with the same toll-free number: 1-888-567-8688. You'll be calling the Opt-In Opt-Out Request Line, and by giving them your information when asked, you kill three birds with one stone.

To be removed from the Publishers Clearinghouse mailing list, simply call 1-800-645-9242.

To stop getting ValPak Coupon packs, call 1-800-237-6266 during regular business hours. You can also go online to www.valassis.com, click on Contact Us, and fill out the online form to stop a bunch of other flyers and various mailings. It'll only take a couple of minutes to do these two things and will save you hours over time, plus reduce your contribution to the landfill or energy required to recycle all that paper.

Another company you might want to contact to have your name deleted is National Demographics and Lifestyles, which collects buyer profiles and sells the information. Write to:

> **National Demographics and Lifestyles**
> List Order Department
> 1621 18th Street, Suite 300
> Denver, CO 80202

Staying away from buyer's clubs or special buying programs is another way to reduce the number of promotions and coupons sent to your home. If you want to join, be sure you ask that your information not be shared with any other company or program. Use these magic words from ecocycle.org:

> **Please do not rent, sell, or trade my name or address.**

Another source that companies use for mailings is the telephone book. Having an unlisted number, or having only your name and number (no address) in the book, is also a good way to cut down on the number of solicitations you receive.

According to www.obviously.com, which outlines a detailed step-by-step procedure for reducing all kinds of junk communications—mail, phone calls, and electronic solicitations—these steps also help:

◆ Whenever you donate money, order a product or service, or fill out a warranty card, write in large letters:

> **Please do not rent, sell, or trade my name or address.**

Most organizations will properly mark your name in their database.

◆ Product warranty cards are often used to collect information on your habits and income for the sole purpose of targeting direct mail. These cards are not required in most situations—avoid sending them.

◆ When ordering on the telephone, say, **"Please mark my account so my name is not traded or sold to other companies."**

◆ Contests where you fill in a little entry blank to win are almost always fishing expeditions for names. If you fill one out at a football game, for example, expect to get a catalog of football merchandise within a few months. Avoid these if you don't want the mail.

Black Hole

If you order or request a catalog from a mail-order company, ask that the company not pass on your information to anyone else. Otherwise, your mailbox will begin to fill up with unwanted junk mail all over again. Make it a habit to "just say no" right from the start. Whenever you get the chance, make a formal request that your name be kept private and that no mailings other than those you specifically request be sent.

Even the post office sells your name and address if you happen to be a business! Didn't know that, did you? When you move and fill out change-of-address cards, they sell your information to bulk mailers. Better to skip those cards entirely and contact your correspondents individually.

Here's the official United States Postal Service policy from its website:

> If you are a consumer, we use an opt-in standard. If you have provided personal information to register for or purchase a product or service, we will not use that information to contact you in the future about another product or service unless you have provided express consent.

> If you are a business, we use an opt-out standard. We assume you are interested in other products and services that could aid you in your business, and so we will provide information to you unless you tell us you do not want to receive it.

So you may just want to "opt out" unless you think you want to spend your time going through junk mail instead of running your business!

And what about those junk faxes? The ones I get are for Florida vacations or health insurance for the self-employed. The way to stop those is to contact the opt-out number at the bottom of the fax. It should be toll-free.

If that doesn't do it, you can file a complaint with the Federal Communications Commission using an online form found at support.fcc.gov/complaints.htm or e-mail the complaint to fccinfo@fcc.gov. You can also write or call:

Federal Communications Commission
Consumer and Governmental Affairs Bureau
Consumer Inquiries and Complaints Division
445 12th Street SW
Washington, DC 20554
1-888-225-5322

See www.fcc.gov/cgb/consumerfacts/unwantedfaxes.html for everything you wanted to know about fax marketing, legal and not.

This may all seem like a lot of effort, but it really doesn't take more than filling out a bunch of online forms and perhaps writing a simple form letter, addressing a few envelopes, and sticking them in the mail. The reduction in unsolicited mail, however, can be dramatic. It's one of those things that you take the time to do once and it will save you time over a period of years. In about 5 years or so, you may find you're starting to get more junk mail again and have to repeat the process, so just keep this book handy and you'll know right where to go to find the information you need to get it done.

Another important paper-reduction technique is to cancel subscriptions to publications you don't really read. Consider combining subscriptions with someone else who shares your interests, or using the library. I'd bet if you had to make a trip to the library to read publications, you'd see in a hurry which ones really mattered to you!

And finally, when you're out and about, get into the "no paper" habit! Free paper is everywhere, just for the taking. You can grab free flyers, brochures, coupons, and publications by the dozens on any given day. Don't! Unless it's something you're sure is really valuable to you, don't touch it, don't take it, and don't bring it home.

Idea 2: Decide Now

When paper in its many forms first comes through the door, you need to make a decision about it right away. Don't allow it to pile up. This is the first step in avoiding the Paper Acquisition Trap. Train yourself to have the Immediate Decision Habit, and I can show you how to set up a system to manage what's left so you'll know immediately where in the system it goes. Probably the single worst thing you can do when it comes to paper is to put off while deciding what to do with it. That's how the piles got there!

Why do we put off deciding about paper? Often it's a result of our anxiety about losing information we might need later or a false sense of security in believing we'll be able to back up everything we do. Well, if you're choking in paper, you won't be able to do either of these things.

Simplewise _____

Because warranty or product registration cards might generate more junk mail for you, consider not sending the card next time you buy something new. You're covered by the manufacturer's warranty whether or not you send it in. If you feel you must send in the card, fill in the bare minimum and indicate you do not want your information passed on. Use those magic words! Keep your receipt along with the product model and serial numbers for warranty and recall purposes.

The antidote for these feelings of insecurity is knowledge. When you know what you really need to keep and have a system for retrieving it quickly and easily, you can liberate yourself from paper pileups.

Sorting Into Three Categories

So how do you decide what to keep? The best way is to sort and do it right away. Make a deal with yourself that you'll implement this sorting procedure starting now with the new paper that comes into your life. That's the first step. Idea 3 will help you sort through the piles already crowding the surfaces and hidden spaces in your home or office. But for now, at least stop the avalanche!

Paper falls into three basic categories:

◆ Action (respond to or file)

◆ Throw Away/Recycle (challenge yourself to send as much as possible directly into the trash barrel or the recycling bin)

◆ Pass On (stuff that needs to be handed or sent to someone else)

An Action might be to read it, do something with it (such as pay a bill), or respond in some other way. It might go into a tickler file, you might need to transfer the date to your calendar and then throw the piece of paper out, or it may need to be filed for reference. Maybe you need to write a letter in response. Whatever the action is, those papers are the only ones you keep. The rest get trashed or given to someone else. But before you make the decision to keep it, ask yourself the following about those papers:

- ◆ Would I miss this? What would I do if it were gone?

- ◆ Can I get this somewhere else?

- ◆ Does having this piece of paper support the goals I've set for myself?

- ◆ Can I reduce or consolidate this?

- ◆ If I decide to keep this, how long will I need it?

- ◆ Where can I keep it so I can find it when I need it? (This last question leads into how you sort and file paper, which I discuss shortly.)

If you have items to pass on to others, decide to do it right away. You may need to set up folders for people you often need to hand things off to. If you need to mail it, gather your supplies (they'll soon be easy to find in your Life Management Center after you work through the next chapter!), and get them in the mailbox.

Don't Open It!

Get in the habit of sorting your mail near the trash barrel and recycling bin. Whatever can go directly into one or the other should go there unopened. This is the ultimate way to "decide now!" This is especially effective with expiration notices for magazines you've decided not to renew, contests, catalogs, and offers. Rip up or shred credit card offers without reading them. Hopefully, because you seriously implemented Idea 1, you're getting fewer and fewer of these. Some of your junk mail should definitely be shredded, and I highly recommend getting a good paper shredder. This is essential in today's world, where identity theft is a real concern.

Anything you're not sure is absolute junk should be opened. You don't want to throw away a check or a bill!

Simplewise _____

Sharing is a great way to reduce the paper in your life and even save money. I share my copies of various specialized magazines with friends in my area and so does my husband, and those friends then pass them on when they're done. Consult professional associates or people with the same interests who might be willing to do the same. Knowing that someone else is waiting for your magazines is also an incentive to get them read and out the door.

Idea 3: Purge, Sort, and Systematize

Idea 3 is the first step in handling what you already have in piles and files all around the house and what's left each day when you've applied Ideas 1 and 2.

Just as you did in Chapter 5, you're going to unstuff your paper piles. First you're going to use the quick-sort technique you've already learned.

Schedule some time on your calendar to apply the sorting process to the piles you have accumulated, a little at a time, choosing the piles that are most in your way. The places where paper is likely most troublesome might be the kitchen counters, the dining room table, your desk, and perhaps the coffee table in the family or living room. Pick the worst one first and work the system.

Set the kitchen timer for 15 minutes, or more if you have the time. Using the categories in Idea 2—Action, Throw Away/Recycle, and Pass On—take a pile and work through it in rapid fire, putting each piece of paper in the trash or the recycling bin, in a pile to Pass On to someone else, or in a third pile that requires you to take additional Action. Use boxes or baskets if you have a big pile.

The Action pile roughly corresponds with the Keep pile from Chapter 5. You want to make it as small as you possibly can in your initial sort, but you have a chance to reduce it even further when you do your final, more detailed sort, which happens next.

Dealing With What Remains

After you make the first set of decisions about what to act on, what to trash, and what to pass on, you need to decide what to do with what you have left.

This is the second sort. Here you need to map out a bit more time. Depending on the size of the pile you started with and what you ended up with that wasn't trash, you may want to set aside half an hour or more. But as before, don't spend more than an hour or so. You didn't get buried in paper overnight, and you're not going to dig out of the piles in a day either. Be realistic, be kind to yourself, and take small steps that add up to big results.

First take care of the Pass On pile. If the item needs to be mailed, get it ready to go. If you just need to give it to someone when you see him or her next, put it in a prominent place so you won't forget. Set up a folder for that person if you often have things to give him or her.

Next you need to refine the Action pile and set up systems to handle the paper that falls in that category from now on. These systems need to be flexible and maintainable. They need to be easy to use so you *will* maintain them, and they need to fit your personality and lifestyle. After a piece of paper enters your system, you need to be able to find it again quickly and easily.

Out of your Action pile, separate those things that need to be filed away for future reference. The backbone of your paper-handling system is your filing system. Depending on your needs, your filing system will be bare bones or it might be quite extensive. In our house, we run three businesses out of our home, so we have more file cabinets than the average household. But just like everyone else, our household filing system is the hub and center of it all.

Black Hole

Be careful about bulletin boards; they can become catchalls instead of organization tools. The items on them can all too easily become strangely invisible. If you must, use a bulletin board only to post material you refer to regularly, and make a vow not to clutter it with anything else.

In Chapter 7, I talk about setting up a central area where you manage your household affairs, the Life Management Center. If at all possible, this is where you want to locate your household files. If it's not convenient, get a rolling file cabinet and set them up there, so you can bring them wherever you make your phone calls and pay your bills as needed.

The contents of your household filing system may vary somewhat from your neighbor's, but generally it will follow the basic categories you use to file your taxes at the end of the year, along with some additional files for receipts and household records that may not be tax related.

I talk at length about household financial files in Chapter 15, but as you sort through the piles, you're going to see some patterns developing. At least begin setting up some preliminary files based on what you find. You want only the current files in this preliminary system. Anything you think you need to keep but goes back beyond the current year or previous tax year (if it's prior to April 15) should go in its own pile. Remember what I told you about prime real estate in Chapter 5? Only your current files should be there.

Set aside regular time for filing, preferably at least once a week, so you don't start another big pile called To File!

Personal Action Items

The next decision level concerns what's left of your Action pile. Decide now how you're going to sort all your personal paper—past, present, and future. The usual categories most people use are To Do, To Pay, To Read, and To File (we've already handled that one, but you'll still need a regular place to keep papers to be filed). Some people add a Pending category as well. That can become a catchall and a black hole for paper, however, so be careful. If you do decide to have a Pending or Holding file, be sure you're going to check it often; if not, skip it.

I have used a stacking basket system for my Action items. I like wire baskets because I can see what's in them. Be sure you label each one. You'll probably want one with four stacking baskets—one labeled To Do, one for bills labeled To Pay, one for items you need to Pass On, and one that's labeled To File. Because I handle bills for two other people for whom I act as caregiver, I have an extra category and separate out those bills. You may have a similar circumstance or may want to separate business bills from household ones. Adapt your system to your life. What's nice about these stacking baskets is you can add or subtract baskets based on what works best for you as you test these ideas for yourself.

The basket system worked for me for many years, but I have since moved to an out-of-sight system. If you're easily distracted or simply like to be greeted with a clear desk each time you sit down to work, you may want to "hide" your sorting system. If your desk has a file drawer or you have a filing cabinet or rolling cart nearby, you can use it for this purpose. Hanging folders with box bottoms allow you to corral a larger stack of papers in one folder. Label the folders the same way you would stacking baskets.

Reading material can go in another basket, or you may want to have something portable for magazines and newsletters, such as a wicker tote or basket that sits on the floor near your desk. This enables you to take your reading material to another location. In nicer weather, I like to catch up on my reading out in our screened-in porch, or I may decide to take the basket with me on a long car trip. Decide now that you'll only allow one basket of reading material to accumulate and no more. If you don't get to it before the next issue arrives, let it go. If this keeps happening, you need to take a serious look at the number of subscriptions you have and be realistic about how much time you can devote to keeping up.

We deal with the To File basket in even more detail when we get to the chapters on work (Chapter 9) and finances (Chapters 14 and 15). What you're working on here are some general systems to get you started. As you sort your Action items, ask these questions to help you get rid of still more paper *before* it finds its way into your system:

♦ Is there enough time to do this, or is it already too late?

♦ Do I really want to do this? Do I *have* to do this? Does this support the goals I've set for myself?

♦ Will doing this really make a difference for others or myself?

♦ What would happen if I never did this (worst-case scenario)? What would happen if I never read this? What would happen if I never filed or replied to this?

Visualize It

Playing the worst-case scenario game is an extremely useful tool when you're trying to break old habits that have held you back from getting clutter out of your life and getting organized: When you're stuck and can't make a decision about a piece of paper, use visualization. Close your eyes and imagine the very worst thing that could happen if the item were lost forever. Really see it happening. Could you call the bank and get a copy? Could you find it in the library or online? Would your lawyer, accountant, or financial planner have a copy? If you can see yourself solving the problem, maybe you don't need it after all.

Decide now to schedule a regular bill-paying day each week or at least twice a month. In our house, Friday is bill-paying and filing day. What's your day?

Next, put all the items you need to call about in a file folder marked Call. For now, put that by the phone and schedule a time to catch up on these. In the future, you'll be doing this each day at a designated time. Think about when might be a good time for you. Experts say the best time to return calls is the half hour before *their* lunch hour and the half hour before *their* quitting time. Keep this in mind when you set your calling times.

Now on to the To File pile. If you have paid bills in the pile, file them. If you don't have a filing system for paid bills, put aside some time to set one up. It took me all of one afternoon to set up my own files. I included both household and business and organized them according to the categories I use in my Quicken personal finance software. These are set up for tax purposes, so they make what used to be an end-of-the-year scramble a breeze.

Simplewise _____

If the thought of setting up a household filing system overwhelms you, help is available! You can purchase a prefabricated system—complete with preprinted labels, tabs, file folders, and even a portable file box or rolling cart—all for less than $100! You'll probably have to tweak it a bit, but at least it's a start. The EasyFile Home Filing System is available at www.easyfilesolutions.com or by calling 386-673-5574.

You may want to look at how your taxes were prepared for some of the categories and then include anything else you'd like to track or need to be able to put your hands on quickly. (I talk more about taxes in Chapter 15.) Adapt and adjust your system to your needs, and always remember you can change and improve it at any time.

Reading Material

So you threw out all those back issues like I told you to, right? If you didn't, be honest with yourself and get all that paper off the floor and off your back. Just let it go. Unread stuff is a burden. It's just that—stuff! Give them to your local library to sell if it has this service like mine does.

Now honestly evaluate the periodicals you subscribe to. Which ones do you look forward to reading when they come in? Which ones always seem to have at least one article you truly enjoy or that pertains to your work or lifestyle? And which ones do you just never seem to get to?

Cancel the last category. Do it now. You can always pick up a copy on the newsstand now and then or check out the table of contents the next time you're at the library. If you're not reading it, you don't need it in your space.

Now that you've pared down what arrives regularly in your mailbox, you need a system to keep up with the reading material you've decided you truly need or enjoy. If you can't stay on top of it, you have too much. You'll never get to it anyway, and when it's in huge piles, you won't want to.

A good rule is to have no more than two or three issues of any one publication at any one time. If it's a publication you need for reference, you need to provide a way to store it, and usually a year's worth is all you'll ever need. Photocopy the table of contents for each issue and keep those copies in a place where you can find them quickly and easily. That way you'll know what's in which issue without having to pull out each publication.

Beyond a year, the information contained in these publications usually becomes out-dated, and you can obtain back issues another way if you really need them. Some online magazine databases enable you to retrieve and print out articles for a small fee. If you're saving magazines with projects for hobbies, remove and store only the projects you really think you'll make, and trash or recycle the rest of the magazine.

Simplewise _____

> Why read when skimming will do? Much of what we put aside to read only needs a quick perusal for pertinent infor-mation. Skim with a highlighter in your hand to mark important infor-mation. If it's something you need to file, maybe you only need a small portion of the article. Keep a pair of scissors nearby.

Use the table of contents to save time. Why thumb through the whole magazine if only one article really pertains to your topic of interest? Besides, you'll miss all the ads (remember the Acquisition Trap?). If you don't have time to read it right away, tear it out and put it in your To Read basket and then trash or recycle the publication right away.

I make a habit of reading through the day's material most evenings after I've put away my work and while I listen to the TV news in the background. Those are two activities I can easily do simultaneously. If certain reading material requires more serious concentration, I might put it on my bedside table and read it before I go to bed or over my morning cup of coffee the next day. What system for your reading material would work best for you? If you commute daily to work, how about using that time to catch up on your reading? If you spend a lot of time waiting for appointments, maybe those can be some "found" moments for catching up on your reading.

Idea 4: Distinguish Between Short and Long Term

We all have paper we need to save for various reasons, but most of us end up hanging on to it much longer than we have to.

Find out from your tax preparer, financial adviser, and lawyer what documents you need to keep and for how long. I discuss this at length in Chapters 14 and 15, but you might want to start asking some of these questions now, because this is the quick-start part of your organization plan. Weigh the cost in storage space and time required for you to hold on to these documents against the costs involved in re-creating them in the event you might need them in the future. What is the likelihood you'll ever need them? How difficult would it be to obtain them again?

Remember, paper is the same as other stuff as far as storage is concerned. What you need at your fingertips should occupy prime real estate. That's the filing cabinet or cart you have in your daily living space. Those are your Working Files. Other paper that needs to be accessible but isn't used as often falls in the Reference Files category and occupies secondary storage. Last, you will have some paper that belongs in the deep freeze, of which there should be *very, very little*. These are called Archival Files. All I keep in the deep freeze is support material for books I've already completed and previous years' tax information. The rest is either active or essential, and those are in systems that are easy to access and regularly purged.

Your Working Files are what you need to function in your day-to-day life. I talk more about them in the next chapter, but basically, they're files for current projects and current financial information.

Reference Files contain information you need to refer to fairly often, but they're not part of your daily life. These files might include information on hobbies, career, housekeeping, your family history—whatever is currently in your life but not essential to the daily workings of your household. If you have room to keep both your Working Files and Reference Files in the same place, that's great. If not, your Reference Files should still be accessible.

The final part of your filing system is the Archival Files, and there should be practically nothing there. In our household, because I'm a writer, we probably have more in this category than most people. I need to keep support files for the books and articles I write. I weed them out, and they go into cardboard bankers boxes and get stored in the garage. As I mentioned earlier, the only other files for the deep freeze are past years' tax records and support material.

Visualize It

Imagine what would happen if everything you own were destroyed in a fire, flood, or other disaster. What would you need to pick up the pieces? How would you identify yourself? If you died, how easily could your survivors handle your estate and other affairs? Visualize what would happen. Then take a look at your files and records, and come up with a plan that would deal with these two circumstances. Consider off-site backup and who should know where things are (and what that person might need). I deal with this in more detail later on, but having this visualization will help get you started in the right direction now.

Be sure to purge your files regularly (every 3 to 6 months) using the guidelines your professional advisers give you. Mark the date on your calendar as an appointment with yourself. I like to key my purging with important seasonal events. I do one purge right after New Year's in preparation for preparing our tax returns. The second purge coincides with midyear cleaning. Figure out what works best for you. It's easy to forget and just allow these mounds of paper to accumulate, and your files can become clogged with useless paper, too.

Don't store what you don't need! Some people think organizing means fitting more stuff into less space. Organization is really having less stuff and creating space! And that goes for paper most of all.

Idea 5: File So You (and Others) Can Find It

There are many filing systems—some so complicated only the person who set them up can use them. But you want your filing system to be easy and simple, right?

Keep your system as streamlined as you can, make it alphabetic wherever possible, label everything clearly and boldly, and be sure it's easy for other people to use. It should be self-explanatory; someone besides you should be able to open a file drawer and "get it" right away. What if you're stranded in Bora Bora and need someone to get a copy of your birth certificate to you? It should be simple for anyone (even the house-sitter) to oblige if your files are set up correctly.

Simplewise

As you sort through your paper piles, you can help speed up the filing process later on by either highlighting a word or two in the document that refers to the filing category it best fits into or by writing that category on the top. This will get easier as your filing system is developed and you get used to using it regularly.

Here's a list of categories I think almost every household should have. I discuss several of them in more detail when we get into organizing your financial life later, but for now, consider setting up hanging folders for each of these categories right away. You want hanging folders, which you never remove from your file drawer, *and* regular file folders. Some people may disagree with this, and if space is really at a premium, you may not be able to do it this way. The reason I like this redundant system is that it practically maintains itself. When you take out the manila file folder, the hanging folder remains in its alphabetic spot. When you go to put the file folder back it's easy to see immediately where it goes. If a file folder is missing, that's easy to see, too!

Now for the categories:

- ◆ Auto (gasoline, loan information, repair records)
- ◆ Bank Statements

- Birth and Other Important Records (copies of birth, marriage, divorce, adoption, citizenship, death, and military records would go here; keep originals in a safe-deposit box)

- Budget

- Contributions/Charities

- Credit Cards

- Heating (fuel and service)

- Home Repairs, Improvements, and Equipment

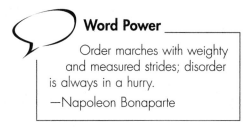

Word Power

Order marches with weighty and measured strides; disorder is always in a hurry.

—Napoleon Bonaparte

- Income Tax (current year and prior year's form as filed)

- Insurance (auto, homeowner's or renter's, health, business, life)

- Inventory (a copy of this should be kept in a safe-deposit box, along with supporting photos and/or video)

- Investments (stocks, bonds, pension, mutual funds, savings; you might want to break this out into separate sections if you have a lot of investments)

- Medical (divided by person; receipts; you might want to include dental or break that out into a separate folder)

- Safe-Deposit Box (information on the box itself, as well as copies of important documents kept there and an inventory of everything in the box)

Some other files you might have include the following:

- Legal (case information, including expenses)

- Pets (this could also be a subcategory of Medical)

- School (transcripts, registration information)

- Social Security

This is just the beginning. Have filing supplies handy and add to your system as needed. In the beginning, you'll probably have to set aside some time regularly as you apply Ideas 1, 2, and 3 to those paper piles all over the house!

Another important point: whatever categories you choose, be sure they'll make sense to you 6 months from now. Start with general categories and refine them later. Keep in mind that you may not be the only person who needs to be able to find something in your filing system. Choosing logical categories for your files that will help you find pieces of paper you need in the future is a key step in setting up an effective filing system.

Don't Forget Computer Records and Documents

Even if your computer records and documents aren't in hard-copy form, they may still be important pieces of information that need to be organized and probably backed up. Make printouts of documents that really belong in your files and would be hard for a person who's not computer-oriented to find.

A man we know died quite suddenly, and all his financial information was on his computer, which no one else in the family knew how to operate. It took months for his widow to learn that she had been well taken care of so she could stop worrying. If you do keep important records on computer, be sure someone else knows how to access them, or back up the critical ones with actual paper printouts that are clearly labeled and filed so anyone can find them.

Here again, file stuff on your computer or disks using filenames that make the information easy to retrieve in the future.

Paper with Deadlines

You already know where to put things such as permission slips, invitations with RSVPs, and anything else that has a deadline on it. It's an Action item and goes in the Action basket. But sometimes these pieces of paper need special handling. The systems you set up depend largely on the needs of your household and what kinds of things are most common for you. If you have kids in school and lots of papers and permission slips to sign, you might consider setting up a special box or basket just for those. Train the kids to deposit these items daily in the designated place so you can handle them by the following day.

If you do a lot of traveling for business, you may want a separate folder for travel documents. I have a Trips, Upcoming folder in the file drawer in the desk where I work, and everything relating to my travel plans goes in there. If you go to a lot of concerts or theater performances, set up a system for keeping track of these time-sensitive events. This may be a good use of that bulletin board for you. This wouldn't work for me. I once spent hours looking for tickets that had been pinned to the bulletin board and somehow became "invisible." But that's me!

To ensure these crucial pieces of paper don't disappear into your new filing system, make a note of the dates connected with them on your calendar in your planner/organizer. Also note where the documents connected with the event are stored. Eventually, when your system is refined and you have it committed to memory and habit, you may not need to take this extra step. But while you're making these initial baby steps to get organized, a redundant system such as this will help.

Idea 6: Keep It Where You Need It

If you use certain information that's on paper on a constant basis, put it where you need it. I keep a file near the kitchen for all my instructions for electric tools and appliances. The file is close to most of the appliances we use, which are in the kitchen, the laundry room, and the garage just off the kitchen. I have a separate one in my work area for all the office equipment and computer stuff I use there. It's clearly labeled, so if someone needs to run the equipment when I'm not around, he or she can quickly and easily find the information.

Keep phone message pads by the phone. Ditto with the family address and phone file and the phone book. You'll be making a User's Manual for your household in Chapter 7, which you will want to keep close at hand. Keep the TV, cable, or satellite guide by the TV. If you have places designated for these things, they're less likely to walk away. Just keep in mind the idea of prime real estate and the importance of location, and you'll find you can lay your hands on the important papers you need when you need them.

Simplewise

If you're most likely to read magazine articles while relaxing at night, soaking in the bathtub, or waiting for appointments, tear them out and keep them where you're most likely to read them and get rid of the rest of the publication. This is one way to help keep magazines from piling up. Ditch the clipped articles after you've read them.

Idea 7: Tailor Systems to Special Needs

Some activities involving paper require special handling. Perhaps you work at home, or maybe you work outside the home but handle the paperwork for your job at home. Some paper just doesn't quite fall into the usual categories; examples include greeting cards, recipes, photos, or your kids' school projects.

As you examine, purge, and sort the many kinds of paper in your home or workplace, these are the items you might not know what to do with. These types of paper may need special systems to handle them in a way that preserves them and makes them easy to get to.

I specifically tackle home office solutions, recipes, and photos in later chapters. You may want to skip ahead if you're really motivated, or for now you can simply start grouping items together in temporary containers until you reach those sections. Boxes from computer paper, stationery, or file folders work great for this. Shoeboxes work well for receipts and smaller pieces of paper.

But please *do* sort them, contain them, and label them. *Don't* just throw them in a jumbled paper pile again!

Idea 8: Use Computers to Cut Paper, Not Make More

You already know that computers haven't eliminated wasteful paper. Far from it! If you're a computer user, you know from experience how much paper it can generate. Luckily, computers can also reduce paper if we think before we print and remember the principles we've already learned in this chapter.

Think seriously before printing out something. It can become a bad habit. Before you click the print button, ask yourself the following:

◆ Can I work with this on-screen?

◆ Do I really need to save this? What are the chances I'll need to refer to it again? What's the worst-case scenario?

◆ Can I archive this on a disk rather than make a hard copy?

Visualize It
Put on your imagination cap, pick a room, and scan it for any paper items that fall into the "special" category. Can they be grouped together in categories? Can they be integrated into the filing system you set up earlier? If not, what storage or display format would make them most useful to you? Consider things such as photo boxes, albums, display cases, frames, magnetic strips or boards, and anything else that might be used for that purpose. Can you think of ways to reduce the quantities and keep only the most meaningful or useful?

A lot of information we used to get in print form is available and, actually, more useable in online form. For example, just this year I stopped several subscriptions and now use online newspapers and magazines to get most of my news. If there's something I want to save or have someone else read, I can print out only that item or e-mail it on to a colleague or friend, but I can be very selective. Sure, I'm generating some paper, but far less than I had with the paper subscription. Are there any areas where this might work for you?

Incidentally, things get lost on disks because of poor filing, just as they do in paper files. The same rules apply to both: purge often, label clearly, and only save what you really need.

Use e-mail to reduce the amount of paper coming into your mailbox. Don't feel compelled to print and save every message. Of course, one of the advantages of e-mail over, say, a telephone conversation is that you can make a hard copy of what was communicated for future reference. This proves especially handy for job-related information, directions, travel information, and the like. Again, ask yourself the important questions, and don't hang on to these printouts longer than you need to. Question whether you need to make them at all.

Simplewise

Be creative when thinking of ways to save space, even when it comes to sentimental things like photographs. Take a tip from a clever quilter who selectively reproduced the most meaningful images of her parents and transferred them using computer technology to a quilt for their fiftieth wedding anniversary. Included in the quilt's fabric were swatches from old dresses, tablecloths, and baby clothes. She chose the best, turned it into something special, and let go of the rest.

With online banking and investing becoming commonplace, much of what we used to do on paper can reliably be done online. Arrange for fixed monthly bills to be paid automatically, directly from your bank account. Use e-bills when available. Still other bills can be put on a credit card monthly so you pay only one bill rather than several. Many banking and other financial records can be archived electronically and printed out only in the event you really need them.

Idea 9: Put Paper in Its Place

Many of the same principles I gave you in Chapter 5 for dealing with stuff apply just as well to taking care of paper. Consolidate and compress. Put it on one sheet. Reduce it with a copier. This technique is especially effective with keepsakes—keep a part of something sentimental, not necessarily the whole thing. Keep the best pieces of artwork your child produced in kindergarten, not all of it. Ask him or her to choose a favorite or two. Choose just a few pictures that are representative of an event, not every out-of-focus shot. Consolidate keepsakes—put them in a scrapbook or album or make a memory wreath or collage.

You decide what paper to keep and set up the rules. That way paper doesn't rule your life. Put it in its place, and keep it there!

When you finish with Chapter 7 and you've set up a Life Management Center, you'll reduce your paper even further because you'll have a simple system for keeping important information in one place all the time. You'll stop putting notes on a zillion different snippets of paper, and you'll learn to have a single place to plan and keep track of details.

Idea 10: Create Mobile Paper Systems

As if the paper piles at home weren't enough, most of us have traveling paper problems, too! Let's see—how are your systems for handling paper between home and office working for you? What does the glove compartment in your car look like? If you travel for your job, how are your systems for handling travel documents and receipts working?

If these minisystems are a mess, they can become real bottlenecks in your efforts to maintain order at home and in the office. After you've got a basic household filing system in place, you'll want to tackle some of these "floating" paper piles before they begin to cause problems for you.

Get a portable file box for files that need to come home from work and go back again. Don't keep these in your briefcase, which should contain what you need for the most current activities.

A small accordion folder that has tabbed sections and fits in your glove compartment is a handy thing to have for documents such as your vehicle registration, insurance information, emergency road information, and directions or a local map.

Keep an envelope for receipts when traveling on business and label them with the trip/client/date and whatever else will help you later when you need to fill out an expense report or file them for the IRS. A little thought and organization upfront will save you time and effort later.

Set aside some time every day at home and at work to do your paperwork. Use small bits of time (remember the power of just 15 minutes and your timer!) to handle paper throughout the day. The amount of time you gain by getting control of paper is enormous. The joy of being able to put your hands on the information you need, when you need it, is real and will make your life better. It will serve you well every single day.

Right now, reward yourself for making important strides toward getting on top of your own personal paper mountain. If paper starts to build up again, stop it in its tracks! Now you know the way.

The Least You Need to Know

- ◆ Paper can support or hinder you in achieving your goals.

- ◆ You can't get organized until you get control of paper.

- ◆ You can reduce the amount of paper you handle every day by stopping it at its source.

- ◆ Set up systems to sort and file paper, keeping it under control and easy to retrieve when you need it.

- ◆ Some kinds of paper need special systems to be handled effectively.

- ◆ Applying the ideas in this chapter regularly helps ensure that you never again end up with a paper pileup.

Part  3

Systems for Getting Stuff Done

In Part 3, you develop systems for accomplishing goals in three crucial areas of daily life. First, you carve out a place at the helm of your ship, a hub or center from which to manage your life. You also create a portable system you can take with you wherever you go. Next, you zero in on your relationships—the people who matter most in your life. And lastly, you focus on your work life, both where you are and where you want to be.

When you finish this part, you'll see even more dramatic changes in your day-to-day life. So roll up your sleeves and let's get to work!

Creating a Life Management Center

In This Chapter

- ♦ Carving out an efficient place to run your life
- ♦ Schedules, lists, and time-management systems
- ♦ Commanding, delegating, and co-managing
- ♦ Taking it all with you

Many people have likened life to a ship on an ocean. And if life is a ship, then you're the captain, and somewhere on board there needs to be a bridge. The bridge of a ship is where the captain (supported by a highly trained and obedient crew) navigates and handles crises. This is Information Central, where all the various departments of the vessel report and get their orders.

To manage your life effectively, you need to create your very own bridge. You can call it whatever you like: the hub, the nucleus, the *Starship Enterprise*, the Office of the President—you may even want to put up a sign so there's no mistaking it. Around our house, we call it the Life Management Center.

Some Room of Your Own

Where you locate your Life Management Center is up to you. Just be sure it's in the center of your life's activity. If you share your space with other people, it needs to be a place accessible to everyone. This is where you funnel all the information about everyone's schedules, chores that need to be done, mail that needs to be sent, bills that have to be paid, and everything else that goes on in your household.

Good locations for your Life Management Center include a spot in the kitchen, your home office or desk, or perhaps a spot tucked somewhere near the main door of your home. What you want is to create a hub or launching pad where you can plan your life and keep track of it on a daily basis.

Ideally, your Life Management Center will be located near a phone, and it will have a good-size uncluttered working surface to write on with some wall space to hang a calendar and any other information that needs to be posted, such as lists of chores and maybe regular daily, weekly, and seasonal routines. If at all possible, your current files will be located there as well. If that's not feasible, consider having a rolling cart you can store elsewhere and bring to your center when you have filing to do or need to refer to something. If you have room for a shelf or bookcase nearby, that's a real plus.

Stocking Up: Basic Life Management Center Supplies

Certainly an effective manager or captain needs to have the right stuff to get the job done. Basic tools and supplies kept all in one place make it more pleasurable to do the job—and more likely you'll want to start it in the first place.

Here's a list of some basic supplies you'll probably want on hand:

- Paper/letterhead
- Business envelopes
- Mailing supplies, including overnight mail forms and supplies if you use those services
- Letter opener
- Stamps in denominations most often used
- Supply of greeting cards, note cards, and postcards
- Ruler

- Stapler

- Glue stick

- Pens and pencils

- Highlighter

- Tape

- Post-it notes

- Paper clips

- Scissors

- Calendar

- Bulletin board for posting schedules and other important information (and nothing else!)

- Dry erase board (optional)

Black Hole

Don't let yourself get distracted by gremlins who take your supplies without returning them. Tell the others in your household that things taken from your Life Management Center need to be returned and replenished. You might even want to consider the more extreme measure of putting a long string on your scissors, stapler, and tape dispenser so they're less likely to "walk away." Make it known that anyone caught with the captain's stuff will have to walk the plank!

If you use a computer for your planning and/or finances, you may want to locate it in your Life Management Center (or locate your Life Management Center where your computer is!). If you have a laptop computer, you can bring it into your Life Management Center whenever you need to, of course. There's always room to adapt your center to your particular situation.

You've Got Mail (or Other Messages)

If handled poorly, phone messages, mail, and written notes from members of the family can be a major source of frustration and even disaster. If members of the household are on different schedules, ensuring that these messages are passed on is imperative because you may not be able to tell them in person.

One thing you can do is set up a message board in a prominent place, either a dry erase board, or a separate bulletin board sectioned off with a space for each person. Or you could use a compartmentalized message organizer like many offices do and assign a slot for each individual. You can also make a board with several large clips, putting each person's name above his or her clip. There they can check for mail, notes, or phone messages whenever they get home. Experiment to find the solution that works for your household, and stick to it.

Whatever method you choose to take and receive messages, be sure everyone is aware of the setup, and give it time to be adopted and become a habit. The more permanent and prominent the message center you create, the more likely it will be a success. Magnets holding up messages on the refrigerator may work for some, but setting up a real communication center for a busy household is probably a better solution.

Simplewise

Lost phone messages can be a real problem. Consider getting some old-fashioned carbon phone message pads. As you write down the message, tear it off, and post it for the right person at your message center, or if it's for you, put it in your Action file (see Chapter 6). If a message gets misplaced or lost in the shuffle, there's always the carbon record to refer to. Put one by every phone in the house. They're inexpensive, and they work!

This Is the Captain Speaking!

One more aspect of setting up a Life Management Center is adapting it to your life situation. One essential question in any enterprise is "Who's in charge?" There can be many answers to this question, depending on your living arrangements. But one thing is for sure—when it comes to your own personal responsibilities and interests, the answer is *you*. You are always the one in charge, and the more you accept and believe that, the more empowered you'll be in your life.

But what about the spheres outside of your immediate influence? Let's take where you live, for instance. If you live alone, the answer's pretty obvious. You decide how everything is organized, what you eat, what color the sheets are, when the bills get paid, and what TV shows to watch. But many of us share our space with someone else. It could be a significant other, a roommate, or an entire family. Now the question of who's in charge becomes a little more complicated.

When you set up your Life Management Center, it's important to consider other people and examine the real dynamics in your household. In our house, for example, I'm pretty much the home manager. When my husband and I were first married, I tried different approaches, but it became obvious that he preferred letting me handle the organizing, scheduling, bill paying, and most other activities involving the running of the home. He liked to be consulted, and he was always willing to help, but he preferred to let me handle the details. At first I resisted the responsibility, but then I realized it gave me a lot of freedom to manage things the way I wanted. I also knew I was probably more skilled in these areas.

If you're "in command," so to speak, you'll hopefully be doing a lot of delegating as well. You may delegate to your partner and children, and you may also delegate to various outside contractors to handle certain jobs that no one in the household wants or has time to do.

In another living arrangement, two or more adults may be more equally involved in the home management process. It's very important here that you consult the other people in your life when you design these basic systems. First of all, they'll be more likely to use them if they've been part of the planning process. Also, they may have some good suggestions for making the system work better. You may need to divide areas of responsibility for it to work effectively.

Add children to the household, and you have yet another wrinkle (or two or three). Depending on the age of the child, you may do more delegating (and following up) or work more in partnership. You need to devise systems they can use as well. It may be as simple as positioning the message board at a lower level, or printing lists and labels rather than writing in cursive script. A system of incentives and rewards will likely become part of the mix as well. Be sure to include children, even young children, in the organizing process.

Schedules, Lists, and Time-Management Systems

As soon as you hear the word *schedule*, does the hair on the back of your neck stand up? Are you unpleasantly reminded of school, or punching a clock, and does every fiber of your being revolt? Try to keep an open mind. I promise we won't divide up every minute of your day. But having schedules and lists, and some kind of a system for keeping track of them, is essential for getting your life under control.

One tool you certainly need is a planner/organizer. Think of your planner/organizer as your mobile command center, an extension of the well-organized Life Management Center hub you've established at home. If you set it up right, it'll give you ultimate control, whether you're at work, traveling, or pushing a cart at the grocery store.

A planner/organizer eliminates all the little scraps of paper scattered all over your desk, in your pockets, on the kitchen table, and stuck to the visor in your car. You'll save hours of time you would have spent looking for little notes and appointment cards, or trying to re-create what happened last week. Everything will be at your fingertips in one central place.

You can buy many prefabricated systems online or at an office-supply store. Or you can set up a notebook of your own if you think that would work better for you. Just be sure it's a size that's portable and flexible, yet large enough to handle all the aspects of life management we're going to discuss.

Simplewise

The major personal planner companies are online, complete with product information and lots of helpful articles and tips—even workshops and webinars. Check out Day-Timer at www.daytimer.com, Day Runner at www.dayrunner.com, and FranklinCovey at www. franklincovey.com.

I've used several different planners over the years, and for a long time, I found one of the smaller versions of the Day-Timer to work best for me. It was large enough to give me room to write, yet small enough to fit in a purse or briefcase. But when I became a caregiver for both my elderly mother and developmentally disabled brother, and became increasingly involved in community and business activities, I found I needed a more detailed system, so I switched to one from FranklinCovey. Both companies and others have many options from which to choose. I recommend you pick the simplest system for your needs, but be open to making changes when and if you need to.

Some paper-based planners are supported by various computer software programs that not only complement the paper planner, but also can be used to print out the forms for them. You'll find contact information for the major companies that offer organizers in Appendix A, so you can check out more information on their products. You can also look for them at your favorite business products supply store. If you can see them close up and personal, by all means do! That's the best way to see which one most suits your personality and needs.

The cheapest alternative to buying a premade planning system is to use a small ringed binder with dividers. However, you may still like the convenience of having predesigned forms you can use however you want. Using the computer or by hand, make up something that works for you, and photocopy more when you need them.

Planner/Organizer Essentials

Whichever system you choose, be sure it has the following features:

♦ It's portable enough to take anywhere.

♦ It's refillable and expandable. (A spiral notebook won't do.)

♦ It's durable and can be kept secure.

- It has a calendar section with options for daily, weekly, monthly, and annual calendars.

- It has calendar pages with ample room for appointments, phone calls that need to be made, and a daily to-do list.

- It has a section that's divided alphabetically with tabbed dividers. (You'll see why in a minute.)

- It has address/phone pages separated by alphabetical tabbed dividers.

- It has a variety of other preprinted forms you can use if you need them, such as expenses, mileage, sources, and notes.

The two obvious uses for your planner are to keep track of appointments and schedules on your calendar and to record addresses and phone numbers. But this isn't using your system as a true life-management tool. Your planner is a way to constantly remind yourself of your mission, your goals, and your priorities. It's also a convenient way to chart your progress.

The alphabetically divided section (the one in addition to your address/phone section) is a sophisticated database. Say what? That's right! It may not need a computer chip or power supply, but it can function as your own personal databank. Think of it as an alphabetic filing cabinet for all the information you want to have at your fingertips, no matter where you are. This A-to-Z filing system can empower you to make decisions on the spot, save you time over and over again, keep you on track, and make managing projects a breeze.

Here's how to make it work for you: make a list of all the information you might need if you were suddenly stranded in a faraway city and forced to manage your life from a hotel room or on the road for the day. Your list might include these categories:

Black Hole

Try to avoid all the extra sleeves, pockets, checkbook organizers, and credit card holders that just add bulk to your planner. They not only can be a nuisance, they can also be costly—if you lose your planner, you lose all your important cards and checks, too.

- Banking (account numbers, phone numbers—don't write your PIN or credit card security numbers, though!)

- Computer information/settings/support phone numbers

- Family (clothing sizes, birth dates, blood types)

- Food (master shopping list, weekly menus, allergies)

- Home repairs (vendor and service tech phone numbers, account numbers, list of what was done and when)

- Investments (list of stocks with symbols, phone number of broker, account information, rollover dates, and so on)

- Legal (attorney's phone number and address)

- Medical (list of doctors and dentists, medical history, health insurance information)

- Auto (mechanic's phone number, auto club information, insurance information)

You get the idea. This list is just to get you started. Add your own data as you see the need. When you begin thinking of your planner this way, you'll come up with more and more categories. I have a personal wish list (filed in the *W* section) for things I'd like to have or accomplish, and I even have a rewards list to remind me of nice things I can do for myself when I've done a job well. That's filed under *R* for rewards, of course!

If you're working on a particular project, or serve in a leadership position in an organization, it's helpful to have the pertinent information all on one sheet. Then wherever you are, you can turn to your planner and handle whatever comes up. For instance, you can go down the list and call or e-mail each member to schedule a meeting. Use the blank sheets provided with your planner creatively, or adapt one of the preprinted forms. Have important preexisting lists, forms, corporate objectives, or records reduced at the copy shop, punch holes (try one of the miniature hole punchers just for this purpose), and file them in your databank.

Pretty soon you'll be relying on your planner/organizer as you would a partner. It adds confidence to know that wherever you are, you can quickly put your hands on all the important information you rely on in your everyday life. It helps you handle emergencies, and it enables you to take advantage of waiting time. Just grab your planner/organizer whenever you leave the house, and you're all set.

The power of any planning/organizing system is imparted only when you use it! If you think of it as your partner, you'll want to consult it on a regular basis. Use it for as many aspects of your life as possible. Make it user-friendly by setting it up in a way that works for you and pleases you. Use forms and paper fillers that encourage you to use them. A little color or graphics may add to your enjoyment.

For starters, you'll want to consult your planner/organizer first thing every morning and at the end of the day. As time goes on and you customize it more, making it more and more useful, you'll find yourself turning to it throughout the day.

As with any filing system, your planner/organizer needs regular maintenance. Go through it periodically (a great use for one of those 15-minute snippets of time I keep reminding you about!) and update or purge information. Put some planning time into your schedule—whatever works best for you. How about Sunday evenings before the workweek begins? Or Friday afternoons, when the week is drawing to a close? Maybe short periods every morning or evening will work best for you.

Simplewise _____

Whatever time you choose for updating your planner/organizer, be sure you add it to your routine. Use it to review your goals, track your progress, and reward yourself.

Electronic Planners/Organizers

Electronic devices for keeping track of calendars, contacts, appointments, and just about everything else have become commonplace. These minicomputers called personal digital assistants (PDAs) actually have more processing power than the ones that took the *Apollo* astronauts to the moon! Not only can these devices help organize your life, some have built-in music players, digital cameras, phones, and voice recorders. You can use them to make phone calls one minute and play poker the next. PDAs let you take notes, store phone numbers, manage to-do lists, keep track of your calendar, and much more.

In addition to PDAs, all the major mobile phone carriers offer "smart" phones. These are essentially a combination cell phone and PDA that can include e-mail and web surfing capability.

Depending on your lifestyle, how technology-oriented you are, and how much you actually have to keep track of, you may find a PDA or smart phone the perfect solution. They can be pricey, however, and complicated to use. For many of us, a paper-based system is all that's needed. In fact, it actually simplifies our lives more than an electronic device would. For others, the reverse is true. The power and convenience of a PDA or smart phone is worth the money and the time to learn how to use it wisely.

Until recently, I have been entirely paper-based for my planning, but about a year ago I bought a smart phone because of the additional responsibilities I have acquired. I use both! But remember, I've been working on refining my organization skills for years and have conquered many of my long-standing challenges. If you're really having a hard time keeping track of your life and you're not already very computer-oriented, starting with a paper-based system is probably the best way to go. You can always move to a PDA or smart phone at a later date. The learning curve with a new electronic device can be steep and could get you completely off your path toward organizing your life!

But if you're seriously thinking of purchasing a PDA or smart phone as a life-management tool and you're certain it's the way to go, do your research. Compare the different models close up and personal. Be sure you have the different choices demonstrated for you and then try them out yourself. Consider functionality, operating system, display, memory, battery options, input options, size, connection options, expandability, and cost.

Simplewise _____

If you're thinking of going digital and purchasing a PDA or smart phone, research your options and fully understand the advantages and disadvantages versus a paper-based system. Several good discussions online cover this very topic. Just put "paper planner versus PDA" into your search engine and you'll find plenty of food for thought to help you make your decision.

The Master of All Lists

One of the most important lists you'll keep in your planner/organizer is what I call the Master To-Do List. You actually started it in your organizing notebook in Chapter 5. This is a type of to-do list, but it knows no priorities and no boundaries. This is where you dump anything that comes up requiring action during the day—tasks you either want to do or feel you need to do that suddenly pop into your head in no particular order. Don't worry about when you'll get to it, or whether it's urgent or not—just get it down on paper. You consult this list when you're actually doing your planning and scheduling. At that time, you set priorities and decide which activities most support you in meeting the goals you set for yourself in Part 1 of this book. This list is simply a repository for all your possible actions.

Your Master To-Do List contains everything from making important business calls to cleaning the gutters, from fixing your daughter's bike to making a doctor's appointment. The purpose of the Master List is to catch the fleeting thoughts you have that remind you of your responsibilities and reveal your motivations and desires. Your brain is working on many different levels, even when you're occupied with something else. It's a powerful computer and is often triggered by associations or visual input in an unpredictable way. The beauty of the Master List is that you capture the thought *and* get it off your mind by putting it in writing.

Some things stay on my Master List a long time. Some things never get done because I later decide they're not important. That's the key word—*decide*. The Master List lets me decide what to do about each item, and that puts me in control.

The Calendar

The rest of your planner/organizer should contain a calendar section. I prefer a form that allows a full page for 1 day. Most planner companies also have a weekly form that lays out an entire week on two opposing pages and various other options. What-

ever your style, you need to have enough room to put down your appointments and things to do. I divide each day into three sections: Appointments, To Do, and Phone Calls. Because I generally make all my phone calls at one particular time of the day, I like having a list of people to call in one place. Record all appointments in your planner, rather than trying to rely on your memory.

Black Hole

Try not to make notes on your calendar pages. For this purpose, use a separate pad or note sheets. This will make your calendar more useful for later reference and keep it easy to use at a glance.

Whichever method you choose, keep your calendar section clean and functional. You never know when you may need it to re-create the past. The one and only time I was audited by the IRS, I brought in my bank records and my planner/organizer. After just a few minutes, the auditor could see I had a record of every trip, every business lunch, and every appointment. He told me to go home, and that I kept very good records. Most of it I could hold in one hand!

Backing Up Is Smart to Do!

Be sure you have a backup for all the essential information you keep in your planner/organizer. Just as you would need to recover from a disaster that destroyed your records at home or at work or in a computer crash, you'd likewise need to re-create the important information in your planner/organizer if it were lost or stolen.

One simple way to back up is to keep a file folder with photocopies of the important information in your planner. For me, these include the telephone/address section (updated periodically to include new additions), specialized phone lists, family information, and a few information lists that I could re-create, but only with some serious time and effort.

If you're working from a computer program and printing out your pages from there or using a PDA or smart phone with computer interface, you can easily create an automatic backup, which is one of the advantages of this arrangement. My only caution here is that you could end up using two systems but fail to have all the information on both. If you're not diligent about transferring information back and forth, it could cause confusion and missed appointments. You need to be sure information is shared between both systems or devices on a daily basis.

A User Manual for Your Life

Just about everything you own has a user manual or instruction book to go with it. How about your life? Well, if not, that's the next project I'm going to ask you to tackle.

Call it your user manual, household management book, control journal, or captain's log—whatever you call it, the binder you're going to create will be an invaluable tool not only for you, but for everyone in your family and anyone who helps you take care of your home.

Get yourself a three-ring binder, some tab dividers, and some plastic sheet protectors. Choose the size binder that suits the size of your family and the amount of information you think you'll have to keep in it. This book will provide you with all the information you, your family, and anyone stepping in to take care of your household might need to refer to. That goes for day-to-day information as well as instructions on what to do in an emergency. This book will become a repository for critical information about your family and home.

Your planner/organizer is for you. Your family user manual is for everyone else. Don't worry about putting this together all at one time. Just get started, and as things come up, you'll begin adding them to your binder. Having the information in your computer makes it easy to revise the various information sheets and print out a fresh copy as needed. Here are some of the categories you'll want to create:

♦ Emergency phone numbers—include cell phone numbers, doctor, veterinarian, hospital, poison control center (add a reminder to call 911 first)

♦ General household numbers—utilities (gas, water, electricity), schools, relatives, plumber, electrician, carpenter, etc.

♦ Security alarm system instructions and information

♦ Pet instructions—who's who, food, walks, litter box, idiosyncrasies, house rules (on the couch or off? outside cat or not?)

♦ House rules for kids—bedtimes, mealtimes, school/homework, TV

♦ Important things to know—turn-offs for water, gas, hot water, electricity; that the furnace makes a weird noise when it turns on and off!

♦ List of important documents (birth and marriage certificates, passports, etc.) and where they can be found (should be a secure place like a safe or safe-deposit box)

♦ Instructions on what to do if you become incapacitated or die—who to call first, where the will is located, the names and phone numbers of your estate attorney and financial adviser

Simplewise _____

Want to get a leg up on putting your family user manual together? At least one company has thought of everything for you. The Family Facts Family Life Organizer (www.family-facts. com) has all kinds of predesigned forms you can use to create one tailored to your needs. It also has a simple paper-based planning system that might be right for you!

You know your life better than anyone. Ask yourself, "What would someone need to know if they had to walk in and take over for me?" Label this boldly and keep it in your Life Management Center. Every family member should know where it is and what's in it. You may want to have an abbreviated version for when the baby-sitter, house-sitter, or pet-sitter comes; put it out for them and explain what's in there. The kids will probably have ideas to add.

Personal Management for Road Warriors

If you're one of those people who spend a lot of time on the road, your Life Management Center will most likely need to be a mobile one. The principles are still the same, however, and you simply need to have a scaled-down system for handling the same tasks.

If you receive a lot of phone calls when you're on the go, you need a way of taking down messages so you don't lose them. If I'm traveling, I prefer to keep everything in one place, including phone messages, so I keep them in my personal planner. That way, there are no little pieces of paper to lose.

You'll also need some sort of portable filing system to keep track of important receipts and papers generated during the day. These could include personal and household items as well as those related to work. Setting up labeled folders in one of those portable plastic file boxes is a workable solution. Instead of having receipts in your pockets or flying all over the car, you'll deposit them in their folders—one for business, one for personal. Of course, you can organize this in whatever way most suits your particular situation, but you get the idea.

If you use a PDA or smart phone and/or a laptop, these can contain a digital version of your Life Management Center. Much of your information can be kept electronically, including personal files, so you can manage both your work and personal life on the go right from your computer. If you're using personal organizing software, this may be the place to keep it, rather than on your desktop at home.

Just be sure whatever option you choose (laptop, PDA, desktop, or paper), you use it consistently and don't have partial information in a variety of different locations. Instead of making life less complicated, this fragmented or duplicated approach can really foul you up. If one system doesn't seem to be working, try another, but commit to one at a time and use it fully and consistently. Simpler is usually better.

You'll also want to be sure your laptop and other electronic devices are secure so if they're lost or stolen others don't have access to your personal information. Always use the security features on these devices and require a password to use them.

Make It So!

Now that you've got control of your ship, you can explore any uncharted territory with confidence. You now have one place to handle your finances, plan the week's menus, check on the kid's soccer schedule, or plot the overthrow of your company's competitors. With your Life Management Center and its satellite, your planner/organizer, you're ready for any mission. And with your family user manual safe at home, anyone can keep the home fires burning and handle just about any emergency in your absence.

The Least You Need to Know

- ◆ Setting up a central place for managing your affairs gives you control and saves you time.

- ◆ Having basic supplies on hand helps your Life Management Center operate smoothly.

- ◆ When setting up your Life Management Center, be sure to take into account your personal living situation.

- ◆ Keeping a personal planner/organizer will make you more effective at home, at work, and on the road.

- ◆ Your family user manual will make it easy for you; your family; and anyone taking care of your house, children, or pets to help keep your life running smoothly, even in an emergency.

Chapter 8

People Who Need People: Interpersonal Systems

In This Chapter

- ◆ Priority one: taking care of yourself
- ◆ Nurturing relationships as part of your organization plan
- ◆ Setting people priorities
- ◆ Keeping track of important dates and events
- ◆ Using organizational tools to have more fun with the people you love

I've spent a lot of time so far talking about organizing *things*. But besides getting control of your possessions, an important aspect of organization that most experts overlook is getting control of your relationships. What do I mean by *control?* I'm talking about establishing successful, rewarding relationships with the people you value most in your life through planning, scheduling, goal-setting, and plain old-fashioned organizing. You didn't think organizing your life could help you with your relationships? Think again!

Who's Looking Out for You?

The first person you need to provide for in your overall organizing program is *you*. The very fact that you're reading this book and taking steps to carve some order out of chaos shows you care about yourself and are trying to make your life better. Let's begin, then, with the premise that you're no good to yourself or anyone else—family, friends, co-workers, *anyone*—unless you're taking care of business with the most important person in your life: you.

Maybe you have trouble thinking of yourself as number one, but you are. You are, and you have to be. Your goals regarding health, mental attitudes, physical appearance, and spiritual well-being all need to be essential parts of any organization plan.

> **Word Power**
>
> Friendship with oneself is all-important, because without it one cannot be friends with anyone else in the world.
>
> —Eleanor Roosevelt

It's also true that people who have chronic problems with clutter and disorganization are also likely to have self-esteem issues. So it follows that the more you learn to love and care for yourself, the smoother your organizing journey will be.

In any discussion about planning and organizing to include the people in your life, it is extremely important to get you thinking about yourself and your own well-being as you engage in the organization process.

One of the side benefits of making the commitment to get organized may well be improving your own health! Let's face it—a chaotic life is a stressful life. By committing to unstuffing and streamlining your life, you are committing to a healthier lifestyle from day one.

Now that you've got a serious personal planner thing going (paper, electronic, or both), you can set health and fitness goals and schedule them into your plan. And hey, soon you'll be unstuffing the whole house, so that exercise equipment you can't get to or the treadmill you're currently using as a substitute for an organized closet will have more of a chance of actually getting used. You'll have time soon for those daily walks with the dog you keep promising yourself (and her). And just a few chapters from now, you'll be organizing your kitchen and setting up food plans to compliment your health and fitness goals. Next you'll create an uncluttered and serene bedroom that will contribute to a peaceful night's sleep. You'll see! Loving yourself and getting organized are two sides of the same coin.

Unstuff Your Relationships

Just as your home or office can be full of stuff that falls into the "junk" category (useless things that only get in your way), your social and emotional life may be filled with junk relationships. This can be a hard thing to face honestly. None of us like to discard people, and we don't want to be discarded. But if we haven't been steering our own ship well in other areas of life, it's likely that our relationships may be foundering on rough seas, too.

There's no polite way to say it—you need to get the people who don't support your goals and share a positive outlook out of your life. You need to learn how to say no to these people and concentrate your time and energy on those people who add substance and sustenance to your life. Most of all, you need to build your life around positive people who will be an asset, not a liability, to the process you've begun with this book.

Relationships, like stuff, tend to fall into three categories. First there are the people who deserve to occupy *prime emotional real estate*. They're the closest to you and often the ones you're most likely to take for granted or ignore. Sometimes they're not as demanding as people who are actually less important to you.

Then there are *secondary* people. You like them and care about them, but they're not fundamental to your existence or your happiness. They're not at the core of your life. This probably includes people you encounter at work, in your community, at your place of worship, or while pursuing your various interests. You enjoy their company, and they play an important part in these particular spheres of your life, but if you were to lose contact with them through a move or other change, you might not see them regularly, or you might lose track of them altogether.

Visualize It

Close your eyes and clear your mind. Visualize the people you spent time with this past week. If necessary, write down a list before you begin this visualization. Put the face of each person in front of you, one at a time. Note how you feel when you visualize that person. Recall what the time spent together was like. Was it rewarding? Do you eagerly await seeing that person again? Is this a person you've identified as one of the key people in your life (see "Creating a Quality Circle," later in this chapter)? How much time did you spend with the ones you love and enjoy most?

Last are the people who are better put in the *deep freeze*. I know that sounds harsh, but I think you know what I'm talking about. It's essential that you have an honest talk with yourself about the people you devote time and energy to who might fall into this category. Do some people you spend time with add nothing to your life? Or do they, in fact, actually suck the vital energy out of it?

I look at it this way: the people who are most important to me are held in the highest esteem in my life. I give them priority over all others. What's left goes to the next level of relationships, and I simply don't have a place in my life for the third kind.

Take a People Inventory

At the beginning of this book, I spent some time talking about your personal challenges and your mission in life. This was a broad-stroke process to help you identify what's important and what you really want. Now I'm asking you to take a similar inventory of your relationships and implement some incremental changes to make them better and stronger than ever before. The goal of this book is not just to help you be an organized person. Plenty of sharply dressed people with tidy offices and showplace houses have relationships falling apart. I want you to have it *all*, and the only way for you to do that is to include it *all* in your Life Plan.

Simplewise _____

When you de-junk your relationships, you have more time to nurture ones with the potential to be more rewarding. With more frequent visits, phone calls, e-mails, or letters, could you grow closer with certain loving and fun relatives and friends who have gotten pushed into the background? You might be surprised what happens when you make the effort!

Take a look back at the past week. Who did you spend time with? How much time? Write down the names and, next to them, the approximate time spent with each. Use the visualization exercise I've given you to help you accomplish this. Now look at your schedule for this week. Who are you planning to see? Add these people to your list if they're not already there. Next make a separate list of the people who are most important to you. Your spouse, partner, or person you're dating? Your children? Your parents? Siblings? Extended family? Friends? Co-workers? List them in the order of their importance. How does what you're actually doing stack up against what you say is most important to you?

Now that you've taken your People Inventory, the next step is to decide what results you want with the people who mean the most to you. To get you started, try asking these questions about the key people you've identified. Again I suggest you write down your answers so you can get a clear overall picture. For each person, ask the following:

- ◆ What's the current state of our relationship?

- ◆ Do we communicate often enough?

- ◆ What are some of the areas between us that could be improved?

- ◆ What would I have to do to make those improvements?

- ◆ How would improving that relationship make me feel?

- ◆ What is one small thing I could do today to contribute to making that happen?

- ◆ How can I use my current organization plan to improve my relationships with this person?

- ◆ Is there a phone call, e-mail, or visit I need to make? A letter or card I really need to send?

Maybe you need to schedule a night out with your spouse. Many people have a regular weekly "date night." Maybe you could improve the interaction between you and a partner or your kids by streamlining some of the daily chores and working together on the process. I bet if you start today to focus regularly on your people priorities and include them in your daily and weekly planning sessions, you'll see some immediate results.

Creating a Quality Circle

In the 1970s, an idea was introduced to American management from Japan that many people believe helps improve productivity and quality, especially in manufacturing. The concept was called *quality circles*, and it has helped build strong project teams and strengthen communications. I'd like to suggest applying a modified version of this concept to your relationships.

Somewhere I read that we can't have quality relationships with more than 10 people at one time. I'm not sure I can even manage 10! That's not to say we can't know and interact with more, but we can only give of ourselves to 10 people or fewer in a deep, intimate way.

Let's look again at your list of the most important people in your life. How many people are on it? Are you certain these are the people who are vital to your happiness, who truly mean the most to you? Are they at the core of your life? Do you hold a similar place in their lives? If not, pare down your list to those relationships that are important for your happiness. I bet when you're finished, you'll have 10 people or fewer by default.

Think of this as your own personal Quality Circle, and nurture it every day. Hold these people in the highest esteem, and give them the best you have to offer. Organize your life around them. They form your support system in difficult times and are the ones you celebrate with in joyful times. Being committed to their happiness and well-being will help ensure yours.

You Remembered!

Just by focusing more on the people you care about and eliminating unrewarding relationships, you'll find it easier to remember and keep track of important events such as birthdays, anniversaries, school plays, or whatever. But if you tend to be forgetful or remember too late to make the occasion as special as you'd like, I have a foolproof method for always being on top of remembering these milestones.

What makes it foolproof is that it actually involves several systems, not just one. It's what in computer jargon is called *redundancy*. Most of the time, organizing involves eliminating duplication, but in this instance, duplication works in your favor.

Here's how I do it: in my personal planner, I keep an events calendar. It's really just a list of regular events that occur each year pretty much at the same time. Toward the end of any given year, I use my events calendar to fill in important dates for the coming year on my daily calendar pages. I put the actual date on the calendar *and* an early reminder 10 days before. I *also* put these dates on the communal family wall calendar for the year, so I can help my husband keep track.

I also have a calendar program on my laptop. My choice is Google calendar (www.google.com) because I can also share it with the key people in my life. Any annually recurring events such as birthdays and anniversaries need only be entered once, and the program keeps them perpetually year after year. I set the program to sound an alarm to remind me, too. Most PDAs and smart phones have similar features with the added redundancy of a backup to your computer. I can synch Google calendar with my smart phone easily. The 10-day lead time allows enough time to order a gift or send a card, and the second reminder the day of the event gives you nudges to call and wish your favorite aunt a happy birthday, too.

If you're strictly using a paper system, one way to create redundancy is to put all these events on both your family wall calendar and your personal planner. Remember to build in the 10-day cushion so you have time to get a gift or send a card by noting that on the calendar as well.

Simplewise

Several e-mail reminder services will send you an e-mail before an important date or to remind you of your goals. Check out the one at www.personalreminderservice.com. It's pretty complete and easy to use. Another popular one is www.memotome.com. If you don't use a computer that often or you need even more of a nudge, consider a telephone reminder service. My Big Dates (www.bigdates.com) will text your cell phone with the reminders you program into your account on their website. And it's free.

Another good idea is to keep a list in your planner/organizer (under *G* for "Gifts") of outings, books, or gifts you hear people say they'd like—their personal "wish list" kept by you. If you come across something in a magazine or on TV you think they might like, jot down the information and transfer it to this list. You could also have this in a file folder if that's more convenient for you, but I find that having it with me in my planner/organizer allows me to act on it whenever the opportunity arises. If I'm in a store, for example, and I have some time to browse, I refer to my list so I have my giftees in mind. At the beginning of the year, I review that list and put out feelers to see whether these things are still appealing to my giftee. If not, I cross it out; if so, I decide whether I need to do some advance planning and build that in to my calendar.

When a new year begins, set aside some time to review special events coming up unique to that year. Note, especially, landmark events such as twenty-fifth or fiftieth wedding anniversaries, decade birthdays, baby's first Christmas, confirmations, bar mitzvahs, and similar once-in-a-lifetime events. This gives you even more time than the usual 10 days to plan something really special. Draw up a plan and schedule various tasks into your calendar.

For example, one year for a special Father's Day, I decided I wanted to do something really different for my husband. I investigated a Jeep tour I'd read about. He's a Western history buff, and the tour involved traveling over some rough road to an old mining town and following a historic Arizona stagecoach route. I found out I needed to book at least a month in advance and had to have a minimum of four people to go on the tour. I had time to invite one of our favorite couples and make it a total surprise. This took some advance planning and organization, but because of my system, I was able to pull it all off without a hitch and in plenty of time. No telling what might happen next year!

Something else that will save you time and keep the pressure off is to buy greeting cards in advance. You can keep them in a box with dividers especially for that purpose. Because you have your personal planner with you, you'll know which events are coming up and who you need to have cards for. If you do buy cards in advance, be sure you have a place to keep them where they won't get soiled or wrinkled and where they're easy to find any time. You might organize them by month and put a sticky note on ones you have specifically earmarked for certain individuals. Then when you reach your 10-day reminder, you'll just go into your box and grab the card you planned for in advance. Don't just buy for specific occasions—have a few extra for those unplanned-for times when a get well, birthday, or thinking of you card would come in handy.

Letters! We Get Letters!

Do people really write letters anymore? Well, *I* do! Granted, I write far fewer letters than I used to, with e-mail being so handy, but there's just something special about a handwritten note, and it's important to create some time for it in my life. When you simplify and organize your life, you have time and energy for some of the social graces that make daily living kinder and gentler.

Simplewise

One way to encourage personal letter writing and make it quick and easy is to have all your supplies—stationery, stamps, return address labels or rubber stamp, stickers, and pens—in a box or basket you can take with you anywhere.

Sometimes I write because I have to clear up a question on a bill or change an address on an account or for similar reasons. This generally falls into the category of business correspondence, and I discuss that in Chapter 9. But on some occasions, a personal note, postcard, or letter is appropriate.

Be creative in thinking of ways to keep up with your correspondence. Sometimes I sit out in the hammock and jot off a short postcard message to a friend with a quote or a thought to let her know I'm thinking of her. You might write letters for an hour or so in bed, just before drifting off to sleep. Or you can bring your basket of stationery supplies and write while others might be watching a TV program you're not all that interested in. Remember those small 15-minute gems of time I mentioned earlier in this book? When you have your letter-writing supplies handy, it's easy to make use of those 15 minutes to stay in touch with your loved ones.

Lots of systems are available for keeping addresses and phone numbers, from the most old-fashioned (a handwritten address book or card file) to the most newfangled (contact software or on your PDA). You decide what's best for you, but be sure your system is portable and easy to update.

Social Media and Other Newfangled Things

So what about social media? Should you join Facebook, MySpace, LinkedIn, or Twitter? There's no clear answer here. But I'd like to offer a word of caution: if you've got your act together, these new avenues of communication can be fun and creative, and they can actually save time if they're used wisely. But if you're a baby on the road to organizing your life, I can tell you from experience that these distractions can easily be a time sink and an aid to procrastination of the highest order!

The good thing about social media is it lets you share the same things with a lot of people at one time. Some of these people are the ones in your Quality Circle, but a lot of them are not. You'll get invitations to be friends from people you barely know. And it's difficult to say no. After all, they consider you a friend!

My advice to you, much the same as my advice about electronic planning devices, is to wait until you've got your act together. Then you can better decide if this is a worthwhile use of your time. Your goal was to organize your way out of the stress and chaos you're in, not get sidetracked with new things that have a significant learning curve and may not serve you at all in your efforts to streamline, destress, and simplify.

Escalating E-Mail: How to Keep Up

With the rapid increase in the number of people who have computers at home and in the office, the use of e-mail has skyrocketed. Depending on how you use and manage it, e-mail can make a big difference in how well you stay in contact with the people in your life who really matter, but who may not be close at hand. If mishandled, however, e-mail can become just one more cluttered mess choking your computer and stealing your time.

The Benefits of E-Mail

I find e-mail indispensable for both personal and business correspondence. Benefits of e-mail include the following:

- It's convenient. You can communicate at 4 o'clock in the morning in your pajamas across any time zone.

- It's cheap, especially if you have an Internet connection for other purposes.

- It's fast. In fact, in most cases it's immediate.

- E-mail gives the people you write to a hard copy at the touch of the button, but only when they choose.

- You can send links to items of interest, photos, and audio and video files as attachments to e-mail.

- You can use e-mail to transmit short messages that would otherwise end up in chatty phone calls, taking far more time out of your schedule.

E-mail is great for firming up visiting arrangements and for transmitting directions and flight information. I urge caution here, however. Print out the information, and always confirm by telephone closer to the date. That's good e-mail etiquette in any case and will prevent misunderstandings.

 Simplewise _____

For a nifty selection of electronic greeting cards, check out Blue Mountain Arts (www. bluemountain.com). It offers something for just about any holiday, including those that might be obscure to many of us, and some greetings are available in French, Spanish, and other languages. Or try www.care2.com. E-cards are green, too, because they significantly cut down on paper in our landfills.

E-mail just doesn't have the urgency or impact that phone or face-to-face communication does. In some instances, it's a great supplement to voice communication, but not a complete substitute.

The Importance of Netiquette

Just as there are polite rules of behavior in other areas of social interaction, there are also rules governing communications in cyberspace. Learn them and observe proper net etiquette, or _netiquette_. Rutgers University offers a nice, concise document with the basics at mmlweb.rutgers.edu/music127/basic/email.htm; a more comprehensive view of the good, the bad, and the ugly of e-mail can be found in the book _Send: Why People Email So Badly and How to Do It Better_ by David Shipley and Will Schwalbe.

Unsolicited commercial e-mail or spam is a growing problem, and it wastes our time every day. Use a spam filter, learn some tips on how to cut down on spam, and fight back at spam.getnetwise.org. Use some of the same techniques with electronic junk mail you learned for handling paper junk mail in Chapter 6. Stop it at the source (ask the people you know, politely, who regularly send irrelevant e-mails to please stop), don't open it, and for goodness sake, don't waste your time reading it!

Simplewise

It's bad enough that your virtual mailbox is stuffed with unsolicited offers and advertising. The other big culprits in creating unwanted e-mail are your friends and family! If you don't want your e-mail stuffed with junk, ask others to take you off their joke-of-the-day, recipe, or other mail list. It's just a waste of your time if you don't enjoy it. Likewise, don't subject other people to your own mail list without their permission.

Putting People in Their Place

What do you do when you really need to tell someone to give you some space or let others know they're intruding on your privacy or time? If you're truly committed to simplifying and organizing your life, this may well be necessary at some point.

Generally, I find honesty is the best policy. If it's not a good time for people to call, say so. If they just drop in without asking, tell them you can't see them right now and ask them to call first next time. If you need uninterrupted time to get something done, don't answer the phone. Let your voicemail or answering machine take it. You decide who has access to you and when. Use the various means available to you to control your time and your life.

Start by registering all your phone numbers on the federal Do Not Call Registry. It's easy. Just go to donotcall.gov and register up to three phone numbers. If you're calling to register, you must call from the phone you want to register; the number is 1-888-382-1222. This doesn't stop calls from charities or political calls, but it's a start. You can even purchase phone call blockers that give you more control by letting you block individual phone numbers in a variety of ways.

I use all the tools available to eliminate calls from solicitors and control calls from people I know who are habitually inconsiderate of my time and my needs. My home is my castle, my Quality Circle is my first concern, and my time is precious. I use every trick I can find to protect them and me. You can, too.

Scrapbooks and Other Memory Devices

While we're on the subject of people, let's talk about the things we tend to accumulate as keepsakes to remind us of special people and important moments we spend with them. These can include letters, cards for special occasions, photographs, memorabilia, and just about anything else that reminds us of a special event or person. But these things can accumulate, and unless they're selectively organized in a meaningful way, they just become part of the meaningless clutter.

The first thing to acknowledge is that a collection of "things" is not the person or the memory itself. By paring down what you keep to remind you of the past, you are not dishonoring it. In fact, by clearing out the clutter, picking only the very best and featuring it in a special way, you are honoring that person or event.

Simplewise

There's really no need to keep negatives anymore. If you want to make a duplicate of a photograph, all you need to do is scan the photo and print it out. And ditch the outtakes, whether in your print pile or in your digital camera. Unless you can make use of them through cropping, cut them out of your life!

Scrapbooking, an old-fashioned hobby, has become quite popular these days. It's a great way to unstuff your life of sentimental clutter and keep only the best or most memorable things … if you actually do it. You end up with an archival-quality album made with acid-free paper, so you're protecting your precious memories from the ravages of time. You can add sentimental value by adding your own personal comments and artistic sense and putting photos and keepsakes into a form that can be passed on and appreciated by the whole family and future generations.

But scrapbooking, like any craft or hobby, can be a clutter trap. Keep scrapbooking materials to a minimum, even though that may be hard to do. Lots of products are available to enhance your scrapbook—stickers, rubber stamps, special papers, glitter, and much, much more. Just keep it simple and basic, and buy only what you need. Put your best photos and mementos in your album, and get rid of the rest. Organize your digital photos, and create something worthwhile with them—a digital slideshow or a scrapbook page.

Another way to pare down keepsakes is to incorporate them into a collage or other display that, again, only uses the best or most memorable objects. Still another idea for kids and adults alike is to keep a memory box. Use the size of the box to limit what is retained, and weed it out periodically so it contains only the most special trinkets and photographs.

I find that my personal journal and the events I write about there often make it less necessary to save these things. An illustrated journal (a few choice photographs can be added to enhance the text) makes an even more personal way to remember the past without cluttering the present and future. Keep your memories of the past, but don't let them become a bottleneck in your present path to organization and achieving your future goals.

Scheduled Spontaneity?

Making an inventory of people in your life and planning time around them may seem too structured, too scheduled, not spontaneous. That doesn't have to be true if you be sure there's unstructured time in your plan. This may seem like a contradiction—planning to be spontaneous? It isn't. By getting physically organized and mentally focused (they reinforce each other), you get the must-do's done more efficiently. You release yourself from the nagging feeling that things are out of control and getting further away from you. You feel confident knowing that you're making time for the people and activities you really care about. This actually allows you to be more spontaneous and provides the emotional freedom to let go.

One important point about intimacy and romance—I believe it's essential to have planned times for intimacy, as well as spaces in your life where the unexpected can happen. Think how much more passionate you can be when you can relax and know that your life is humming along on an organized plan. You'll feel strong and energized knowing you're well on your way to achieving the goals you've set for yourself. Bet you didn't know that being organized can be sexy!

My friend Karen and her husband actually schedule at least half an hour every day to snuggle. They usually set time aside each evening at 5:30 P.M., when they're both done working for the day, to connect with each other. It's absolutely precious and jealously guarded time for them. No phone calls, please!

Simplewise

Want some terrific ideas for gifts (many of them nonstuff ones) you can give the one you love? Get a copy of Gregory Godek's *1001 Ways to Be Romantic,* and after you've worn out that one, try his sequel, *1001 More Ways to Be Romantic.* They're like a quick course in romance anybody can love!

People Time, Alone Time

There's a time to be with people and a time to be alone. And time alone spent in silence is especially healing and renewing. Remember, the top dog in your Quality Circle is *you!* Be sure you schedule time each day—yes, I said *day*, not *week!*—to listen to your own inner voice. That's how you know if you're on the right path and you've got your goals and priorities in the right place. That's how you know whether your people time is being spent wisely. Call it your daily happiness check.

Tend to the people you care about most, but always leave time for solitude and having important (or even frivolous) conversations with yourself.

If You Can't Have Fun, Why Get Organized?

Getting your life in order may seem like hard work. And in fact, it *is* hard to honestly assess what you're doing that isn't working for you and change old, deeply ingrained habits. But as I'm sure you're beginning to see, the rewards are enormous. Granted, cleaning out your dead files; throwing out old newspapers; and getting a PDA won't automatically make you spouse of the year, Super-Dad, and Mega-Friend.

But let me ask you a question: if you have more time to spend with your loved ones, if you're more relaxed when you're with them because your life is under control and if you're making sure you include them in your overall Life Plan, could this possibly *hurt?* I think you know the answer!

The Least You Need to Know

- Your own health and well-being are the center around which your entire organization plan revolves.

- There are three types of relationships. The first is most important and occupies prime emotional real estate; the second is maintained with what remains; and the third should be eliminated entirely.

- A redundant reminder system ensures you never again forget an important recurring event.

- Correspondence is easily managed by assembling all the supplies in a central place and making use of small blocks of time.

- E-mail can be an effective way of keeping in touch if you observe a few basic rules.

- Spontaneity (and even romance!) is made possible by organization and planning.

Chapter 9

Work Systems: Getting Ahead Without Getting a Headache

In This Chapter

- Organizing your work life and career goals
- Unstuffing your office
- Getting control of the paper piles in your office
- Organizing your home-based business

When people are disorganized at work, they live every day feeling overwhelmed, ineffective, and pressured. Not sure whether you're disorganized in your job? Check whether any of these has happened to you recently:

❏ You missed an important appointment or meeting because you forgot or lost track of time.

❏ You forgot to return a phone call, and the caller had to phone you a second time.

❏ You had to do something over because you couldn't find the original work.

❏ You missed an important deadline.

❏ You spent hours looking for a piece of paper you needed in a hurry, only to find it sometime later in a pile on your desk or stuffed in an obscure file folder.

❏ You passed up an opportunity for a better job or promotion because it was too much trouble to put your resumé in order.

❏ You spent evenings or weekends working at home because you couldn't get the job done during regular business hours.

If you checked one or more of these, you probably have a less-than-perfect work life. If you checked three or more, it's probably darn near out of control and you're likely way more stressed out than you want or need to be.

Never fear. Together, you and I can conquer the work front the same way we began whipping things into shape at home. So stop making excuses, stop procrastinating, roll up your sleeves, and let's get to work on work.

Goal-Setting Fine-Tuned

More goal-setting? Absolutely! Only this time you're moving into advanced goal-setting, fine-tuned specifically for work and career. Let's start with a few questions first:

♦ How satisfied are you in your current job? Do you plan to be there a year from now?

♦ If you're dissatisfied with where you are now, what are you specifically dissatisfied with? Could any of these be related to your own performance or lack of organization? How could getting organized improve your present job satisfaction?

♦ If you plan to seek a new job in the next year, how would getting organized right now support both your job-hunting efforts and your goals in your new position?

♦ What are your broader career goals? Where do you want to be 5 years from now? 10 years? 20? What additional skills, education, or experience do you need to realize these goals? How would getting organized support you? Do you have a career strategy or plan for getting where you want to be? What would one look like if you did?

♦ Look at your current working environment. What feelings does it create for you? Which elements do you have the freedom to change? (Look at "Designing Your Work Environment" later in this chapter for some specific areas to consider.)

◆ Can you take the basic principles of organization you learned in Chapters 5, 6, and 7 and apply them to work? (Don't worry if the answer is no on this one. You'll be getting some additional help!)

Visualize It

Would thinking of yourself as an entrepreneur, even though you work for someone else, have an effect on your attitude and ultimately your results at work? Close your eyes and visualize your present job position as your own small company, with you as president and CEO of your job. Imagine you're solely responsible for making the company grow and all the people you work with are part of your corporate team. Imagine you're responsible for motivating these people to help you grow your business. How does this feel? How does this shift in viewpoint change the way you see your job? Act on this shift in perception, and see if it doesn't improve your attitude and performance.

Unstuffing: The Work Version

Before you get organized at work, you need to get rid of the clutter that's getting in your way. (Sound familiar? This unstuffing stuff seems to apply to *everything!*) Commit to getting rid of the clutter and junk around you and streamlining your workspace, just as you've already begun to do in other areas.

Start by mapping out some time. Come in an hour early, or stay an hour late. Use your lunch hour or a series of breaks to get started. Whenever you choose to make time, focus exclusively on implementing your organization plan, and don't allow any interruptions.

Remember the boxes for sorting you used in Chapter 5? You're going to use the same basic system for unstuffing your workspace. Label your boxes Trash (or just use a large wastebasket), Put Away (this is stuff that doesn't belong in your office—most likely you'll be taking it home), Pass On, and Keep.

Do the same thing here you did earlier with your living space. Tackle one small area at a time, be it a drawer, cabinet, or shelf. Remember the power of "just 15 minutes"? Use the same double-sort technique, too. Bring your kitchen timer to work and use it to do an initial quick sort. That should leave you with a full trash can, a box of stuff to get to other people, a box (small, I hope) to take home, and a box of stuff to keep.

As you do your initial sorting, ask the same basic questions you asked when you unstuffed your home space:

♦ When was the last time I used this?

♦ How often do I use it?

♦ If I don't use it very often, could I borrow it the few times I might need it?

♦ Is it a duplicate? If so, which one works best? How many copies do I really need?

♦ Is it out-of-date?

♦ If I didn't have this anymore, what impact if any would it have on my work? What's the *worst* thing that could happen if I tossed this and then found out I needed it?

As you answer these questions, more items should be finding their way into the Trash or Pass On bins or boxes. Be ruthless. Remember, just because someone sent it or gave it to you doesn't mean you have to keep it.

Next, follow the "directions" on your Trash and Pass On bins. That's easy—just do it. Now let's take a look at the Keep box. Chances are you're dealing mostly with paper here, but there will also be supplies and personal items. Are you hoarding things such as artwork, knickknacks, photographs, funny calendars, souvenirs, sneakers, umbrellas, food containers, or coffee mugs? For now, group these personal items in piles of similar items and put them aside.

Black Hole

Besides taking a toll on your own mental and physical well-being, both the reality and the perception of you as a disorganized person may be keeping you from a promotion or from moving into the career you really want. How likely would you be to trust additional responsibility to someone you thought of as disorganized and scattered?

Take a look at your pile of supplies. You may find you actually have three rulers and two staplers. Look for duplicates, keep the best one, and either pass on the others or trash them if they don't work well. Decide on a place to keep supplies. You'll probably end up with two places: one for what you need right at your fingertips such as tape, a stapler, staple remover, and pens, and one for supplies you don't need very often such as tape refills and extra staples. Keep the prime real estate—the drawers, shelves, cabinets, and surfaces closest to you—for the most frequently used things. If your secondary storage space is limited, keep only a bare minimum of extra supplies in your office and go to the supply room when you start to get low.

Even if your company won't supply you with a rolling cart, you may want to consider buying one for supplies. I use this in my home office and couldn't be without it. It cost about $30, has 5 drawers, and sits on casters so I can move it out of the way when I don't need it. Remember to label the drawers on the outside so you don't have to rummage through each one looking for a pair of scissors or a letter opener.

Simplewise _____

Appendix A lists lots of mail-order and online companies that sell office and organizing supplies. Filing supplies, rolling drawer carts, rolling file carts, baskets, racks, office furniture, phone equipment, and just about anything else you can think of to help organize your office space are just a click or a phone call away.

If the rolling cart idea doesn't work for you, consider drawer dividers and step shelves for cabinets to maximize your storage space. Again, if your company won't pay for them, it's worth getting them yourself. You can always take them with you, and when others in the company see how well they work, you may even be reimbursed.

Keep personal items in your office or cubicle to a minimum. Make them simple and meaningful.

What's left in your *Keep* box at this point is probably mostly paper. In this second sort, divide into the same categories you did at home—To Do, To File, Pass On, and To Pay. If you own your own business, you may actually have bills to pay at your office. Otherwise, these should be sent to the proper department or individual. If you found more paper that needs to go to someone else, pass it on. That leaves you with To Do and To File.

Your Files Aren't Another Trash Can!

How much of what's in your files is outdated or no longer useful to you? Probably about 80 percent, according to the people who know these things! As you clean up the stuff strewn around your office, file only what you really need. Then set up a time to go through your existing files and do some serious weeding out. When that's done, commit to purging them at least twice a year; more often if you can. Perhaps you can key those purging sessions to events such as the New Year and a midyear spring cleaning. You don't have to do your file purge all at once. Take 15 minutes and do a little every day. Before you know it, you'll have more file drawer space than you ever imagined possible.

Another important issue is whether it's easy to find something after you file it. My advice is to keep your filing system simple. Not only does it save you time, it also makes it easier for someone else to handle things in your absence. In fact, when you get that promotion, it'll make it easier for the next person in your position to take over!

Let's go over some tips for improving your filing system, starting with alphabetizing. Don't separate individual files into various conceptual divisions and then alphabetize within them. If it makes sense, use separate drawers for broad divisions such as Projects, Personnel, and so on, and alphabetize the whole drawer. Of course, sometimes you may need to use another type of system, but for most filing, alphabetic is the way to go. If you must use subcategories, alphabetize those within the main category, too.

Label clearly and boldly so you can read the subject headers quickly and easily, even from a distance. Black and bold is best. Label programs are available for your computer, and handy labeling machines enable you to select an easy-to-read font in any size and print out labels whenever you need them.

For each item you're filing, ask what word comes to your mind first and use that as your category. Use a noun for file categories. For example, "Files, Organizing," not "Organizing Files." Remember that the word you choose to be first determines where the file goes alphabetically. File so you can find it!

And be careful you don't duplicate categories—Records, Medical and Records, Health, for example. Pick one and be consistent. Use the same file names for both paper and files on your computer. At least in the beginning, consider keeping a list of all your file categories. That'll prevent you from creating duplicates and make the system easier to revise.

Black Hole

Avoid labeling files Miscellaneous or Other. These are paper traps, and you usually can't remember what you put in them anyway.

Use a hanging folder and a regular folder for each subject. This may seem like extra work, but in the long run it isn't. Never take the hanging folder out of the drawer and you'll file the manila folder in the same place every time. Filing will be quicker and easier, too. Guaranteed!

File the most recent document in the front. When you open the folder, your documents will always be in chronological order.

Consolidate and compress wherever possible. Can you make a list on one piece of paper and eliminate several sheets? Can a document be reduced or copied double-sided? Can several short paragraphs relating to the same project be taped together and copied on one sheet?

Don't forget to unstuff your computer files while you're unstuffing your paper ones. Many of the same principles apply—file things under names you'll find easily, avoid catchall filenames such as Miscellaneous or Stuff, consolidate files, and avoid duplicates. Use the search or find function to find files when you can't, and organize them so you'll be able to find them better next time.

Save files that are secondary or archival to a CD, DVD, or external hard drive to save disk space. You should have mostly working files on your main hard drive. Regularly defragment your hard drive to optimize space. Keep your computer desktop clean and uncluttered, just like your physical desktop.

And Speaking of Paper ...

In Chapter 6, I talked at length about controlling paper at home and gave you ideas to help. Now how can you apply what you learned to handling paper in the workplace? Let's review.

Stop It!

Get rid of as much junk mail at work as you can, using the techniques I've already given you for the home front. Ask to be taken off mailing lists. Stay away from surveys and questionnaires. And when you subscribe to a publication, send a form letter requesting to be kept off mailing lists and not to sell your information to anyone else.

Another way to stop the proliferation of paper at work is to review your subscriptions to see whether you can't cut them in half. Be realistic about the time you actually have for reading. If you've got reading material backed up for more than a week, trash it and start fresh. What reading is truly essential for keeping up-to-date with your job and your field?

Can you use an electronic or paper-clipping service or specialized, closed Internet mailing list to stay on top of subjects you need to track? I use Google Alerts when I'm working on a particular subject and want to track any new developments or stories on the subject. Is there a printed or electronic industry newsletter that does a good job of summarizing the latest developments in your field? Even though some of these options may seem somewhat expensive initially, in the long run they'll save you precious time and money. (Add the cost of all those subscriptions, for instance.) In addition, information is often easier to absorb on one particular subject when it's gathered in one place.

Simplewise _____

If your name is on a publication pass-on list within the company, request to be taken off the list if the information in the publication isn't crucial. If there's a political reason why you need to stay on the list, simply scan the publication's table of contents and read or scan only what's absolutely necessary. Most likely you don't need to read every word.

If you have a secretary, see whether he or she can open and sort your mail before you get it. Deal only with priority mail during the business day, and quickly sort through the rest at the end of the day during your homebound commute (if you don't drive to work, that is), or during your afternoon break.

Don't be a paper generator. Limit memos and letters whenever possible. Try to avoid getting into the CYA (cover your you-know-what) habit. Most of the time this causes unnecessary accumulation of paper to prove something actually occurred in case you're asked to defend yourself. If this is really a constant necessity in your job, you might want to think about changing jobs.

Finally, don't print e-mail messages or online information unless it's absolutely necessary. Whenever possible, file it digitally.

Sort, Sort, Sort

When you sort through mail or other papers, put them into categories right away. Be ruthless. The paper in your hand either gets trashed, is passed on, or goes in one of three compartments: To Do, To File, or To Read.

If you decide something needs to be filed, be sure it's something you really need to keep. Keep it only if it meets one or more of these criteria:

 ◆ Can't be found elsewhere

 ◆ Supports you in the goals you've set for yourself

 ◆ Has been reduced or consolidated as much as possible

 ◆ Is up-to-date

File it where you can retrieve it when you need it. Have a clear idea of how long you really need a particular piece of paper. If you purge your files every 6 months (or more often if you can manage it), you'll be pitching it in the circular file after a particular item's usefulness has passed and freeing up space on a regular basis.

File So You Can Find It

Treat your files at work the same way you do at home. You should have your current working files, secondary or reference files, and archival files—the deep freeze! Keep your working files close at hand in your prime real estate. You may even want to consider a rolling file or a divided holder next to your desk. Secondary files that you only refer to periodically can be less accessible than working files. Archival files should be put in storage, preferably out of your office, and should be kept to an absolute minimum. Find out your company policy for handling archival file storage.

Whatever you use for current project files, be sure it's not a catchall. In Chapter 6, I talked about a stacking basket system or in-drawer system, and I mentioned I prefer to keep my working files in my desk filing drawer. In the morning, the desk is clear and I can focus on whatever tasks I decide should get my attention first. I put away everything off my desk at the end of the day for a fresh start in the morning. And because I'm easily distracted, having a clear desk keeps me on track. I've tried both systems and found both have advantages and disadvantages. You decide.

File everything in alphabetic order using a hanging folder first with an identically labeled manila folder within it. If there's more than one subdivision within a hanging folder, file the manila folders alphabetically as well. That's the simplest and quickest system I know, and it works best for most people. In some cases, depending on the nature of your work, you may need to use a chronological or numeric filing system instead.

Black Hole

Before you make any radical changes in the way you handle and store files and records, review your company's policy (and that of your department) to be sure you comply with its financial and legal requirements.

Be sure your documents are dated and the source is identified before you file. This is especially important when clipping newspaper or magazine articles. Should you later need to quote the piece or place it in a chronology, you'll be glad you took the time.

Observe good filing practices in your computer as well. Use color coding only if it really helps. Keep files and folders off your desktop and tucked away under pertinent category folders on your hard drive. Key them as much as possible to the same categories you have in your paper filing system. Purge often. Put as much in the trash as possible, use portable media to store big chunks, and organize the rest on your hard drive. Don't duplicate digital files with paper files unless it's absolutely necessary. Choose the file form that makes the most sense, preferably digital!

Dealing With Spam

Spam. You know what it is, the junk e-mail you see in your inbox far more often than you'd like. This fast and cheap way to target consumers has lots of e-mail subscribers up in arms. It takes valuable time to download, open, read, and then trash those useless messages, and it overloads online resources already pushed to the limit carrying important stuff we really want! (I talked briefly about spam in your personal e-mail in Chapter 8.)

If the sender gives you a way to "opt out" in the message, do so. (It should be the other way around—we should decide whether we want to receive the stuff in the first place!)

Black Hole

Avoid registration forms and surveys on the Internet. If you fill out one to access a site, give as little information as possible and tell them you don't want your information to go anyplace else.

Ask your company to address the sending, forwarding, and receiving of spam in their e-mail policy, if they haven't already. Know your company's policy on spam.

Learn the "dead giveaways" for spam, and use them to filter out the spam that makes its way to your online inbox. Scan the subject and address lines. Clues to spam are misspelled words spammers use to outwit filters, numeric address formats, and names in the address line similar to yours.

Complain to your Internet service provider (ISP)—but find out who the right person is first! Some ISPs have standard addresses for this purpose, such as postmaster@*yourisp*.com or abuse@*yourisp*.com. You can ask your provider to install a junk e-mail filter, which will filter out spam from known offenders. Most ISPs are already doing this and putting suspected spam in quarantine so you can trash these unwanted e-mails without reading them.

Turn on your e-mail program's junk e-mail filter. In Microsoft Outlook, this is done under the Tools menu. Go to Options and select the Preferences tab. Then click on Junk E-mail. If you're using another e-mail program, the process is probably similar, but refer to your help files if you need to.

Internet activists are attempting to get Congress to regulate online marketing and the proliferation of spam. Until they do, you can at least take some steps to reduce the amount you get clogging your e-mail box by following these steps and looking regularly for new and better ways of controlling spam.

Back Up or Else

We all know we should do it, but most of us back up sporadically at best. One study a few years back showed that 9 out of 10 PC users don't back up regularly. Media choices for back up include CDs, DVDs, USB flash drives, and several different types of external hard drives. Your company probably has backup systems for critical data, but you still need to back up your personal files.

If you have a home business, I suggest you have two methods of backup for your files. Keep one in your home office so you can recover from a crash or equipment melt-down, and store the second off-site. Especially if you own your own business, having a backup for your files can mean the difference between surviving and going under in the event of a fire or other disaster. Media devices with removable disks give you some simple options, such as storing your backup in a safe-deposit box and replacing it with an updated set each week. You may even want to consider a commercial online Internet remote backup service. Data Deposit Box (www.datadepositbox.com) and IDrive (www.idrive.com) are two popular ones.

If you tend to forget to back up your files (and who doesn't?) why not make it a ritual? How about every Friday afternoon? I generally use Fridays for "housekeeping" in my office—filing, tidying up, bill paying, and nonurgent correspondence. This is my time to do a weekly backup. On important documents, I back them up to an external hard drive every day. Software is available that automatically reminds you to back up. Symantec offers several options, and free programs are available online as well. If you have an off-site service, you will most likely have automated backup as part of the package. Whatever you do and however you do it, remember to back it up!

A final note: be careful about taking digital or paper files out of the office without adequate backup. Think of the hardship it would cause you and your company if these files were lost or damaged. Keep duplicates of absolutely critical files.

Life Management Center: Work Version

In the office, you'll have a different version of the Life Management Center than you set up at home. This one is specifically geared toward supporting you in your career goals. Depending on what kind of work you do, it may involve a planning board, a project calendar on the wall, or other specialized tools.

You also need a way to integrate the schedules of other people in your department and overall deadlines. Some companies do this through software on a networked computer system. If yours has one, learn how to use it effectively, and train others, too.

Get Out Your Planner/Organizer

The planner/organizer you set up in Chapter 7 is still an indispensable tool. This is what integrates all the things important to you in your life and helps you keep a balance between work and home. Enter everything that comes to mind you need to do on your Master List as you think of it. You can keep a separate one for work and home if you like, but I prefer to keep everything on one list so I'm sure to include both when I'm planning. If you use a paper planner/organizer, use a pencil for writing down appointments and to-dos that may change. Try a colored pen or highlighter to emphasize important appointments or reminders.

Your Master List is simply a databank of things you want or need to do. You're the sorter. Review your Master List whenever you do your planning (I recommend daily mini–planning sessions first thing in the morning and last thing in the evening) and see what should be transferred to your daily to-do list and when. Include deadlines and phone calls you need to make (or times you've asked others to call you) as well.

Prioritize the tasks on your daily to-do list. Some people like the A-B-C method:

A   Top-priority items.

B   These things are important but don't absolutely have to get done today.

C   It would be nice if these things got done, but they could probably be put off indefinitely.

I don't think any C items should be on your list at all. Keep them on your Master List and only add them to your daily one when you decide they're important enough. If they are things I know I may never get to but I might like to do someday, I put them on my Someday/Maybe list, as recommended by productivity guru David Allen in his book *Getting Things Done.* There are more wishes than actually things to do, but I like to keep track of them nevertheless. Dreams are important, too, you know!

So all that's left on your list are A's and B's. I number them in order of priority, from number 1 to whatever. Anything I don't get to at the end of the day gets put on the next day's list and most likely gets a high-priority number.

Assigning a task number 1 priority doesn't necessarily mean it's the one you do first. It simply means that of all the tasks on your schedule for that day, it's the one that you most want or need to get done. Take advantage of your peak performance times for tasks that require the most concentration or creativity.

Black Hole

What seems to be most urgent is not necessarily what's most important. Keep repeating this over and over to yourself. Don't let only the squeaky wheel grab your attention. You decide what's important.

Remember, what determines priority is the place a particular activity has in supporting you in your goals, not whatever comes up first or shouts the loudest.

Use the organizing principles you learned in Chapter 5. Group like things together when you plan your time. It's often more efficient to do all the things that require certain tools or skills at one time, such as writing letters or making phone calls, than it is to scatter them throughout the day.

Don't forget to write down planning time on your schedule, block out time to be with family and friends, and make appointments with yourself to take care of your needs for relaxation, learning, and spiritual development. Always keep in mind the whole picture of who you are now and who you're aspiring to be, and integrate that into your daily work planning and organizing.

If you're not accomplishing all the tasks you set for yourself in a day on a regular basis, that usually means you're wasting time, asking yourself to do too much, allowing too many interruptions, or suffering from the big P: procrastination. If it's the latter, go back to Chapter 3 and review the section on procrastination. You can't afford not to conquer it.

Tickler Files

In conjunction with a planner/organizer, some people have a "tickler" file. A tickler file is simply a set of 31 numbered files representing each day of the month and a set of 12 files for each month of the year. As invitations, tickets, conference brochures, memos, or anything with date-specific importance comes through your hands, you can file it in your tickler file. When the event draws near, you have all the information you need.

I had never used one of these until I ran for public office a year ago. There were so many events to attend, with attendant directions, instructions, and support materials, this was the only way to keep track, and it worked beautifully. But now that my schedule is less hectic (I didn't win, but I sure put up a fight!), I find I don't need to use it anymore.

Simplewise

A tickler file system should occupy prime real estate (as in, right under your nose), and checking it must be a habit. This system only works if you use it regularly. If you forget to check it, things can get lost, and you can forget to take important actions when needed.

Be sure to file the information in the file for the date you need to act on it, *not* when it's due. If you get a memo about a project that's due 2 weeks from now and you don't intend to work on it for another week, for example, put it in the numbered file for 7 days from now to remind you to start on it. Keep information for later months in the 12-month folders.

Be sure to check your tickler file every day. It's not a bad idea to check ahead for the following week on Monday morning and Friday afternoon, as well.

Tickler files don't work for everyone, but if your work is very date-oriented, it might be the right system for you.

Designing Your Work Environment

The environment you create in your workspace has a direct effect on how well you work. That applies to offices away from home as well as home offices. Often, if you work for someone else, you simply accept the environment you're given and fail to realize how much you can actually do to adapt it to your own needs and working style. It's time to take a look around your office or cube and ask yourself some questions.

What's the furniture in this room really like? Is it functional? Is it in the best spot? Is it attractive? Is your desk the right height? Your computer keyboard? Do you have space to spread out? Is there ample room for you to stretch out your legs or lean back? How comfortable is your chair? What are your options in this company as far as furniture is concerned? Can you make changes? If not, what can you do to adapt what you already have using add-on drawers, step shelves, desk pads, chair pads, or other removable accessories?

What are the predominant colors in this room? How do you respond to them? Is there a way to add color through wall decorations, furniture choices, or office accessories?

How does this room filter out sound? Is there a way to improve it? How does sound affect you when you work? If music is piped in, does it help or hinder you? Can you eliminate it if you want to? When might you need to do that? Is there a quieter place you can retreat to when noise becomes a serious distraction? Can you use noise-filtering headphones?

Where are your light sources? Is there any natural light? What kind of blinds or curtains do you have to control natural light? What kind of light fixtures do you have? Are they adequate? Are they located in the best places? Are they fluorescent or incandescent? (Incandescent is easier on your eyes.) If you have a fluorescent fixture, does it buzz? (If so, the ballast may need to be replaced.) What are the strength and type of lightbulbs in your fixtures? What are your options for changing and improving your office lighting? Can you improve the lighting in your workspace in any way?

What's the temperature in your office? Is it too cold? Too warm? Does it fluctuate? Can you control it in any way? Can you control the sunlight into your office? Would the addition of a small fan or space heater help? Would wearing layered clothing make a difference? Do you include getting some fresh air as part of your daily routine? Is there a way to get fresh air into your workspace?

How about humidity? Is it too damp or too dry? Would the introduction of a room humidifier or dehumidifier be an option?

What's the location of your phone jack? Is it conducive to where you want your desk and computer to be? Can you have your phone jack moved or an additional one put in? Can you go wireless? How about electrical outlets? What are your options here? Can you get extension cords or power strips? (Be careful about overloading electrical circuits, protecting critical equipment, and the safe locating of cords and wires.) Would the addition of a headset, cordless headset, or speaker phone enhance your comfort and efficiency?

 Simplewise

To find good suppliers of office phone equipment, check out your local business-supply store or chain such as Staples (www.staples.com) or Office Max (www.officemax.com), Radio Shack's Duofone products (www.radioshack.com), and the Quill business-supply catalog (www.quillcorp.com). Some excellent sources specialize in headset phone equipment, such as Headsets.com.

Do you store food in your office? How does that affect your working environment, and does that support you in your health and fitness goals? Does having food nearby distract you or encourage you to procrastinate? Do you tend to eat lunch and take breaks in your office rather than resting your eyes and your wrists or stretching your legs?

What comforts or accessories can you add to make this a better workspace? Can you get a better chair, a cushion, or backrest? Can you purchase a wrist pad or more ergonomic mouse for your computer? An antiglare screen? A mat or footrest? How about a rolling cart for supplies or a rolling file cart?

Do you have your space set up to maximize your movements, and have you allotted prime real estate to the things you need for the tasks you perform most often? Are all the supplies you need to perform a task located in the right place? Can you obtain more or better storage to accommodate your needs? Can you make better use of vertical space (think *up!*)?

Have you managed your total work environment to bolster your energy level and help you stick to your health goals? Are you taking regular breaks from your computer screen or other work? Are you getting up from your desk regularly and moving? Have you considered buying equipment such as an air filter, ionizer, or aromatherapy diffuser to enhance your work environment? (Be sure these things are allowed before bringing or purchasing them.)

Have you given consideration to the care and feeding of your mind, heart, and soul when you survey your work environment? What's your overall sense of well-being in your current workspace? Are your goals, dreams, and visions somehow projected and presented for you on a daily basis?

By the time you're done asking yourself these questions, you'll probably have a list of things to do and requests for your purchasing department or office-supply center (or you may need to buy things personally). Don't delay, because these environmental improvements can have an immediate impact on how well you perform your job and how you feel about it. These things are so easy to take for granted or ignore. Take a few minutes today to focus on them, and make the necessary improvements.

People Power

Being organized reduces stress, not only for you, but also for the people around you. Order increases efficiency and promotes creativity; it has a definite effect on your ability to perform and your level of satisfaction. Let's look at some strategies for increasing your people power.

Delegate. Delegating means giving other people the authority and freedom to do a task that you might otherwise do yourself. Be sure you thoroughly explain the task, communicate what's expected, and empower the person you've asked to do the task to perform it thoroughly and well. Agree on when and how progress will be reported and reviewed. If you learn to delegate effectively, you'll have more time to attend to higher-priority tasks, and the person you've delegated to will have a valuable opportunity to learn and grow.

Network. Use your friends' and colleagues' knowledge and experience. If you're asked to do a project or implement a program that others you know have done, pick their brains. And make yourself available to them for the same purpose. I regularly let my writer friends know what projects I'm working on. Because they see a lot of information daily on a variety of topics, just as I do, they often pass on news or magazine clippings or make me aware of experts, books, or websites I should know about. I reciprocate in kind.

Collaborate. A "buddy system" often makes tasks easier or helps you stick to a particular project. Can you work with a colleague? How can you make it to his or her advantage to do so? This technique is effective at work but can also be applied to many other areas of your life.

Prepare. Organize and plan carefully for meetings ahead of time. They'll be more productive and take half the time. If your department has regularly scheduled meetings, try eliminating one and see whether it really makes a difference. You may just be meeting out of habit, rather than need.

Listen. Apply this rule from the book *The 7 Habits of Highly Effective People:* "Seek first to understand, then to be understood." By listening carefully and fully comprehending the problem before you try to give advice or attempt a solution, you'll save time in the long run and be much more effective in your dealings with people in all areas of your life.

Learn to say no. Just because someone calls, walks in your office, or asks you to do something doesn't mean you have to give him your time right then. Make decisions about how to organize your time, and be firm about not allowing other people to sabotage your efforts. Be polite, but don't be afraid to say, "No, I can't do that," or, "I'll talk to you about it later." If it's something you want or need to do, but you're busy with something else, schedule a time then and there when you'll meet with or call the person to discuss it. Thank the person for respecting your time.

Visualize It

Saying no is very difficult for some people. Close your eyes and imagine yourself in various situations (be as specific as possible) where you might be asked to do something where saying no would be a good idea. See yourself saying no firmly and politely. Say it out loud when you're by yourself, and hear yourself taking control of your time and what you need to do. Repeat the process over again until you really feel comfortable doing it and then try it out. Notice how powerful the word *no* is. If you have trouble thinking of the words, you can turn to professional organizer Ramona Creel's tip sheet called *20 Ways to Say No*. Find it at www.onlineorganizing.com/ExpertAdviceToolboxTips. asp?tipsheet=16.

If you already have too many commitments, resign or beg off of some. What committees or boards are you on that don't really serve you or make the best use of your time and resources?

Look for Shortcuts

What can you streamline? Standardize? Customize? Computerize? Look for ways to standardize forms, formats, routines, and checklists. Create procedural manuals whenever possible, and be sure it's kept up-to-date. (This saves time with new employees, too.) Create form letters and e-mails for regular types of correspondence. You can change them slightly if need be, but you won't have to put in the mental energy creating a new letter each time.

Simplewise

Write thank you and follow-up letters and e-mails while you're on the road (a great way to use flight time), or at least do a draft, which you can tweak later. You can address envelopes ahead of time, too.

Set up style sheets for regular correspondence or flyers in your desktop publishing or word processing software so you don't have to reformat each time. Keep a file with directions to your office or meeting place and send it with confirmation e-mails, or print out and send a copy with written correspondence. This eliminates those "How do I get there again?" phone calls and e-mail messages. If you have a smart phone, have them saved as a text document there as well.

Use checklists. When you travel, use a packing checklist. When you make a sales call, use a checklist or a phone interview sheet to be sure you've covered everything. Create a fax cover sheet and store in your computer. Copy enough to have on hand when you need them.

Use binders when they make sense. A binder can be used to organize business cards, slides, computer disks, specific business trips, newsletters, professional organization information, and any sheets of paper you want to last a long time. You can use all kinds of inserts and plastic sheets to customize a binder to suit any number of purposes.

Learn how to use all your fax machine or fax software features to their fullest. That goes for all the office equipment you use regularly. Some time spent in self-training upfront will save you time every day.

Make an effort to really learn your computer's capabilities. Take the time to read software manuals to help you understand program features. You'll be amazed how little of your computer's power you're actually using! Get help with a tutorial, a book, or a class that addresses your particular software. It's not cost effective to spend $500 for a program and only know how to use a fraction of its features. When you know what it's capable of, you can make an intelligent decision about which features are most useful for you.

Ring Around the Workplace: Phone Control

The telephone is a tool. In fact, it is your servant! So how come it feels like it rules your life? Do you walk around with a cell phone or Bluetooth glued to your ear? Take charge and use these techniques for a happy, productive phone relationship. Get control of your phone, and you get control of one of the greatest sources of interruptions and wasted time.

Have a specific time for making and returning phone calls and a specific time when you can encourage other people to reach you in your office. If possible, have your answering machine, voicemail, or secretary take messages at other times.

Change your voicemail message as needed to let people know your schedule and when they should call. Then be sure you're available when you say you'll be. Don't answer except at the allotted time. Do the same for returning calls, and keep your word.

When recording a phone message on someone's answering machine or voicemail, leave a specific time when he or she can call you back. Always give your full name and repeat your phone number, even if you think he or she already has it.

Black Hole

Don't let disorganized phone time eat up your day. Set up telephone appointments just like in-person appointments. Say, "I'll call you at 2 P.M." and do it. Just because you have a cell phone doesn't mean you have to be available to everyone all the time.

Do phone messages have a way of disappearing? Use a two-part carbonless phone message book available from business-supply stores. This ensures that if someone misplaces the original message, there's always a backup.

If you make a lot of telephone calls or make extensive notes from your calls, consider buying a telephone headset for your land line and a Bluetooth headset for your cell phone. These free your hands to do computer file maintenance, open mail, write short letters, or sort papers while you're on hold, and it beats scrunching the phone between your shoulder and ear. Your neck will thank you!

Learn to make phone calls quickly and get to the point. Answer phone calls the same way. Decide on the focus of the call, prepare (make a list of points to cover before you dial or use your checklist), and stay on track. If you know you're going to be calling someone who tends to chat a lot, make the call just before lunch or a few minutes before quitting time. Hunger or the desire to go home can be great motivations for keeping it short. This is also a good time to call someone who's difficult to reach.

Treat e-mails and faxes the same way you would other mail or phone calls. Pick specific times to go online and collect your e-mail (twice a day is the minimum). Respond immediately to anything you can, and add to your schedule those that are really a to-do. If an e-mail message contains information you need to retain, file it in a computer folder or print it out and put it in the To File basket or folder right away. (Do this sparingly!) If you need to pass it on to someone else, do so promptly. The same applies to faxes. They either go in the To Do basket or folder or they get filed, passed on, or discarded.

Business Correspondence Made Easy

Now let's move on to organizing your business correspondence. I've talked a little bit about e-mails and faxes, which, along with letters and memos, make up the bulk of your correspondence. You can apply your basic sorting system to all of them. Some go directly in the trash. Some might need a short notation and can then be returned to the sender or passed on to the appropriate person. Some may simply need to be filed. And some require action, which might include a more extensive reply. Throughout the day, think of these categories—Trash, Pass On, File, To Do—and continually get things off your desk or desktop and into the appropriate place.

When only a brief reply is needed and the original doesn't need to be kept on file, return the original letter with your reply noted at the bottom. That gets it off your desk, saves paper, and reminds the sender what was said originally.

Simplewise _____

Make your daily commute count in your quest for organization and peace. Use it to set up for a great day and to start unwinding the moment you leave your office. If you drive, give some creative thought to providing an orderly, pleasant environment each morning and evening. If you use public transportation, organize yourself so you can use that time to prepare for the day, relax, or pursue a favorite hobby. And don't use your morning commute for breakfast. Get up as early as you must to prepare a nutritious breakfast at home. You'll save money, eat better, and help your digestion!

Use e-mail to reply whenever possible, rather than a written letter. It's quicker to write, doesn't generate paper, and is cheaper and instant. However, be sure the recipient is someone who checks his or her e-mail frequently if your message is urgent. Keep a backup in the sent file until you're sure the recipient has gotten your e-mail.

Schedule time to fully learn your e-mail program. These programs are being updated all the time, and newer versions may have powerful features you may not even know about.

When you have a choice between a written letter, a fax, and a phone call, choose the telephone. When you have a choice between an e-mail and a phone call and the e-mail will work just as well, choose e-mail.

Write e-mails in clear, concise English using action verbs and nouns. Write short sentences and paragraphs. Poor communication wastes time—yours and everyone else's!

Simplewise _____

Need some quick help with your writing style? One of the best books I know on effective business writing is Robert Gunning's *How to Take the Fog Out of Business Writing*. You know if your writing can use help. If it can, get it!

Don't create more information in your written communications than anybody needs! Don't write a 10-page proposal when 1 page will do. Aim for tighter writing. It promotes clearer thought (you have to focus and be clear yourself to write concisely) and results in greater understanding.

Don't print e-mail messages unless you really have to. Enter the information in your planner if it's about an appointment or a meeting. File electronically whenever you can. If you must file a hard copy, print it out and put it in the To File bin immediately.

Visualize It

Imagine yourself in total control of your work environment. See yourself using your time effectively, meeting your deadlines and handling crises. Make it real. What are you wearing? How do you feel? Visualize yourself walking through your workday with all the right tools at your fingertips. What does this picture do for your self-confidence? Where can you imagine it leading? List all the ways not being organized and confident has cost you, financially and emotionally. List all the benefits you'd gain by organizing your working life.

Taking It on the Road

Travel for both business and pleasure creates its own organizational challenges. The boundaries of the office are blurring into a 24/7 world of laptops and smart phones.

Going on a business trip to a trade show or an industry convention doesn't have to mean coming back with a backlog of paperwork, tons of phone calls and correspondence, and a general feeling of disorganization and inefficiency. Technology can help you stay on top of things as you go along.

Simplewise

Don't carry home literature you've accumulated from trade shows—mail it home! Trade show companies sometimes provide boxes and mailing points specifically for this purpose. If you only need to glance over some of the literature and have room for it, read it over on the flight home and dispose of it at the airport when you arrive.

Use travel time and evenings in your hotel room to keep on top of it all. Have folders that duplicate your office sorting system in your briefcase: To File, To Do, To Read, Pass On. As you sort through paper for filing, especially if you can't do it right away, highlight or jot down the filing category on top. This speeds up filing when you get back to the office. I use a portable business card reader so I don't even have to take all those little cards home with me.

On your first day back in the office, schedule time to deal with the accumulation of mail and paperwork. Don't put it off, or it will soon grow into a mountain instead of a small hill.

Keep an envelope for your receipts, and write notes on them while the purpose or other details are fresh in your mind. Write notes on the back of any business cards you get right away. Note anything you've agreed to do, where you met the individual, or any other pertinent information. Then transfer the card information to your computer contact software using a card reader or manually, or put the card in your office card file after you've taken any necessary action.

Add any deadlines or promises you made to your planner/organizer. Any other ideas that come up can be added either to your idea list or your Master List of things to do.

Choose a hotel with a high-speed wireless Internet connection. Write snail mail letters and e-mail them to your secretary to mail out while you're gone. By the time you return, you'll either already have a reply or will have one shortly. Don't forget to send thank you notes and e-mails. E-mail is also a good way to reinforce your commitments to employees when you can't be in the office.

Use e-mail to keep in touch with family when schedules conflict and a phone call doesn't synch. It's not a substitute for a personal chat, but can be a great way to help keep the home fires burning when you're far away.

If you can manage it though, young children enjoy talking to Mommy or Daddy in real-time on the phone, or even seeing them via webcam. If you can set this up, it's a great thing. My son-in-law travels all over the world on business, but videos with his two young boys whenever he can coordinate it with time differences.

E-mail and online technology are just one more way of keeping your people priorities straight. Learn to use them to your full advantage.

When Home Is Your Office

If you're new to working at home or just considering it as a possible alternative, you need to realize it takes time to adjust to this new lifestyle. You have to set all sorts of limits on other people—like the neighbor who figures that because you don't have a "real" job you can let in the plumber and walk her dog. This includes your own family as well.

In the beginning, allow yourself room to experiment. If at all possible, plan for becoming a home-based worker in advance, set up your workspace, and ease into at least a partial routine before you give up your off-site job.

If you can, get your equipment and supplies, design your office space, write your business plan, and have your stationery printed before you quit your job. Consider using your days off to try things out and get a handle on the challenges you'll face. Take notice of your energy patterns, what distracts you, and where your time goes. It might help to keep a log of these things at first.

Go through the questions in the "Designing Your Work Environment" section earlier in this chapter, and broaden them to take advantage of the freedom being a home-based worker affords you. You can repaint, remodel, accessorize, and furnish to your heart's (and budget's) content. It's up to you to make the choices and keep your focus at the same time.

Because someone else doesn't structure your workday, *you* have to define it. Use your Life Management Center and your planner/organizer to give your work life structure. Set regular hours with room for planned deviations built in. Create routines and rituals that help you stay focused. Some experts suggest dressing a certain way for work, even if it's just wearing a particular sweater or pair of tennis shoes. If you wore a suit to work before and it puts you in the "work mode," wear a suit at home, at least in the beginning, until you establish some kind of routine. One man even got dressed, walked out the door, got in his car, drove around the block, and came back to work in his home office to get himself in gear. Hey, whatever works!

Simplewise _____

If you're thinking of setting up shop at home or even if you already have, I highly recommend *Working from Home: Everything You Need to Know About Living and Working Under the Same Roof* by Paul and Sarah Edwards. It's the bible of the home-based business movement.

Set regular deadlines for yourself. If all you have is the deadline for the completed project, break it down into smaller, manageable chunks and assign deadlines to those. Add them to your planner/organizer.

Define your work area. If at all possible, physically separate your office from the rest of the house. You can possibly turn a spare bedroom, a rarely used dining room, a large closet, garage, attic, basement, or finished porch into the perfect office space. It helps if it has a door you can close or even lock or some other way to mark off a separate space and indicate that you're working and don't want to be disturbed.

Working at home is about taking full responsibility for your work life, especially if you're self-employed as well. So take responsibility for ...

- Preventing interruptions.
- Creating a supportive working environment.
- Getting the right tools.
- Creating the image you want for your business.
- Learning about and using new technology.
- Keeping up with your field or industry.
- Finding local services and vendors and establishing good business relationships.
- Making a business plan and reviewing it regularly.

- Finding a good business lawyer, tax preparer/accountant, and financial planner.

- Filing the appropriate papers and obtaining necessary licenses, such as a local business license, resale certificate, seller's permit, employer ID number, business name registration, partnership agreement, or articles of incorporation—find out from your lawyer what you need, and get it!

- Investigating and using telephone company services such as call forwarding, call waiting, voicemail, and built-in (often free) accounting features if these will help you run your business better, stay focused, save time, and help organize you.

- Backing up important print and computer files.

- Preparing your business for fire, flood, theft, or other disasters.

- Making time to dream, plan, think, and create.

- Rewarding yourself and sharing your success with others.

Take responsibility for your own success. You wanted to be in charge. So take charge!

Black Hole _____

If you work at home, you don't have to go overboard devoting permanent space to meeting with clients or colleagues. If there isn't adequate space at home, meet at their location, at a rented suite (in some areas, office suites can be rented by the hour or the day), or in a restaurant or club. Even a park can be a meeting place if the client is amenable.

On the Lookout for Your Next Job

How prepared would you be if you got fired or laid off today? Perhaps this has already happened. If you're currently working at home, what if you decided to get an off-site job? How quickly could you begin to make the transition? What if a head hunter called with the job of your dreams but you needed to get a resumé in today's express mail? Or what if a job opening was announced today within your company that you really wanted? Would you be able to act on it in a hurry?

An important benefit of being organized is that it allows you to be proactive, rather than reactive. *Proactive* is really just another word for "prepared." If an opportunity arises, you don't need to "throw something together"—you've already *got* it together.

Have a file both at home and at work that contains your employment records, references, letters of praise, and an up-to-date resumé. If you don't have a resumé, write and design one. Microsoft Office Online even has a selection of resumé templates you can use (office.microsoft.com/en-us/templates). Get professional help if you need to.

Review your job readiness every few months. Set up a plan to have enough money in the bank to cover 4 to 6 months of unemployment just in case. If you're not in a financial position to do that right now, start working toward it. Chapters 14 and 15 can help you. Even if you switch jobs, you still may need extra money to make the transition between your last paycheck at your old job and the first at your new one.

Keep a diary of your job accomplishments with specifics. How much did you actually save the company? How many people did you oversee on that project? What were the results? Who? When? What? Where? How? Why? You'll have everything you need at your fingertips if you need to back up a request for a raise or for your next job interview.

Simplewise

Buy or borrow *What Color Is Your Parachute? 2009: A Practical Manual for Job-Hunters and Career-Changers* by Richard Nelson Bolles. This is the classic guide to career planning and job hunting. You'll probably want to reread it periodically because it's so informative, entertaining, and uplifting. It turns "looking for work" into "discovering your life's work."

Don't just organize for the job you *have*; organize for the job you *want*. Think of the peace of mind you'd have today just knowing you could handle any change in your job situation and respond to any opportunity.

Your work life is also your life. Identify how it fits in to your mission statement. Make it part of your overall organization plan, and you'll not only be more productive, you'll also be a happier person.

The Least You Need to Know

- The same principles and techniques you use to organize yourself at home can easily be applied to work.

- Using a planner/organizer effectively helps integrate your work and home lives and keeps larger goals in front of you.

- Even if you work for someone else, you can customize your office space to make it more comfortable, efficient, and enjoyable.

- Working at home offers more freedom and creates unique challenges. Taking responsibility is a key element in being a successful home-based worker.

- Keeping up with basic organizing tasks on the road makes your first day back in the office a snap.

- Being prepared for unemployment or new job opportunities alleviates worry and creates possibilities.

Part 4

Room by Room

Each room in your home plays a different role in your overall organization picture. In Part 4, we examine them one by one, taking a close look at their form and function in your organized life.

Imagine how different your life would be if your kitchen supported you in your health and fitness goals. What if your bedroom was a serene retreat and your bedroom closet filled with attractive, wearable clothes that flatter you and that you love? Well, together we can make over every space to give you breathing room and good vibes every time you enter it.

Chapter **10**

Morning Routines: Strategies for a Better Launch

In This Chapter

- ◆ Starting the day the organized way
- ◆ Saving time on grooming and makeup routines
- ◆ Keeping a lid on clutter
- ◆ Cluttered handbags no more!

Houston, we have a problem.

Does this describe how you begin your day? Are you scrambling around in the morning trying to find something to wear? Are you fighting with cords and cabinets overflowing with half-full shampoo bottles and outdated prescription medicines just so you can get ready for the day? Do you skip breakfast because you run out of time and the kitchen is a mess anyway? Is your day filled with stress before you even begin? You deserve *better* than that!

This chapter helps you create a launching pad for the day that gives you a fighting chance to meet whatever the world throws at you. You learn how to pare down and devise a simple morning routine that continues to work for you throughout the day and beyond.

Your Day Begins the Night Before

The last things you do before you lay down your weary head to rest help determine how things go when you open your eyes in the morning. Now I must say I resist too much regulation and routine, but over the years, I have become a big fan of setting up some basic routines and sticking to them. As a result, I've had great results in my own struggles with organizing my life and managing my time.

Before You Go to Bed

Here's what I consider the bare-bones must-do nighttime routines to help create a smoother launch and landing for life:

Check out your calendar for the next day so you know what lies ahead and how to dress for it. One of the side benefits of getting organized is you'll have a better chance of looking good instead of frazzled.

Before going to bed, lay out your clothes for the next day. This way, when you're groggy and in a hurry in the morning, you won't have to think twice about what you're going to wear. Besides, if something needs ironing or mending, you can either do it the night before or find something else to wear.

Simplewise

While you're laying out your clothes the night before, also get out anything else you need to take with you and put it by the door or somewhere you're sure not to forget it. Some people literally put it in front of the door so they can't leave the house without it!

Take care of yourself! Brush your teeth, wash your face, take your vitamins—whatever you need to do for your health and well-being.

Be sure your dishes are all done and the kitchen is picked up. I can't go to sleep with dishes in the sink! I just can't stand to start the day with a sink full of dishes staring me in the face. And if there's anything you can do to prepare for breakfast or make lunch to take, do it before you go to bed.

Finally, get to bed at a reasonable hour!

Good Morning!

Now let's go over a few morning-routine things I recommend you make non-negotiable, without fail, to give your mornings a positive lift-off.

First things first, take care of yourself! You're going to read these words a lot throughout this book. Take your vitamins, brush your teeth, wash your face and put on some moisturizer with sunscreen, do your hair and makeup, or whatever it is you do when you want to greet the world with your best face on. This applies whether you're staying home all day or meeting the president of your company. And eat a nutritious breakfast—that's an order!

Next, get dressed. FlyLady, a.k.a. Marla Cilley, says to get dressed to your shoes—and she means shoes that lace up! If that helps to give you a cue that you mean business and this day is going to mean something, then by all means do it! I find that a good pair of sturdy shoes does seem to help put a spring in my step much better than the shuffle of slippers or the bang of flip-flops.

Empty the dishwasher and do your breakfast dishes before you leave the house. Just get into this habit. Turn on the slow cooker if you want dinner waiting when you get home (more on this in Chapter 11). Think about it: a clean sink and a hot meal waiting for you at the end of the day—what more could you ask for?

Finally, add to your routine anything that helps you get off to a good start in the morning and makes it easier to unwind in the evening when you may be tired. For me, that means cleaning the cat pans and running a brush around the toilet. With our hard Arizona water, I find if I just hit the toilets every morning with some vinegar and water, I don't get the ring that's so much harder to remove if I let it go.

Get these few regular habits down in the very beginning of your organizing journey, and make them automatic. You can always add to them as you go along. As you do, I promise, things will get better overnight!

Unstuff the Bathroom

One of the first places (if not *the* first) you go to when you greet the day is the bathroom. Most bathrooms are booby-trapped, with bottles and tubes of goo tucked everywhere—some of it from another decade. It may be hard to find the sink, you have to duck when you open the medicine cabinet, or maybe the vanity is a jungle of pomades and potions and tangled electrical cords.

Because it's one of the smallest rooms in the house and its purpose is pretty clear, the bathroom is a great place to start flexing your organizing muscles. So set aside some time, grab your timer and your boxes, and let's get going.

Out It Goes!

Step one is to go through your cabinets, bathroom drawers, linen closet, medicine chest, dressing table, bureau—wherever you keep various personal-care concoctions, bath brews, face paints, nail polishes, hotel samples, hair tools, etc. Clear them all out (bet they'll fill a clothes basket!), clean the drawers and shelves, and start to weed out the pile using the sorting method you learned in Chapter 5.

Sort into Trash, Keep, and Put Away. You probably won't have much to pass on to charity, but you might have some knickknacks or appliances you no longer need. Or you may have some things in the bathroom that don't belong to you. So have a Pass On/Return box as well.

Do the initial sort quickly with the kitchen timer ticking away—15 or 20 minutes should give you a great start. Then refine the Keep pile by putting like things together. You can use boxes, bags, or baskets to start. Some may work as they are, or you may need some containers or dividers to corral the things you're going to keep.

Get rid of old cosmetics and personal products. I'll bet a majority of them are far past their prime anyway. Creams and lotions, for example, can be kept up to 2 years. Pump-type dispensers are best because your fingers never touch what's left in the bottle, so there's no risk of contamination. Otherwise, dab what you need on a cotton ball.

Black Hole

Don't get duped into buying single-use products. By choosing products with multiple uses, you can cut down on bathroom clutter. For example, as most outdoor enthusiasts know, Avon's Skin-So-Soft bath oil does double duty as an effective bug repellent. Petroleum jelly has a host of applications. And many moisturizers and makeup bases have sun protection built in.

Sunscreens usually have an expiration date. If none is listed on the container, ditch it if your guess is it's older than 1 year. And when you head for the beach, remember that the sunscreen should be kept in a cool, dry place—not in a hot glove compartment or basking in the sun.

Mascara is a real villain for transmitting bacteria that can cause infections, so don't keep it more than 3 months. Use a permanent marker and write the date you bought it on the tube. You can do the same for toothbrushes, which should be replaced every 3 months. (Store them so they dry quickly—dampness breeds bacteria.) If you're not sure how old something is, toss it out.

Foundation, cover-up, lipstick, eye shadow, blush, and powders are generally safe for 1 year. Why not make an annual purge on New Year's Day or just before the holiday season?

Nail polish may thicken or separate with age, and usually all you have to do is shake it to blend. If that doesn't do it, you'll know it's time to toss it.

Hair color has an expiration date on the package. It should be kept out of light and heat.

Finally, remember these three general points when doing your bathroom purge:

◆ If you can't remember when you bought it, throw it out.

◆ Get rid of duplicates, broken items, and those that just don't do the job.

◆ Toss expired medicines. And never, *never* transfer prescription medicines to different containers. The results could be dangerous or even fatal. (For safe medication disposal tips, check the federal guidelines at www.whitehousedrugpolicy. gov/publications/pdf/prescrip_disposal.pdf. Many communities have local programs for this purpose.)

Stow It! Bathroom Storage Solutions

Now that you've unstuffed your beauty and grooming products and sorted them by type, you need to find a better way to store them. We all know bathroom cabinets and drawers were devilishly devised to make it impossible to retrieve what you want, when you want it. Small things get lost in deep cabinets and at the back of drawers. Let's take a look at some storage suggestions that may work better for you.

Store regularly used products such as shampoo, conditioner, and cleanser in the shower. In a smaller shower, consider an over-the-showerhead organizer. In a larger stall, a spring-loaded floor-to-ceiling unit with multitiered shelves works well.

 Simplewise _____

Can't seem to find any more space in the bathroom? Try hanging a shoe caddy on the back of the bathroom door to store small things you need at your fingertips. Be sure the compartments are clear so you can see what's where without rummaging around, and group like things together in one compartment.

One way to organize drawer contents is by assigning each drawer or drawer section to a particular part of the body. How about one drawer for hairbrushes, combs, and accessories; one just for the man of the house's shaving paraphernalia; and another just for special pampering accoutrements—complete with bath oils, scrubs, and moisturizers? If you don't have that many drawers, do the same thing with baskets on shelves or in cabinets. Divider trays in drawers keep smaller items under control. To clean the drawers, just remove and wash the trays.

In some instances, a tackle box, art-supply caddy, or box made especially for holding cosmetics or grooming products might make the most sense. This is especially true if you're sharing a bathroom with other people and need to look for an alternate place to get ready when the bathroom's occupied. You can take your box anywhere, even when you travel.

In cabinets, consider a lazy Susan to move things easily from the back of the cabinet to the front.

Hang hair dryers, curling irons, razors, and electric toothbrushes in special caddies or racks specifically made for affixing them to the wall.

An old-fashioned vanity or dressing table gets you out of a shared bathroom for certain parts of your morning routine. Be sure it's well lit; has a good mirror; and has places for all your makeup, perfume, and hair-grooming supplies.

Routines Revisited

Nighttime and morning routines help you every day in every way—I promise! And there's more good news: you can apply the same bottom-line principle to your daily grooming routine.

The best way to make your morning production smooth is to standardize what you do. By creating a routine, you'll save time, narrow down the products you need, and won't be faced with making new decisions each morning. Do the same steps each day, and your morning ritual will eventually become second nature. Write down the steps to start with, if you need to.

To start, decide what you need as a minimum to look neat and well groomed every day. A clean face goes without saying. You'll probably want to use an astringent and a moisturizer (with sunscreen, if you please) at the very least. An easy-to-maintain hair style is invaluable to getting off to a quick start.

When creating your makeup strategy, find a selection of products that work for you and get rid of those that don't. Practice applying them (plenty of books and magazines can show you how) until you have it down to a quick set of steps. You might even consider making an appointment with a cosmetician or color consultant (something to add to your Rewards List!) with the idea of finding a simple routine that makes the most of your makeup time and your best features. Assemble *only* the products you need for your daily makeup routine, and keep them in a caddy. Put away everything else for special occasions.

Black Hole _____

Resist the urge to buy makeup in large palettes or ensembles. Invariably, you'll like only a few colors and the rest just sit there unused and take up space.

Allow yourself enough time for your makeup routine. Applying mascara while driving is an absolute no-no! At the very least, you could soil your clean clothes. At worst, you could have an accident or blind yourself.

And one more thing—take care of yourself! Protect your skin and hair from sun, wind, and cold. Make that a part of your morning routine. And of course, makeup can only go so far. There's no substitute for regular exercise, adequate sleep, and healthful food. Good health is the prettiest makeup of all!

Don't let cosmetics or personal-care salespeople load you down with more than you want or need. Find your own routine and stick to it, using the products you've determined work best for you.

If you keep what you use in a box, divided tray, or zippered bag, you won't have to hunt for what you need. Add duplicates of your major makeup products to your handbag, in smaller sizes if they're available.

Routines Revisited—Redux

For those longer, more involved beauty rituals such as manicures, hair coloring, hair treatments, masking, bleaching facial hair, and the like, why not make them an opportunity to pamper yourself? Make it a regular Friday-night end-of-the-week treat, a relaxing Sunday get-away before the week starts, or a midweek pick-me-up. A little imagination can turn it into a special occasion, when you can indulge yourself at the same time. Start with a good soak in a bubble bath, complete with relaxing music and a mug of special tea, something bubbly, or a fruit juice cooler.

Assign monthly tasks to a particular time of the month—say, the last day or the first day of the month. Or get creative and schedule your magical beauty rituals for the full or new moon! You might even enjoy experimenting with the natural fragrances and health benefits of aromatherapy. Some excellent, easy-to-follow books and reasonably priced, high-quality oils are on the market now, so you can experiment with some simple, mood-enhancing and healing scents. And always remember my order: take care of yourself!

Create routines for bathroom cleaning. It's the job everyone loves to hate, but let's face it—you've decided a dirty, unsanitary bathroom is just not an option anymore! You're taking better care of yourself, remember?

I've seen YouTube videos that show you how to clean a bathroom in 3½ minutes. Maybe … maybe not. It shouldn't take any more than 15 minutes if you create a routine, have all your cleaning tools and products grouped together right there, and just do it. If you're not sure how or want to do it better, plenty of books, websites, and videos on cleaning are available. Or next time you check into a hotel, watch how the maid service does it—after all, they don't have time to fool around!

There are five basic steps to cleaning anything:

Simplewise

Get a shower squeegee for every shower in the house, and hang it in a prominent place in the shower. If you squeegee down the shower after each use, you'll save a heap of work later.

1. Remove
2. Wash
3. Rinse
4. Dry
5. Replace

Move things out of the way, wash the surface down, rinse it, and dry it so you don't leave any spots. Then put back what goes there. Simple, right?

Cleaning expert Don Aslett says to clean from top to bottom and from left to right in a clockwise direction. I get the top-to-bottom thing—if you clean the ceiling fan after you vacuum the floor, that's not going to work well—but I'm not sure about the left-to-right thing. You decide. And that's the key work—*decide*. Pick the products, the tools, and the method, and stick to it. You can always refine it or make it better later. Just start somewhere.

A good cleaning once a week should suffice. Add to that daily toilet swishing if you need to, a quick cleaning of the bathtub after each use, and a wipe of the counters every morning and evening, and your bathroom should stay in good shape. Once a month you can do a more thorough cleaning and keep up with purging any outdated products and returning any items that don't belong there to their proper homes. Decide now—and enlist your family's cooperation—that towels and clothes on the floor are no longer acceptable.

Just as you have your self-care and grooming routines down to a few easy steps, do the same with cleaning your bathroom. Do a little each day wherever you can. And for a more thorough cleaning, find the best products and tools, set the timer, turn on some bathroom-cleaning music, and get it done!

Give Your Handbag a Hand

I always marvel at women who can carry a tiny purse. You know the kind—they barely hold a lipstick, $20, and a credit card. Heaven forbid you should need a tissue or a nail file! I'm afraid most of us just can't pare down quite that much. But I do have a system for keeping your handbag from becoming a catchall for everything under the sun. Friends who've tried it say it works well for them, too.

Simplewise

Several purse inserts are out there, and one of those may suit you just fine. I have used one that was advertised on TV for years for things I always carry and then add my modular cases as I need them.

I've developed what I call a "modular system" for handbag paraphernalia. Which module I use depends on where I'm going, for how long, and what I'll be doing. I choose the size of the handbag I carry according to what my needs are. The basic modules in my system are as follows:

Module 1: Makeup. This module includes the basic neutral shades I use for my everyday makeup routine. It duplicates what I have at home on my vanity. Add what you might need for hair emergencies (bobby pins, a hair elastic), a small tube of hand lotion, some lip balm, an emery board, and maybe some clear nail polish for pantyhose emergencies, and you're good to go.

Module 2: Emergencies. A few simple first-aid or medical supplies (including aspirin, eye drops, a small tube of sunscreen, a small tube of antiseptic ointment, a couple of Band-Aids, and a couple of antacid tablets) are in this module, plus a small sewing kit. This fits into a very small pouch, and I always keep it in my bag.

Module 3: Mini-office. In this pouch I have a couple of pens, a highlighter, some Post-it notes, extra business cards, some stamps, and a small roll of tape—anything I might need on a business call or if I expect to be waiting and might be catching up on my reading or correspondence. This is basically a companion to any clipped articles or a book I might take with me to read, my planner, or something I'm working on. (By the way, I always carry some business cards in a holder in the small zippered pocket of my handbag. This module just has some extras as a back-up.)

Module 4: The bank. This one has my cash, credit and membership cards, checkbook, and a credit card–size calculator. (You could use your cell phone's calculator instead if it has one.) I've used both a zippered bag and one of those all-in-one wallets as my bank. It's your call. Use whatever works for you so you can grab "your bank" and have your money matters in hand in an instant.

By using these modules, I never have loose stuff floating around in my pocketbook. Most of the time I just have the bank in my handbag because I'm probably running to the grocery store or dropping off a shipment at the post office. If I'm going out for a business meeting, I add the makeup module, the one for emergencies, and the mini-office. An evening out might mean just grabbing the makeup module and stuffing a little cash in it. If I'm going for a day trip in the mountains, I might take them all!

Your modules may be made up of different elements, but at least give the modular system a try. Don't forget to periodically go through each module and restock or weed out unnecessary items. It's easy because you've already grouped like things together. And it makes a weekly clean out of your handbag a snap. If you're going to be doing a lot of shopping or are going on vacation, throw in another pouch for your receipts.

Oh, and what to do with that age-old problem of finding the keys? One solution is to get a clip-on key chain that hooks to an outer ring on your handbag. Because I don't have any other loose things in my bag (the modular cases hold everything), I find just dropping them in one compartment isn't a problem. They're easy to find among the zippered modular cases.

Happiness + Good Health = Beauty

To risk sounding like a cliché, beauty really does come from the inside out. If someone's relaxed, happy, and smiling, he's attractive, no matter what his actual facial characteristics. There's no remedy for a frown, a harried look, tiredness, or bad humor.

With your life organized and your most important goals being achieved on a daily basis, people will notice a difference and start asking you what you've been up to! Happiness comes from fulfilling your dreams, and there's nothing more beautiful than confidence and success.

Good health is another friend to beauty. If you drink plenty of water, eat a balanced diet, and get adequate rest and regular exercise, you're going to exude something no one's been able to bottle yet. So keep the commitments you've made to yourself, follow your routines, make your bathroom a place to create an orderly and relaxed beginning, and report back at the end of the week. You look better already!

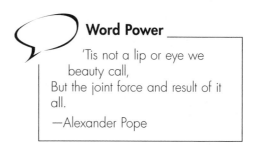

Word Power

'Tis not a lip or eye we beauty call,
But the joint force and result of it all.

—Alexander Pope

The Least You Need to Know

- Daily, weekly, and monthly rituals save time, help you focus on what's important, and can be important opportunities to pamper and reward yourself.

- Weeding out cosmetics and personal-care products not only makes them easier to organize, it helps ensure products are fresh and free of bacteria.

- A modular system using separate zippered bags is one way to keep confusion in your handbag to a minimum.

- The beauty that's generated from good health and a happy life is dazzling. It's the best makeup ever made!

Chapter 11

The Kitchen: Systems for Getting Your Daily Bread

In This Chapter

- ◆ Setting food goals
- ◆ Creating a well-organized kitchen
- ◆ Cutting shopping time with lists and menus
- ◆ Cooking made simple
- ◆ Organizing cookbooks and recipes

Whether you're a gourmet cook or you eat on the fly most of the time, the kitchen is one of the most time-consuming spaces in your home to keep clean and organized. Yet it's one of the most important rooms to tackle. The kitchen is where we congregate, communicate, nourish ourselves and our families, create, offer hospitality, and share our abundance. Clutter and chaos in the heart of the home spreads to the rest of your world, and having an efficient, well-laid-out kitchen can mean the difference between enjoying preparing a nourishing meal and dreading it.

First Things First

Before you start moving stuff around or giving away half your appliances, let's first take an inventory of where you are with regard to food and decide what matters to you about the daily rituals that surround putting healthful, pleasing meals on the table.

You Are What You Eat

Take the time right now, before you start your kitchen reorganization, to ask yourself some revealing questions. What you're looking for here is insight into the role food plays in your life and helping you decide whether you want to make some changes. Your answers will help you make informed decisions about what to keep and what to dispose of based on the goals you identify. You'll probably want to write them down, so get out your planner/organizer or your organizing notebook, make yourself a cup of tea, and begin by asking these questions:

◆ What place does food occupy in your life? Do you just "eat to live" or are you a "foodie" for whom food preparation is an enjoyable and social event?

◆ Do you eat out or order in most of the time? Do you cook at home but use a lot of prepared foods? Or do you cook largely from scratch using fresh ingredients? What, exactly, did you do for supper each night last week? Can't remember? Keep track for a week, and the patterns you discover may surprise you.

◆ How would you assess the quality of the food you eat? Do you eat a lot of junk or fast food? Do you use a lot of prepared or frozen food? Do you consider your diet healthful, or would you say you need to make some improvements in that area?

◆ Do you need to lose a few pounds? Are you battling a blood pressure, blood sugar, or cholesterol problem? Do you have food allergies? What other special dietary or nutritional needs do you have, if any?

◆ Do you usually eat alone or with family, friends, or housemates?

◆ Are you expected to cook for your family, or is meal preparation a shared activity? Would you like to see some changes in that area?

◆ Do other people share your kitchen? What's their schedule? How is that working for you?

- Do you eat on a regular schedule or whenever you can grab a bite? Does your family have regularly scheduled mealtimes?

- What are some things about your cooking or eating habits you'd like to change?

How, when, where, and what you eat goes a long way toward setting you up to have a good or bad day. Food can affect your mood, your energy level, how you sleep, your general sense of well-being, and your long-term health. This is a book about organization, not nutrition, but this isn't a bad time to consider the fuel your body depends on to help you accomplish all the things you plan to do now that you're on the road to organizing your life.

Taking a Closer Look

As you probably know by now, I strongly believe that before beginning any worthwhile task it's good to see it in a larger context—to know its purpose and ask whether it supports you in what you want in your life. Now may be a good time to see a nutritionist or your doctor and take an honest inventory of your health and the role your eating habits have in keeping you healthy or making you sick.

If everything's okay, you may only need to look at your kitchen layout, work flow, and convenience. If, however, you want to make some major changes in the way you eat, you need to scrutinize these things, as well as which foods you have in your pantry and even the kinds of cooking equipment you use.

After examining the way you eat now and thinking about changes you'd like to make, write down two or three goals for the way you plan, shop for, prepare, eat, and clean up after your daily meals. Perhaps you'd like to begin eating at home a little more often. Maybe you'd like to get on a more sensible

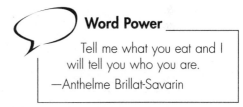

Word Power

Tell me what you eat and I will tell you who you are.

—Anthelme Brillat-Savarin

eating program that includes more fruits and vegetables. Do you need to face up to some diet-related health problems and take action to correct them? Would you like to entertain more but find yourself putting it off because cooking for company is such a hassle or you're ashamed to have anyone in the house looking like it does? Would you like to rein in your budget and feel you could save money by changing your eating and cooking habits?

Whatever food goals you set, choose two or three and write them down in your planner or notebook. Keep these goals uppermost in your mind as you revamp your kitchen. Read through this chapter, decide on specific actions to help you accomplish your goals, and add them to your Master List in your planner/organizer.

Confronting Your Kitchen

You can confront the kitchen in an all-day session or work on it piecemeal, one small area at time. Those 15-minute sessions can be very powerful if you keep doing them every day. Whichever method you choose, you need to understand the design and layout of your kitchen as it is now, be conscious of how you currently function in the space, and analyze how to minimize your movement and maximize the space available to you.

Simplewise

Not enough space in your kitchen cabinets for food storage? Consider a free-standing cabinet or piece of furniture. If you have the wall space, you can install narrow wire racks designed especially for canned goods and other food packages. Or try a rack that fits over a door. Look for space in unconventional places!

Now let's take a look at your kitchen space from a distance. What works and what doesn't? Are you short on counter space? Cabinets? If there's too much clutter to tell right now, take a fresh look after you go through the unstuffing process (that's coming up next). Where are the catchalls—places where clutter just loves to live? Do certain things bug you about your kitchen? Is it a one-person kitchen, or can two or more people prepare a meal together? Do you find yourself making lots of steps to get a meal on the table? Just make a note of these things and move on to the next step.

Unstuff Your Foodstuffs

After setting your goals and analyzing your space, the next step is to unstuff your kitchen, using the routine you learned in Chapter 5. If you can, begin to clear out the space in your kitchen you've decided to reorganize first. A good place to start is with any food you have stored in your kitchen cabinets, pantry, refrigerator, freezer, or any other food storage area.

Toss out any food that's passed its expiration date. Separate foods that need to be used up shortly. These will go in the front of the cabinet or pantry shelf when you put them away. If you have a lot of one item, evaluate whether you can use it up before it expires. If not, pass some on to someone who can. And give or throw away food that doesn't fit your nutrition objectives.

If you tend to store a lot of canned goods, put the oldest cans in the front, and when you shop again, put the newer cans in the back. Make a written inventory, and plan meals around what you already have.

Clean out your refrigerator and freezer; throw out food that's bad or stale or freezer burned; and put the remaining food back, grouping similar things wherever possible. If you have freezer items not kept in original packaging, label them with the name of the food and the date. Make a written inventory of what foods are left in your refrigerator and freezer so you can plan meals around them.

 Simplewise _____

If you anticipate doing a major revamping of your cabinets and drawers, adding shelving or buying inserts and dividers, you may want to put your nonperishable foods into boxes labeled according to category for a short while and put them back when you've finished adding your storage solutions.

Group your packaged and canned goods into categories: staples, baking ingredients, vegetables, fruits, meats, sauces, beverages, and so on. Store food using the same basic principles you've used for everything else: put most-used items in the prime real estate right near where you prepare and cook, and set least-often-used items farther away. Group like things together, and consolidate and compress using various containers and storage options.

Pare Down Your Pots and Pans

Now move throughout your kitchen and continue unstuffing. Use your sorting boxes: Trash, Put Away (for things that belong elsewhere in the house), Pass On, and Fix. Go through cabinets, shelves, and drawers, and look at dishes, pots and pans, appliances, and utensils. Ask yourself the following questions:

◆ When was the last time I used this?

◆ Do I have another tool that can do double duty in place of this one?

◆ Are there any duplicates? Which one works best?

◆ Does it need to be fixed?

If you come across kitchen tools that just don't do the job, get rid of them and replace them with ones that work well. Buy quality kitchen equipment and learn how to take care of it. A few excellent knives kept sharp are far more useful than a drawer full of the other kind, and they take up less space. Learn how to use a sharpening steel properly so you can maintain your cutlery. Many kinds of resources are available online to show you how, including several excellent videos on YouTube.

Have a few high-quality and easy-to-clean pots and pans in the most common and convenient sizes. When you buy new ones, don't keep the old. Seriously, how many frying pans do you really need if you're not running a restaurant?

The same is true with appliances. Buy quality, not quantity. And don't overbuy. If a small chopper is all you need, don't buy a professional-size food processor with all the attachments.

Simplewise

Before you toss broken appliances out for good, check for replacement parts at RepairClinic.com or by calling 1-800-269-2609. This site even offers appliance repair tips and help.

If you're having trouble deciding what kitchen equipment and utensils you really need, pack up everything (as if you're getting ready to move) except the bare essentials you need to prepare your daily meals. Locate the boxes somewhere else temporarily. As you need specialty items, go get them and find a home for them in your kitchen. Whatever's left after a month or so, you obviously don't use. Let it go!

Unstuffing a kitchen that's been out of control for a long time can be a very big job. If your kitchen is Chaos Central, break up your sessions into manageable bites. If you've been thinking you really need some professional help, this would be a time to call in a professional organizer (I tell you how in Chapter 17). The impact on your everyday life would be enormous. Or consider making this a family project, or rely on your "buddy system." Whatever gets it done.

Now that you've pared down and have familiarized yourself with what you have to store, let's talk about how your kitchen is laid out and what you can do to make the most of its design.

Make Your Kitchen Do the Work

I'm not a contractor, so I'm not about to guide you through a major remodeling of your kitchen. If you have the money to do extensive remodeling or build a new kitchen from scratch, go for it. Lots of good books and plenty of experts can help you design your custom kitchen. However, I suggest you consult an organization expert *as well as* a contractor! For now, though, we're going to work with what you already have, which probably has a number of design flaws, and make it the best it can be.

To plan how to use available space to its greatest advantage, divide your kitchen into activity areas or centers. You need the following:

◆ Preparation Center for cutting, chopping, and mixing ingredients

◆ Cooking Center that revolves around the stove

◆ Serving Center

◆ Cleanup Center that basically involves the sink and dishwasher (if you have one)

When you look at some kitchens, you can't help wondering if the designer ever tried cooking in it because these areas aren't clearly defined or efficiently located. So where do you generally do these activities now? Just make a note of it, and let's move on to see if you're currently using your kitchen space as efficiently as you might be.

Simplewise

Short on storage for pots and pans? Look up! Check out some of the beautiful racks that hang from the ceiling for suspending cookware. If you have some wall space, you can hang them from a grid system or brackets instead. Or look in mail-order catalogs, online (try stacksandstacks.com), and in culinary stores for other ideas.

The Preparation Center

In the Preparation Center, lack of counter space is the most common problem. You need adequate surface area to lay out your ingredients and use a variety of tools and small appliances at one time. This center should be located near the sink to allow for rinsing foods and washing off utensils. Locate items such as knives, bowls, cutting boards, and food preparation appliances near this area.

But first, get as much off your counters as possible. Keep your counters for work, not display, especially if your counter space is limited. Store appliances that aren't used every day in cabinets or on shelves. Consider appliances that mount under cabinets if you're short on space. If you still don't have enough counter space, see whether you can make a fold-down counter, the kind you often see in RVs or campers, add a kitchen island, or purchase a movable cart with a butcher-block top.

The Cooking Center

From the Preparation Center, you want to be able to move to the Cooking Center, which includes the stove and any nearby counter space. A triangular layout between preparation area, stove, and refrigerator works best. If you can rearrange your appliances so they give you that pattern of movement, try to do it. The items you use most should be located in the storage within that triangular area.

If you can't arrange things in a triangle, a rolling work cart may be the only solution. You can assemble items from the refrigerator, roll them to the work area, and take prepared ingredients to the cooking area the same way. This should save you some steps and spills along the way.

Pots and pans, hot pads, spices, and other items used regularly during cooking should be located in the Cooking Center, too.

The Serving Center

The Serving Center is best located near where you actually sit down to eat, and your dishes, eating utensils, and serving pieces should be located there if at all possible. I have a counter divider between my kitchen and the dining area, so that's where I set things to be served. The silverware drawer and cabinets that hold the dishes are right next to it, which is also near the Preparation Center.

Just notice how far away your dishes and serving bowls are from where you eat your meals. You may want to consolidate them and locate them closer to where you eat.

The Cleanup Center

The Cleanup Center is usually best located next to the Preparation Center. That way you can clean up as you go, while you're preparing a meal, to save work at the end. When you finish a meal, have a designated place to put dishes. To one side of the sink is usually a good location. Making too many trips from the eating area to the kitchen during the clearing process may indicate that you need to rethink how you're doing things.

You might want to have a tray handy or a rolling cart for stacking dishes and taking them to the kitchen to be washed and put away. It helps if others in the household know where to put dirty dishes as well. There's no sense having them move dishes to one spot and then you have to move them to another. The clearer the instructions and the easier you make it, the more likely others are to help!

Keep one side of a double sink or a dishpan full of hot, soapy water ready to put dirty dishes and utensils in as you cook. This avoids clutter and makes the dishes easier to clean later on. If you keep up with dishes, they'll be less of a problem. Unwashed dishes that have been sitting require more elbow grease and water, and if you're using a dishwasher, they sometimes won't even come clean without prescrubbing. If you can't get to them immediately, at least rinse them or put them in water to soak.

Now this may seem like a no-brainer, but one of the things you're most likely to see in a disorganized household is a sink full of dirty dishes. I know. I've been there. Just repeat to yourself, "We don't allow dirty dishes to pile up in this house! I deserve to see a clean sink!" You and I both know there's nothing more depressing than to wake up in the morning to a sink full of dirty dishes, so wash them as you go and make this one of your bottom-line commitments.

Advanced Kitchen Storage

Now that you've figured out where to locate the main areas of activity in your kitchen, the next thing to tackle is the storage located in each. You want to create storage solutions that save you steps and make the most of the time you spend in the kitchen. After all, you have other things to do!

Some cabinets have adjustable shelves. If yours do, you've got a lot more options. Racks, step shelves, and slide-out drawer units can make your existing cabinets more efficient and flexible. Check out Appendix A for products, organizing-supply and container stores, websites, and mail-order catalogs to help you plan. If your cabinets are very deep and things tend to get lost, a step shelf along the back, a lazy Susan, or a slide-out unit should help.

Don't overlook walls and ceilings or the backs of doors as possible storage components. Grid systems for wall storage (or you might consider pegboard, which can be painted), racks that fit along the backsplash, over- and on-the-door racks, and various fixtures for hanging pots and pans from the ceiling are all available to help. Just be sure not to hang anything where you'll bonk your head! Also consider hooks under cabinets or shelves for cups, or one of those racks that hold stemmed glasses upside down. There will need to be adequate space, however, to work underneath without hitting them.

Simplewise

The small space above a door between the doorjamb and the ceiling can be used for cookbooks or other smaller, uniform items just by installing a shelf.

Make a list of storage problems you've identified in your kitchen. Then take a series of field trips to organizing, hardware, discount, and decorating stores. Be sure to take measurements of your cabinet spaces with you, and bring a tape measure. Take notes and check what you find against online or mail-order options. Find solutions to maximize your cabinet and shelf space, and look for options that make items easy to reach and easy to put away.

While you're there, talk to the store employees. Professional organizers know all the best tricks and products for kitchen storage, and home stores sometimes have knowledgeable sales people who can help as well. Take along some photos of your problem areas if you can.

But I must remind you: the more you "unstuff" your kitchen, the less you're going to have to do to find additional storage space. If you got down to basics in the beginning of this chapter, you may just find you have all the storage space you need!

Kitchen Strategies

One of the few things you may want to give a permanent home to on top of the counter is the kitchen utensils you use all the time. Consider getting a large crock that will hold the spatulas, slotted spoons, etc., right next to the stove or preparation area. I find this solution is easier than having them in a drawer, but with drawer dividers and lots of drawer space, you may prefer storing them there.

When choosing decorating materials, appliances, fixtures, and equipment, think about functionality and ease of cleaning. Keep hardware such as faucets, knobs, handles, or pulls simple. The fewer nooks and crannies there are to get dirty, the better. Paint or wall coverings should stand up to kitchen grease and grime, and avoid fancy curtains or other decorating elements that can give you cleaning headaches. Don't forget to put up backsplashes where they're most needed—behind the stove and your preparation area.

Don't let your food storage containers sit in a drawer—use them. You probably only need a few pieces for leftover food storage. You may need a few more if you're doing bulk cooking (coming up later in this chapter), but limit what you store to what you really use.

Get rid of containers you never use or have too many of in one particular size. Ditch those without lids, or use them under plants to catch water or to sort similar items in drawers if they're low enough to fit. They also make great storage for crafts and office supplies, among other things. Just get them out of the kitchen if you're not using them. Relocate and reuse them, and they're no longer clutter!

Keep little-used and seasonal items in the high, hard-to-reach cabinets above the stove and refrigerator (even if you need a step stool to reach them), or get them out of the kitchen altogether.

As far as that dreaded under-the-sink area goes, be sure you do a thorough unstuffing job of that catchall, as well. There are probably cleaning products lurking there you haven't seen in years! Get rid of those you don't use, consolidate wherever possible (can three half-full bottles of window cleaner be poured into one?), and keep your cleaning products and tools to a minimum. Restrain yourself from trying every new cleaning potion, scrubber, or dishwashing cleanser that comes on the market. Find one you like and stick with it.

Black Hole

Be careful what you store in the cabinet under the sink and in all low cabinets, especially if you have pets, small children, or entertain folks with little ones. Many cleaning products are highly toxic or at least can create a nasty spill. Get a child-proof locking device if you must store questionable items there.

When you're done unstuffing and relocating, be sure anyone else who uses the kitchen knows where stuff is and will be kept from now on. You might even consider making up lists in large type and taping them to the inside of cabinet doors or on drawer faces until everyone gets with the new system. At least once a year, do a thorough cleaning of your kitchen storage areas. Get rid of unused items just as you did in this first session. Reevaluate your work flow from time to time, and move things that don't seem to be in the best place.

Simplewise

Ever notice how much stuff ends up in the kitchen? The kids' backpacks, Dad's keys, packages from the store, tools, toys, mail, school papers—you name it—somehow it finds its way onto the kitchen counters. Find all these things homes—elsewhere. Have a place for Dad to hang his keys when he comes in the door. Create an area for kids to keep their school stuff. A cubby system, cupboard, or series of hooks (make them strong!) can help, too. When accumulation starts to take over, rally the team and do a quick put away. Make it a game. Set the timer, grab the kids, and see who finishes first!

When your kitchen is done, you will have pared down to only those things you use regularly and that work well. Each will have a home. You will have located everything so you can prepare a meal with a minimum of steps. Survey your domain and smile!

Shop but Don't Drop

Now that your kitchen is organized and efficient, the next question has to be: is there a way to make shopping easier?

I believe there is, and the way to do it is to standardize. You and your family probably enjoy eating a few basic meals on a regular basis. Maybe it's chicken and dumplings or pot roast. Maybe you just love a particular pasta dish, soup, or stew. Or perhaps you grill regularly. I bet you could make a list of 15 meals you prepare over and over again, probably on a monthly basis. I call these my "rotation meals," and I keep the recipes for them all in a binder, plus a Rotation Meal list in my planner/organizer. I know them so well I can pretty much name the ingredients from memory. What would your rotation meals be?

In addition to your list of rotation recipes, you need an ingredients list. This is a list of all the major ingredients you use in your everyday cooking, including those rotation meals, a kind of master shopping list. That way, if you're out running errands, you can just scan your list and see whether you've forgotten anything. I have mine on my computer to print out whenever I need to, and I also have one in my planner/organizer. If your cell phone has list-making capabilities, you could keep it there, too. Keep a running list for other items that come up in a prominent place where the whole family can add their shopping reminders and requests. A dry-erase board is handy for this.

Simplewise _____

Do your menu planning with your calendar at your side so you can plan easy dishes for busy evenings and skip planning meals altogether for evenings you'll be out. Don't forget to plan to use leftovers, too!

Do you plan menus for the week? If not, it's time you start. You might not cook exactly what you'd planned on the day you planned it, but it takes the guesswork out of answering the inevitable "What's for dinner?" question. You can plan slow cooker meals for the days you know are going to be long and hectic. You'll use up leftovers because you've planned for them in your weekly menus. You'll save money shopping because you'll know what ingredients you really need, and you'll make fewer trips to the grocery store because you've planned ahead. Research proves that fewer shopping trips equals smaller grocery bills!

Buy in bulk when it's practical. If you're cooking for only one person, you obviously can't eat a bushel of apples before they go bad, but you could make applesauce and can or freeze it. But will you? Know what you're really capable of using and don't overbuy.

Also be sure you have storage space for bulk purchases. Buying in quantity cuts down on the time you spend shopping and can save you money, but it's no bargain if you can't find what you bought or it goes bad before you use it.

Some items to buy in bulk if you do have the storage include paper goods, cleaning products, nonperishable staples such as vinegar and baking soda, some personal-care products (cotton balls, Q-tips), canned and bottled foods, and some dry foods such as legumes and pastas that keep well. You can store up to a 6-months' supply in a fairly compact area, and you'll save time, effort, and money. Having at least a small supply of canned goods and dry ingredients is also handy in an emergency. Make an inventory, post it near your bulk storage area, cross off items as you use them, and add them to your shopping list.

Crafty Cooking Strategies

Too busy to create yummy home-cooked meals? Nonsense! I'm going to give you three strategies that make it easy to put tasty, nutritional homemade meals on the table with the least amount of effort. They save you money, too! Try them on for size. You can always mix and match!

Cook Once, Eat for a Month

A few years ago, I made a fabulous discovery. It wasn't a totally new idea to me, because when I was a single parent, working full-time and going to school, I devised a scaled-down version, but I had never seen it systematized and explained quite the same way before. The method I'm talking about goes by many names—once-a-month cooking, freezer cooking, bulk cooking, frozen assets, investment cooking—but they all use the same strategy of bulk buying, marathon cooking, and freezing ahead. If you're serious about using this method, it helps to have a separate freezer, but it's possible to do a smaller version with the freezer in an average-size refrigerator.

Simplewise

Why clean your kitchen every day? With bulk cooking, you only make a major kitchen mess once a month. One good scrubbing after your monthly marathon session and it stays clean until the next time, except for daily touch-ups and dishes.

The basic idea is that you plan your menus for a month, do all the shopping in a day or two, do all the cooking in another couple of days, and forget about it for a month. I especially find this method helpful when I'm heavily embroiled in a book project and don't want to be burdened with thinking about "What's for dinner?" It's also great when I have lots of visitors. My mental and physical energy can go toward other things because I took the time to think out our eating plan ahead of time, and all the work is done.

Bulk cooking comes with many benefits. For example, major shopping is only necessary once a month. You cut down on trips to the supermarket and the extra hidden cost of impulse buys and children constantly asking "Why can't I have this, Mommy?" The fewer number of trips, the less you spend. And you save on gas!

You can take advantage of restaurant-size cans and quantity buys on fresh fruits and vegetables from wholesale clubs, farmers' markets, or food cooperatives. This saves lots of money and often means higher quality. Plus, because you're cooking ahead and freezing, you can make the most of seasonal foods and buy ingredients when they're the freshest and least expensive.

Meals are all planned and prepared so you don't have to think about it. You can concentrate on other things! And if there's an emergency, you're covered at home.

Because you're cooking several meals all at once, there's less waste. After cooking whole chickens for several meals, for example, the remaining carcasses and defatted drippings become the base for a soup or sauce. Trimmings from fresh vegetables can be used to make vegetable stock. More dollar savings!

In addition, you can concentrate on tasty and nutritious side dishes, like fresh salads or vegetable dishes, because the main meal is already prepared. You even have time to whip up a special treat for dessert now and then. And with dinner in the freezer, you're less likely to order pizza or stop for fast food. So you not only save money when you go to the grocery store, you also save money throughout the month.

With bulk cooking, you save energy because you're using appliances for large batches rather than many small batches. In warmer weather, you heat up the house less, especially if you use your slow cooker to thaw and heat your dish earlier in the day. And you'll actually *use* appliances such as food processors, mixers, grinders, slicers, blenders, vacuum sealers, and slow cookers on a monthly basis. It will be worth your while to pull them out of cabinets and off shelves—*and* clean them!

Simplewise

Bulk cooking is environmentally friendly, because bulk buying means less packaging.

You can get the whole family involved in the various tasks associated with bulk cooking, such as chopping and slicing. Or you can join with other folks of like mind and cook together or swap dishes for greater variety.

Having your meals planned and prepared means you're less likely to "throw something together" and eat foods you're trying to avoid. You can plan better to stay on track with the nutrition goals you set at the beginning of this chapter. And dinner is always in the freezer when you're caught with unexpected guests or a neighbor is ill and could use a home-cooked meal. In fact, you might actually find yourself asking, "Why don't you stay for dinner?" more often.

In Appendix A, I list several good books explaining various versions of the bulk cooking method. One that gives you a total plan you can adapt to your own nutrition goals is *Once-a-Month Cooking* by Mimi Wilson and Mary Beth Lagerborg. You'll also find some of the best websites to teach you this way of cooking.

The only disadvantage I've found to bulk cooking is that my family and I sometimes get tired of frozen foods, even if they're yummy and homemade from scratch, so we just extend our freezer stash with grilling and "quick-cook" meals from freshly bought ingredients. (You learn more about this method in a moment.)

Quick Cooking, Easy Cleanup

Another way to get control of meal preparation is to learn quick-cooking methods. Quick-cooked meals involve a minimum of ingredients that can be easily assembled, are often cooked in one pan or dish, and usually take fewer than 20 minutes from start to finish. Several quick-cook cookbooks can give you plenty of ideas, including ones from Rachael Ray and Martha Stewart. I've listed some in Appendix A.

Supper on the table in 20 minutes? Impossible, you say? Not at all! Especially if you have some of the ingredients prepared and waiting on hand in the refrigerator. Here's another use for that seldom-used slow cooker! Put a batch of whole grains such as brown rice in the pot, add the appropriate amount of water, and let it slow cook while you do other things. Use part of the batch for dinner tonight, and save the rest for another meal or two during the week—or freeze it for later. One dish might be a sauté, another could be a casserole, and a third could be a cold vegetable-and-grain salad. Having precooked grains on hand makes quick cooking even easier.

To encourage you (and others) to eat your veggies, put some carrots, onions, summer squash, and zucchini through the food processor using the shredding disc, and store the mixture in a plastic bag in the fridge. Then when you get home from work, you can toss some of your "vegetable medley" in a wok with a little oil, slice some chicken breast or throw in a few shrimps or scallops, add some cooked noodles or brown rice, season, and you'll be sitting down to eat in a flash. For a meatless meal, leave out the chicken breast or shellfish and substitute some tofu. If you don't feel like cooking, toss the vegetable ingredients with some salad dressing and some canned chicken, tuna, or shrimp, and you have a tasty cold dish.

You can probably come up with lots more easy combinations like these on your own. Scan cookbooks and magazines for ideas to add to your collection. You don't even have to follow the exact recipes—just gather combinations of simple ingredients for a quick, healthful meal. Add these to your Rotation Meals file or binder.

Apply a similar strategy to breakfast and lunch. Use leftover rice, some raisins or other dried fruit, a splash of milk, a little cinnamon, and honey, and you've got a nutritious and *fast* breakfast. Toss leftover noodles with a bit of soy sauce, some toasted sesame seeds, and green onions for a quick, healthful, and inexpensive lunch. Add an orange or apple on the side, or a handful of dried fruits and nuts, and you're all set. Simple food takes less time, costs less, and is almost always better for you.

Simplewise

If refrigerator and freezer space is at a premium, the quick-cooking method works especially well. Plan out your week's menus, chop or precook as many components as possible, and shop two or three times a week for fresh ingredients as needed. Just be sure to stick to your list and avoid those impulse buys.

For this cooking method, you want to stock in your pantry certain easy-to-add ingredients that require little preparation. Stock up on items such as chopped canned tomatoes and cans of mushrooms, soups and broths, corn, bamboo shoots, water chestnuts, beans, and chili peppers. It would be handy to have items such as salsa, corn or flour tortillas, prebaked pizza shells, and quick-cooking frozen vegetables that can be added direct from the freezer, such as peas, chopped broccoli, or spinach, too.

Here are some advantages of the quick-cooking method:

◆ You're cooking with the freshest ingredients on a regular basis.

◆ You have ultrafast preparation time.

◆ Required food storage space is minimal. If you have a very small refrigerator/ freezer and very little pantry space, this is a great option.

The main disadvantages are that this method requires more frequent trips to the grocery store for fresh ingredients and it doesn't take advantage of the cost savings of bulk buying.

Slow Cooking: Ready-and-Waiting Meals

Another great way to cut down on cooking time and preparation is to make skill-ful use of your slow cooker. I own six in different sizes, and I use them all the time. As I already mentioned, a slow cooker can be a very helpful tool if you're following the bulk cooking strategy, but you can use it to simplify meals day-to-day, even if you don't choose this method.

Wouldn't it be great if the moment you came home, the splendid smell of a complete, nutritious, home-cooked meal wafted from your kitchen—without ever having to light the stove? How do sweet-and-sour beef, chicken Polynesian, or three-bean chili sound to you? Again, planning is the key, but in this case you're planning your meals around your kitchen powerhouse, the slow cooker.

Use your slow cooker for entertaining, for making delicious gifts such as chutneys, jams, and jellies, and for concocting scrumptious desserts. You can even bake in your slow cooker with the right accessories and instructions from the recipe book that probably came with your appliance. Make it your business to learn how to use this marvelously versatile piece of kitchen equipment, and if you don't have one, you might want to whisper in someone's ear!

When I was working outside the home, I used my slow cooker to make our weeknight meals, and then cooked more elaborate meals on the weekends. The advantages of using the slow cooker include the following:

◆ A hot meal is ready and waiting for you when you get home.

◆ The slow cooking method makes the best of less expensive cuts of meat.

◆ The slow cooking method keeps all the juices and nutrients in.

◆ Cleanup is minimal.

◆ Slow cookers take very little energy to run and they don't give off a lot of heat, which is a real plus in the summertime.

As with frozen meals, sometimes you want a break from slow-cooked ones. Just plan on having some variety and this method will hold you in good stead. I might add that my slow cooker makes Thanksgiving dinner a snap. I do the sausage stuffing in one so the bird cooks faster. Everyone raves about how moist and delicious it is. A second slow cooker holds the mashed potatoes. Yet another slow cooker cooks a pumpkin pudding for dessert and a fourth has spiced cider simmering for before or after the meal. Or did I just make that so the house smelled like Thanksgiving? I'll never tell.

There are lots of great slow-cooker cookbooks around. One of the best comes with your appliance and I highly recommend the *Fix-It and Forget-It Cookbook: Feasting with Your Slow Cooker* by Dawn Ranck and Phyllis Good. The authors also have versions for entertaining, light cooking, and cooking for diabetics, and they're all good.

If you don't want to add to your cookbook collection (and I'm all for that), there are several excellent sites on the Internet for slow-cooker recipes. Try crockpot.cdkitchen. com and one of my favorites, a blog by Stephanie O'Dea called A Year of Slow Cooking at crockpot365.blogspot.com. I'm wheat intolerant, and Stephanie has to cook gluten-free for her family, so this was a really great find for me. Type "slow cooker" into your favorite search engine, and you'll find lots more!

Be on the lookout for systems, strategies, and methods that save time. Use the resources and tools you already have to their best advantage. Adopt strategies that support you in your nutrition and health goals. You won't regret it. Mastering this important part of everyday life will reward you in more ways than you might imagine. To your health!

Emergency Food Storage

There's a saying that goes something like this: "There are no emergencies for some-one who's prepared." The Boy Scouts teach it, and experience bears it out. Whether it's a natural or man-made disaster or something personal such as a financial setback, tough economic times, illness, or sudden unemployment, having a store of food and water, and planning for self-sufficiency in an emergency, gives you peace of mind and can actually save your life!

If you're without power, the Red Cross recommends you first eat up the food in the refrigerator, then the freezer, and finally turn to food in your long-term storage. You'll want a small camp stove or gas-fueled burner to heat things up, but make sure to exercise caution about operating these with proper ventilation. If you have a wood stove, this might be an option in a cold weather emergency.

No long-term food storage? Well, perhaps you should consider building some. Having three to six months of food and water for your family buys an incredible amount of peace of mind and security. It's a lesson our ancestors knew well. They canned and dried food, dug a root cellar to overwinter vegetables, stored grains, and always had a "rain barrel." In our fast-food society, we've all but forgotten what it means to "put food by," but with recent hurricanes, tornadoes, floods, and even terrorist threats, people are rediscovering its wisdom.

You want to set up and locate your system based on the particular circumstances that relate to your region. Are you in a tornado region? A flood plain? An earthquake area? Are there alternative sources of water, or is water a problem where you live?

You don't need a lot of expensive provisions and you don't need to add to your clutter to prepare for an emergency. You can handle just about any crisis with forethought, planning, skills, and knowledge. Just remember to "store what you eat and eat what you store," rotating your provisions regularly. A fun family project is to throw the breaker for a whole day and night or two and see how well you're able to cope with the lack of electricity. No fair hopping in the car and going to the local fast-food restaurant! We did this for a day and it became clear right away what worked, what didn't, and what we had but couldn't find when we needed it. It was a valuable lesson.

Simplewise

If you want to learn how to create an effective emergency food-storage system, a good place to start is *Making the Best of Basics: Family Preparedness Handbook* by James Talmage Stevens.

Handy Recipe Rationale

Recipes come from a variety of sources: cookbooks, magazines, newspapers, television shows, friends, and websites. Of all the recipes that come into your hands, how many do you think you'll ever actually try? This is another time to do some soul-searching and examine your true ambitions as a cook. I'll bet right now you could eliminate two thirds of your recipe collection, if not more. And, hey, if you really need another cheesecake recipe in the future, I'm sure you can find one in the library, in a magazine, or online!

I already mentioned rotation meals and having recipes for those. These are the tried-and-true dishes that everybody in your family loves. If you have recipes you use regularly, and especially if you're trying one of the cooking methods described in this chapter, you want easy access to them. But before you do anything, go through your boxes, drawers, file folders and binders and dump those recipes you've had for years and never tried. Then go through your cookbooks and purge, purge, purge. When you're done choose a way to store your recipes so you can find them.

There are several ways to keep the recipes you really use to make them easy to find and less bulky.

Recipe Binder

One way to keep track of recipes is to use binders with plastic sheet protectors, "magnetic" sheets (used for holding photos), or just paper for pasting onto, as in a scrapbook. You may want to have several smaller binders, with each covering a particular food category, such as one for meats, poultry, and fish; another for desserts; a third for appetizers; and so on. Using sheet protectors or magnetic albums allows you to rearrange or take out recipes, which is an advantage over a more permanent scrapbook. I personally have two recipe binders. One is strictly for holiday and special-occasion dishes and it's part of a larger holiday binder that includes other activities for the holidays besides cooking. The recipe portion of this binder is small because it only includes our favorite holiday dishes and recipes for food we make as gifts. The other contains my "rotation meal" recipes. See what makes the most sense to you for the way you cook and entertain.

Recipe Box

This is the old-fashioned method for keeping frequently used recipes, and it works as well as ever. A new twist might be to laminate the recipe cards so they hold up better and can just be wiped clean. If it's a recipe you clipped from a magazine, just cut it out, paste it on a file card, and laminate it. If it's from a cookbook, photocopy it, cut it down to size, paste, and laminate. Because my grandmother and my mother both kept their recipes this way and many of the cards are handwritten by them, I still use this method. There's something about making my mom's lemon meringue pie from her original recipe card that tickles me. It's simple and efficient, and it doesn't take a lot of time to keep up or take up a lot of space.

Recipe File

A filing folder system is another way to keep track. But remember to purge it regularly, as you should any file drawer, and only save those recipes you honestly think you'll use. Depending on how much you cook and like to experiment, you may set aside part of the household filing cabinet for this purpose. I tried this method and it just became a catchall for recipes I forgot I had. I ditched it. But that's not to say it might not work for you.

Recipe Database

Proponents of the computer school of recipe keeping have a point. Why struggle with cumbersome cookbooks, cards that get dirty, binders, or file boxes when you can put everything on the computer? The powerful cookbook software available today comes with several digital cookbooks and then, of course, you can add your own recipes. You can create menus and shopping lists and keep track of cholesterol, fat, and calories. Best of all, they're searchable, so you can find that recipe in a flash. If you want a fresh copy, just print it out. If you have a laptop computer, you can just bring it along to the kitchen. Just keep it away from the sink and the stove!

Typing in your own recipes can be time-consuming, which is a disadvantage. But if you're limiting yourself to your rotation meals and special occasion recipes, it may be worth it to enter them once and for all. According to TopTenReviews.com, the three highest-rated cookbook and recipe software products on the market are *Big Oven Deluxe Inspired Cooking, Living Cookbook,* and *MasterCook Deluxe,* in that order. All have import/export capabilities so you can easily download recipes from online sources into your digital cookbook. You can also print meal plans, shopping lists, recipe cards, and even create whole cookbooks, plus these programs make it easy to e-mail recipes. There are user forums for each program as well.

So if you're thinking of taking the digital option, you'll have plenty of information to help you decide which program is the best one for you.

Organizing Your Cookbooks

It's honesty time! Time to unstuff your cookbooks! Gather all your cookbooks together. You may have to search the whole house to find them all! Now quiz yourself about when you referred to each one last. If it's been more than a year, you can probably live without it.

Keep the ones you use the most; if you have some cookbooks you refer to regularly, but only for a couple of recipes, why not copy the recipes and ditch the cookbook? You can also get so many recipes online now, that if you're looking for something new to fix, you'll never be at a loss. Consider paring down your cookbooks to only a few and you'll gain some breathing room and shelf space.

Now arrange your cookbooks in a way that makes the most sense to you. It can be alphabetically by author or by type of cooking or by title. Just be sure it will make it easy to find what you want, when you want it.

When culling recipes from cookbooks, magazines, or your recipe files, apply the "quality not quantity" principle. Why have 60 recipes for brownies when you always use Aunt Fanny's recipe because it's the best? Maybe there are a couple of brownie variations you want to try, but save Aunt Fanny's recipe and let most of the others go.

Now breathe in the smells of wonderful things coming from your spacious, orderly, and shiny kitchen. Doesn't it do your heart good to have the "heart" of your home beating strong?

The Least You Need to Know

- ◆ A good time to look at your eating habits and see whether you need to make any changes is when you decide to reorganize your kitchen.

- ◆ The first step toward putting your kitchen on the right track is paring down food, utensils, dishes, appliances, and equipment.

- ◆ Simplify shopping and meal planning using a Master Shopping List and rotation meals and recipes.

- ◆ Cooking ahead and freezing for 2 weeks or a month saves time shopping and cleaning, and is a boon when entertaining. Other time-saving methods are quick cooking and slow cooking.

- ◆ Purge your recipe files and cookbook shelf of recipes you will never use. Organize what you have left onto index cards, into binders or file folders, or in your computer.

Chapter 12

The Bedroom: A Haven for Your Spirit and a Home for Your Clothes

In This Chapter

- ◆ Making your bedroom into a relaxing retreat
- ◆ Determining your clothing style, designing your wardrobe, and shopping smart
- ◆ Unstuffing your closet so it helps you look good
- ◆ Keeping your clothes in great shape

Although this chapter is about the bedroom, in most homes we're actually talking about organizing more than one. There's usually a master bedroom (an adult space), perhaps a guest bedroom, and as many other bedrooms as there are occupants needing a place to sleep. In this chapter, we focus mainly on the master bedroom, but the principles can be applied to any bedroom in the house. We also tackle the bedroom-adjacent closet.

Master Bedroom Savvy

Let's start with the master bedroom. Walk into yours and think about how you feel. Is it truly an adult space? If you have children, do they respect this space, or is it filled with their things? Do they feel they can come in anytime, or do you have rules about privacy? Does it feel serene and inviting? Is it comfortable? Is it peaceful? Does it invite sleep? If you were ill, is this a place you would want to go to heal? When you need to renew your spirit, is this a haven where you can spend some private time and relax? Is it quiet?

Visualize It

Close your eyes; take a long, deep breath; and imagine your ideal bedroom. What color or colors would it be? What would the furnishings look like? What kind of sheets and other bedding would dress the bed? Would there be lots of pillows or only a few? Would it have a reading nook with a comfortable chair and a good reading lamp? How about the lighting overall? What personal things would be there to look at? What mood would the room evoke? Add as much detail as you can. How do you feel when you open the door to this imaginary room? Don't think right now about cost, just about what you'd ideally like to create in this special room.

What is a bedroom? Stripped down to basics, it's a place to sleep and dress. But considering that you spend at least one third of your life in this room and it's the place of intimacy, romance, self-nurturing, and dreams in your life, it's so much more. For many people, the bedroom is also a place for entertainment. They may watch TV there or read. Maybe they knit or sew there or even do bills or other kinds of household paperwork. I like to limit a bedroom to sleeping, dressing, and intimacy, with a corner for quiet relaxation if at all possible.

I strongly recommend against having a TV in the bedroom, but in some households this is the only place where busy parents can get away to watch their own programs and relax. If you must have a TV in your bedroom, try to house it behind closed doors when it's not in use. Many beautiful armoires and entertainment centers with doors work well for this, or you can build a unit to hide the TV or find some other way to cover it.

I also recommend that you not have a phone in the bedroom. In your busy world, there should be someplace you can go and escape the ringing and clatter of everyday life. The bedroom seems to me to be the perfect refuge if you can set limits and create that space.

So what are the functions for the bedroom space you're trying to organize? This is the first thing you have to decide. If it's a room that has to do double duty, you have to include all the tasks going on there in your organization plan.

If you currently have to do work in your bedroom, can you set up anyplace else for paying bills or computer work? If not, you need to create a separate zone for "the office" and be sure it stays contained and organized and doesn't spill over into the rest of the room. After you organize the room as a whole, give some serious thought to creating a separate area for these other tasks that doesn't intrude on the most important purpose of the room—rest, relaxation, and romance.

But before you can create your perfect bedroom, you have to get out the clutter and take back the space.

Back to Basics, Bedroom Style

Remember the "unstuffing" method you learned in Chapter 5? Well, here we go again! This is the skill you'll be using over and over to organize every area of your life. The more you practice, the easier it gets.

First, let's do a quick sort of the bedroom itself. We'll get to the closet later. For now, just determine what you're going to keep that belongs in there and put it aside. You can start a separate Keep box just of the closet if you like. I suggest you start with the area you can see from the bed and also the fastest route to the bathroom. If the floor is strewn with stuff, start there and work up. You should be able to move around your bedroom without tripping over stuff, especially in the dark!

Grab your timer and sorting boxes. Challenge yourself to work fast and make decisions immediately, and ask yourself the questions from Chapter 5. Keep in mind the vision you have for this room. You're going to decide what to Toss, what to Pass On (to charity or someone else you know who can use it), what to Put Away (in another room), and what to Fix. What's left is what you Keep. Anything you're not sure of goes in the Keep pile (for now).

Simplewise

If you feel you can keep going, give it a try. If you can devote a day or a half a day to this project, all the better. If having a buddy by your side helps, then arrange it. The rewards of an uncluttered, organized, inviting bedroom are worth whatever you have to do to make it happen.

Ready, set the timer for 15 minutes (more if you can), and go!

Now get rid of what you can from the first sort. Empty the trash box or bin, take the stuff that needs to be put away to the appropriate places, and bag or box up the stuff you've earmarked for charity and put it in the car. How does that feel? Better, I bet.

After you've gone through stints of quick sorting what's on the floor, in the nightstands, on shelves, and in dresser drawers, what you have left is your Keep pile. As you do a deeper sort of that pile, separate what you're finally going to keep into two piles—one for items that need to find a home in the bedroom on shelves or in drawers, and one for items that normally belong in the closet. As you do a more detailed sort, put like things together. If you need additional containers to do this, find some bags, boxes, or baskets that will help.

Adding Furniture

Now put away what you've decided to keep, making sure everything has a definite home. If you need to add a piece of furniture, make a plan for that. Look for solutions that are both attractive and functional. A nightstand with at least one drawer helps contain bedside items you use often. Or you might consider a "sidekick" organizer made of fabric that fits between your box spring and mattress. It has pockets for your glasses, some tissues, a magazine or paperback, and a few other odds and ends so everything is right by your side when you're in bed.

Perhaps you need to add a small shelf for pictures. Several kinds of under-the-bed storage containers are available, including those that have wheels to make them easy to move. I like to keep the space under my bed open and airy (it's a feng shui thing!), but if you need space to store things that would otherwise clutter the room, then go for it.

Simplewise _____

Your headboard can also provide storage space. But if you pare down your clutter and choose your other furniture wisely, you may not need one of these—they tend to be somewhat large and bulky and can give a heavy feeling to the room. Do whatever you can to maintain a light and airy look and feel in your bedroom for a relaxing atmosphere.

Organize your dresser drawers as you would containers, putting like things together. If you need to further subdivide drawers, look for dividers or containers to fit. There are some great diamond-shaped drawer organizers for individual pairs of socks, for instance, that you can just cut to size.

If you read in bed, have a basket nearby for magazines or books, but don't let any more paper build up than what the basket can hold. Use the size of the container to contain the clutter, and set limits for what you allow in the room and your life.

You might want to consider adding a dressing table or vanity to your bedroom if your bathroom is small and you have room for it. Just be sure it has adequate storage space for things such as cosmetics and hair-care items so they're not spilling out onto other surfaces.

Decide on drawer dividers, baskets, or anything else to contain your final items, take measurements, make a list of what you need, and be sure you acquire them right away. Remember, what you have left should be things you use and things you love. This is not a storage locker—it's your *bedroom!*

Behind Closed Doors

The single greatest source of clutter in a bedroom is usually clothes. Somehow they end up on the bed, on the floor, over a chair—everywhere but in the closet. But why? Are we just lazy? More often it's the "domino effect." The closet is so stuffed full of clothes it takes too much effort to hang them up! Many of the clothes taking up that valuable prime real estate are hardly (if ever) worn because they're outdated, they don't fit, you don't like them, or they need repairs. For one reason or another, these clothes just don't make you feel good when you put them on, but still, there they hang.

Imagine getting dressed on any given morning when you can walk into your closet and everything in it is ready to wear. Everything fits, it's clean, it's in season, and when you put it on, you look and feel your best. Not quite the current picture at your house? There's no reason why it can't be, if you commit now to making some decisions about what kind of clothes really work for you, doing some serious wardrobe weeding, and possibly investing in some new hardware or storage units for your closet. Add to that an easy plan for doing laundry and keeping up with mending and ironing, and voilà! You're ready for anything.

What's Your Style?

Before you can unstuff your closets and dresser drawers, you have to establish criteria by which to judge what to toss and what to keep. Think of the people you know who always seem poised and well dressed. They don't necessarily look like they just walked out of the boardroom or the pages of *Vogue* or *GQ* magazines—maybe their look is quite casual—but their clothes suit their personality and their activities. They're well groomed, and their clothes look that way, too. They seem comfortable and natural in whatever they're wearing. What they wear "fits" them. They have a personal style.

In addition to understanding your own personal style and how you like to dress, consider the activities you engage in. If you're a jeans and T-shirt type but your job demands a three-piece suit, you're obviously going to have to make some compromises. Your off-hours wardrobe might be more of an expression of your real clothing personality, and maybe you can add touches to your otherwise staid work outfits that hint at the other side of your life.

Visualize It
If you had unlimited funds and could start from scratch, what would your wardrobe look like? Think about the colors you like. Imagine the textures, cut, colors, and fabrics in your ideal wardrobe. If you were to pick one word to label your ideal dressing style, what would it be? *Classy? Casual? Sporty? Ethnic? Romantic? Dramatic? Nonconformist?* Keep the picture you just made in your mind (or better, jot down a description of it) and refer to it as you begin to design a wardrobe and organize your closet. When you see pictures in magazines that fit your style, tear them out and keep them with your wardrobe design ideas.

Take out your organization notebook, planner/organizer, or a sheet of paper, and make a list of the activities you engage in during a typical week. You'll probably have things on your list such as work, play tennis, jog, garden, houseclean, work outdoors, hike, date, go out to dinner—whatever. Add to this any special occasions or seasonal activities you might expect to come up in a given year. These might include a formal dinner/dance, holiday parties, skiing, or swimming—anything that isn't part of your regular routine.

Now go into your closet and group your wardrobe into four categories: Work, Play, Dress Up, and Specialty. (Don't forget the piles of clothes on the floor from your purge, and what you found laying around in the rest of the bedroom.) The first three categories are self-explanatory. The last category would include seasonal items (the sweater with the big Santa Claus design, for instance), Halloween costumes, formal wear, and clothing that's especially for a particular sport or other activity, such as a ski jacket or hiking boots.

Unlike some of the other organization projects you've done so far, I don't recommend you break this one up into small sessions if at all possible. Allow at least 2 or 3 hours for your clothing/closet blitz with a couple of smaller follow-up sessions to accomplish some of the redesign projects you choose to implement. Tackling this task all at once will give you a good overall picture of your wardrobe, and investing this time now to get your closet in shape will have a huge impact on your everyday life.

Clothes, Clothes Everywhere—and Not a Thing to Wear!

Next, you're going to unstuff your closet and later your dresser drawers or anywhere else you keep your clothes. After this process, everything you have in your closet will be clean, ready to wear, flattering, and will make you feel good when you put it on. You'll also be weeding out what no longer fits your personal style.

Ask these questions as you look at each wardrobe item:

Does this fit you *now?* If you plan to lose 30 pounds and are actually on a weight loss program, you may want to put aside one favorite outfit that doesn't fit you now but will when you're done dieting. However, don't fall into the trap of having different wardrobes for different weights. Keeping "fat" clothes gives you permission to get fat again. Keeping "thin" clothes mocks your efforts and erodes your confidence.

Simplewise _____

Think of ways to express yourself without compromising your career objectives. For example, one woman who likes lacy, romantic, vintage-style clothes but needs to dress in a more conservative, corporate style at work wears a variety of antique lace handkerchiefs tucked in her jacket pocket, secured with a vintage pin to express her style.

Does this go with anything else? Is it an odd color or style? Is it *your* color or style? Consider having your colors done by a color consultant, read a book on the subject, or ask a fashion-savvy friend to help you determine what your best colors are. Focus on one or two neutrals, a signature color, and one or two complementary colors, and build your wardrobe around those. I did this and it makes putting an outfit together and shopping for clothes so easy.

How long has it been since you wore this? Why?

Is this too complicated to wear? Is it too fragile (silk, sequins, fur) or does it require too much special care?

Does this need to be ironed? Mended? Washed? Dry-cleaned?

Is this in season *now?*

Does this flatter you? You may want to get a buddy to work with you on this. Sometimes we think certain things look good on us when they simply don't. Pick a friend who'll tell you the truth, and be open to what he or she says.

Black Hole

Be careful of the "If-I-keep-it-long-enough-it'll-come-back-in-style" trap. Even if it does (sort of), the trend won't be quite the same or it won't really fit by then, so get rid of it! Besides, if your wardrobe is full of classic, high-quality pieces, you'll always be in style.

Is this comfortable? Does it pinch, ride up, or bind?

Is this a duplicate? How many other items like this do you have? Of the similar items you have, which do you like best or wear most often?

Does this sock have a mate? Do these hose have a run? Underwear stretched out? Stains? Tears? You know what to do with them!

Do you have clothes hanging in the closet still in dry-cleaning plastic? If you're protecting them from dust, you're probably not wearing them often enough to keep them!

As you go through your closet, take out the things that don't fit or flatter you and put them in one pile. If you have four black blazers, decide whether you really need them all and put the least-attractive or lower-quality ones in the Pass On pile.

If an item needs to be mended or ironed, put it in the Fix pile. Decide first whether it's really worth the effort. One reason you may not have gotten around to it could be you didn't really miss it. If that's the case, put it in the Pass On pile. As a reward for all your hard work, consider taking your mending to a tailor and have it done all at once. Vow to keep up with mending from here on in. Set aside things that need to go to the dry cleaners.

If you're not sure about a piece of clothing, put that in a separate pile. This may include items there's nothing wrong with—you like them, they fit you well, they're of good quality, and they don't need fixing—but for whatever reason, you just haven't worn them in a long time. Ask yourself whether the reason you don't wear a particular item is that you don't have anything that goes with it. If that's the case, you may want to set it aside and purchase something that will bring it back into your regular wardrobe. Put whatever's left in a bag or box, and try living without it for a week or two. If you don't miss it, pass it on!

A good time to seriously reevaluate your wardrobe is any time you experience a change in lifestyle. I went from being a corporate professional, wearing high heels, suits, and pantyhose every day, to a work-at-home entrepreneur. I don't wear high heels anymore, ever! So guess what you won't find in my closet!

I also moved from New England to the Southwest, so I don't need a down jacket or heavy snow boots either. Have you experienced a lifestyle change but your closet hasn't caught up yet? Look at what you've hung on to from old activities, locations, and lifestyles. Think about the way you live now, and get rid of clothes that no longer make sense.

If you have room, put off-season clothes in the least accessible part of your closet or in another closet altogether. Be sure what's upfront in your closet is right for *now*. I've pared down my wardrobe so much that I actually have all my clothes in my closet for all the seasons integrated together. In Arizona, this makes sense because the seasons are not that extreme and we dress in layers a good deal of the time, adding or shedding layers when needed. In a more extreme climate, it makes sense to separate warm season clothing from winter clothing.

Do this for each type of clothing you've identified—Work, Play, Dress Up, and Specialty. Put a limit on clothes you keep as "grubbies" for grungy jobs. One or two sets of clothes for outdoor work or painting should be enough.

Now all you should have hanging in your closet are items that make you look and feel good and are in good condition and ready to wear. Continue this process with your shoes and accessories and anything else in your wardrobe.

You can organize your clothes as you hang them. I have mine organized by type: tops, jackets, skirts, and pants. Then within those categories I have them divided by color. Some people like to put outfits together, but I find that limits how I think of the individual items and how they might go together with other things. I've identified my best colors, so I have the most clothing in my "signature color," which is in the turquoise and teal family, filling in with my two complementary colors and my neutrals, bright white and black. Easy!

> **Word Power**
>
> Know, first, who you are; and then adorn yourself accordingly.
>
> —Epictetus

Now back to that last pile of clothes that seem right in every way except you just don't wear them. The question here is, "Do I *love* this?" This should be the final criterion for your clothes. Having a closet full of well-fitting clothes in good condition that you only feel so-so about isn't good. The final goal is to have a closet full of clothes you love and that you feel great in.

I challenge you to live with only 2 weeks of outfits or less in your closet. Make them all things you love, that combine well in a variety of ways, and that can be classified as the "cream of the crop." Put the rest away in a safe place, but give yourself some time to try this pared-down system. See whether it doesn't make your life a lot simpler. You may actually need fewer clothes than you think.

Take the Pass On pile and give the clothes to charity or whomever you think can use them right away. Box them up. Do it now! Put them directly in your car so you can drop them off the next time you're out and about. If you leave them around the house, they just may creep back into your closet. Do the same with the Fix pile if you're taking these items to the tailor. If you're going to do the mending yourself, schedule time in your planner/organizer this week and just do it.

Take a look at what's left in your wardrobe and notice the colors and styles. Does this match the earlier picture you came up with of your dressing style? Make a list of a very few quality purchases that would make better use of what you have and add a little more of your personal style to your wardrobe. Something as simple as a new blouse or shirt or some color-coordinated accessories might pull together several elements and make them more versatile. If you have a lot of neutral colors, you might want to add something with more color pizzazz. Or perhaps you need some more basic pieces to enhance the usefulness of what you already have.

Now that you've organized your closet space, reward yourself with some extra touches. Make the inside of your closet even more pleasant by adding scented sachets between clothes, lining walls with attractive postcards or art posters, and using scented shelf papers. Colorful hatboxes or baskets work well as organizers. Have an attractive box, basket, or hanging bag in the closet to keep clothes that need to be dry-cleaned, one for delicates that need hand washing, and another for mending. With all the space you've created in your closet, each of these should have a home!

A-Shopping We Will Go

When you go shopping for new things for your wardrobe, it's best to keep some basic points in mind. First, don't buy anything just because it's on sale. Have a list in your planner of things you need to make your wardrobe more complete (keeping your style and colors in mind, of course!), and stick to your list.

And stay away from clothes that are too trendy. Generally, fads disappear after a short time, and you're left with clothing "junk." The classic styles never change much because they're flattering, easy to wear, and go with everything. If you must keep up with the latest trend, try to limit your purchases to accessories, not major wardrobe items. And invest in quality when it comes to your wardrobe basics. Buy the best you can afford because they'll last and look good for a long time. You get more than your money's worth.

Buy clothes that are easy to wear and easy to care for. Check for care instructions before you buy. Bunch up some fabric in your hand and release to see if it wrinkles easily. Even if you like it and it's the right color and style, do you really want the extra work you'll have to do to keep it looking good?

Buy any needed accessories when you buy the outfit. That way, a new item won't sit in the closet waiting for the right pair of shoes, a complementary tie, or the right scarf or pin. You have something ready to put on the moment you bring it home.

When you go shopping, wear clothes that are easy to remove and, if possible, have on the same shoes and undergarments you intend to wear with the item you're planning on buying. Don't wear much makeup or jewelry. And if there's enough of a seam allowance, clip a small amount of fabric from the item you're trying to coordinate accessories with, or bring the item with you so you get a perfect match.

Shop at thrift stores for around-the-house clothes. Who says everything you buy has to be brand new? Second hand is fine for painting or gardening, and you may even find some items for your other wardrobe needs.

 Black Hole

If you buy something that needs to be dry-cleaned after only a few wearings, you'd better love it because it's going to cost you a bundle! Avoid clothes that need ironing or special washing. Read the label!

Check over new garments when you get them home. Reaffix buttons that appear loose, and reinforce seams in problem areas like the back seam in pants or underarm seams of blouses or shirts. Be sure hems are secure, and cut off all loose threads. This will save you lots of mending time down the road. While you're at it, sew extra buttons on an inside seam allowance so you always have an extra if you need it. Lord knows, you'll never find it in the button box!

The idea is to end up with a wardrobe full of clothes you love that work well together, flatter your figure, suit your lifestyle, express your personality, and are ready to wear right now. Don't let a wardrobe just happen. Plan it. By using these guidelines, you're less likely to end up again with a closet stuffed with clothes you don't wear.

When there's a change of seasons, go through what you're about to put away and apply the same process. No sense in saving a lot of useless garments until next year. Do any laundering and mending so they're ready for next year with only a little touch-up pressing. Dry-clean woolens and store them properly before putting them away to avoid moth damage.

When you pull out the current season's wardrobe, decide, sort, toss, and fix again. If you do this every 6 months, when you make your seasonal wardrobe change, you maintain your clothing organization system without really trying.

The Great Hang-Up: Closet Design Basics

Now that you've got your wardrobe pared down and in working order, the next thing on our list is taking a hard look at your closet itself. Go through this checklist and then concentrate on those areas you've checked off as needing attention.

Yes	No	
❏	❏	Does your closet make the best use of space?
❏	❏	Are there areas for hanging long garments as well as short ones such as shirts and jackets?
❏	❏	Can you double up on certain areas with a second rod placed halfway down? Can you add additional shelving at the top?
❏	❏	Is your shoe storage effective? (If there are piles of shoes all over the floor, check No!)
❏	❏	Do all special items (such as pocketbooks, ties, jewelry, and hats) already have their own storage solutions?
❏	❏	Can nonclothing items such as sports equipment or luggage be stored in the garage or attic, if appropriate? If not, decide where these items are going and remove them from the closet. Put them away when you're done organizing.
❏	❏	Are your hangers well used? Good-quality plastic hangers are far better than wire ones. Even better are the hefty wooden ones. Even though they take up more space, they give better shape to your clothes and keep you from cramming your closet.

Yes	No	
❏	❏	Do you have special pants and skirt hangers? If not, put these items on the shopping list in your planner.
❏	❏	Can you clearly see what's contained in boxes or other storage containers? If not, consider labeling the boxes or transferring the contents to clear containers. Or affix an instant snapshot of the contents to the outside of the box. Add any containers or supplies you need to your to-do list and shopping list, if necessary.

A number of companies offer custom closet makeovers, and others allow you to design your own closet with help from an in-store salesperson. If you choose either of these options, you will want to completely empty your closet and start from scratch. Closet design systems can double or even triple your closet capacity. If you decide to go this route, be sure to get several estimates. Ask the closet company the following questions to help you evaluate:

- Do you remove old rods and repair any wall damage?

- Are special hangers needed for your system?

- How do hangers fit into the system? (Don't opt for a system where each hanger sits in its own groove or grid section and clothes can't be slid along a rod. This is very limiting and very annoying when you're looking for something.)

Simplewise

Put a towel bar or two on the back of your closet door to hang flat things such as scarves. Look for places to put up hooks for nightclothes, hats, belts, and handbags, or a drawstring bag to hold delicate items for hand washing.

- Are the shelves and any slide-out units sturdy? Put some weight in drawers and be sure they still slide out easily when full. You want to see an in-store sample.

- Will the system you design work with each season's wardrobe? Don't go ahead unless you're sure.

- Are there ways to add flexibility to the system with free-standing units that roll out or with adjustable shelves? Can it be changed?

If you don't have the money to go the total redesign route, start out by measuring your closet and doing a layout on your own before you buy any additional shelving or organization aids. Measure the length of your longest jacket, skirt, shirt, or blouse before you install double rods. That will ensure they're the right distance apart to accommodate all your tops and bottoms. Stores such as the Container Store, which sells do-it-yourself storage systems, will do a free consultation. Don't hesitate to ask. Check Appendix A for companies that offer closet design products and services.

Or you can simply add some easy fixes to your existing closet configuration. A rod that hangs from the upper rod, for instance, can be used to create two shorter hanging areas for shirts and jackets. Make a field trip to your local do-it-yourself, hardware, and department stores to see what's available and then take a trip through the online closet world for comparisons and more options. Keep your closet and clothing measurements with you, and don't be afraid to ask questions.

Also look for various specialty hangers if you have the space. (Now that you've purged your closet of all the things you don't love, you probably do!) Special hangers are available for scarves and ties, and multiple-skirt and -pants hangers might increase your closet space still more. Slide-on shelf dividers help keep sweaters and other folded items in their place on closet shelves. These come in clear plastic or wire and are designed to work on wood shelves.

Even with your pared-down wardrobe, are you still hurting for closet space? Then consider an armoire. Especially in older homes that have smaller closets, this versatile piece of furniture can be a lifesaver.

 Simplewise

> A great way to keep stacks of folded clothes from toppling over is a product called Fold 'n' Stax. These flat dividers are smooth on one side and have a gripping surface on the other, enabling you to stack your clothes neatly and keep them upright. Use the divider as a template when folding to create uniform stacks of folded clothes. These are sold in sets of six at www.stacksandstacks.com and other organizing products stores.

It All Comes Out in the Wash

What's it like at your house on laundry day? Do you even have a regular system for getting your clothes cleaned, ironed, and mended? If you don't, it's time to get that part of your life organized, too.

First off, if it isn't dirty, don't wash it! Sounds simple, doesn't it? Yet many of us automatically throw whatever we've worn in the hamper at the end of the day. If we're in the habit of throwing clothes all over the room, we're not sure what's clean enough to wear again. Now that your closet is organized and you've gotten in the "hang it up" habit, this is no longer a problem for you, right? So before you throw it in the wash, stop and look first! A simple airing might be enough. Carefully fold or hang the article of clothing right back where you got it from this morning, and save yourself some work. Train family members to do the same.

My mother and her mother always did their laundry on Mondays. Monday was Laundry Day. Try as I might to emulate them, it just never worked for me. The system I later devised is a simple one, and the reason it worked so well for me is that it's visual—even a child can use it. In fact, I devised it to teach my daughters to do their own laundry when they still lived at home.

The first thing we did was get in the habit of sorting as we went along. I bought three kitchen-size plastic garbage cans. Each held one washing machine load of clothes. One was labeled Darks, one Lights, and one Whites. A separate basket was sufficient for hand-washable items. As the kids undressed at night, we sorted the clothes together. Soon they did it automatically, peeling off their clothes and putting them in the appropriate bins. I taught them to look at labels for dry-clean or special-care items. When a bin was full, it was time to do a load. Come washing time, they helped in the laundry room, so they could see how the machine worked and how to measure soap powder and pretreat stains.

As they got older, they grew into doing a load when the "garbage" can got to the top. The next step was teaching them to sort out their own clean clothes, fold them, and put them away. They were more motivated to do this because they had a limited number of clothes in the first place and needed what was in the load.

The last step was teaching them how to mend and iron, which took a little more of my attention. Basically, my children were doing their own laundry by age 7 or 8. If young children can be taught this system, why not use it yourself? My daughters are now grown and have families of their own, but my husband and I still use the garbage can system. Now we have a convenient laundry sorter on wheels with removable canvas bags. When a bag is full, we do a load of laundry. As part of your morning routine each day, ask yourself, "Do I have a load of laundry?"

If you don't adopt my system, come up with your own routine and make it a habit. Maybe your family generates a load every day. In that case, it may make sense to build doing a load of laundry into your daily routines.

If a once-a-week laundry system makes more sense in your life, do it that way. Especially if you live in an apartment building and don't have your own washer and dryer, this may be the only logical solution. Presorting will still save you time, even at the Laundromat.

Stain Busters

Knowing how to take care of the clothes you love will keep them looking good for a long, long time. All it takes is a few basic principles, a "stain-busting kit" containing a few important ingredients, and fast action. (Stains are harder to remove after they've set.)

Treat stains as soon as you notice them. Learn something about the chemistry of stain removal. It will save you lots of money and time. Get yourself a plastic container. (We use one the size of a shoebox.) Label it "Stain Kit," and put it in your laundry area. Have on hand the following products for fighting stains, and learn how to use them:

- *Acetone.* Good for taking out glue or nail polish. Get at your local hardware store; don't use nail polish remover.

- *Bleach.* Both the kind for whites and for colors. Removes the stain's color but not the actual stain.

- *Club soda.* Excellent for removing pet stains and odors. Just saturate and blot up.

- *Color remover.* Get at the fabric dye section of your supermarket.

- *Enzyme presoak.* Biz, for example. This "digests" the stain with powerful enzymes. Use on protein stains such as blood and chocolate.

- *Glycerine.* Used to soften and dissolve "set" stains, especially on wool and fabrics that don't take kindly to water. Get at a pharmacy.

- *Hydrogen peroxide.* Another bleaching agent.

- *Lemon juice.* Use as a very gentle bleaching agent on delicate fabrics. The effect is intensified by exposing the fabric to sunlight while it's saturated with lemon juice.

Simplewise _____

Don Aslett's *Stainbuster's Bible: The Complete Guide to Spot Removal* or a similar reference can tell you how to remove just about any kind of stain from any kind of surface. Don's book also explains all the household chemistry involved and even gives advice on avoiding stains in the first place.

◆ *Low-alkali soap bar.* For example, Woolite or Ivory. For delicate fabrics and wool.

◆ *Oil solvent.* For example, Carbona or K2r. Use for oil and grease stains.

◆ *Oxalic acid solution.* For example, Zud. Used to remove rust stains.

◆ *Paint remover.* Be sure to store this safely!

◆ *Petroleum jelly.* For softening up hardened grease and oil stains.

◆ *White vinegar.* For removing hard-water stains and any other alkaline deposits.

Ironing, Mending, and Other Unfamiliar Subjects

To have a closet full of useful, ready-to-wear clothes, you have to maintain them. This is one of those tasks that takes only a little effort each week but can become daunting if it's left to pile up. You can handle part of the problem upfront during the buying process and immediately after taking your purchase home. Take time to read the labels *before* you buy. Ask yourself whether you really want to iron that cotton shirt or wash that silk blouse by hand every time you wear it. Consider the dry-cleaning bill if that's what it takes to keep it clean. Look the garment over carefully and reinforce any buttons, seams, or hems *before* they come apart.

You'll still have to do some ironing and mending, but you can save yourself time and effort, while keeping your wardrobe in tip-top shape. For example, learn how to use your washing and drying machines. Read the manuals and follow directions. Select the right cleaning products for your appliance and water type. (You might want to have your water tested and may need to purchase a water softener or add softening agents to the wash cycle if it's especially hard.)

Dampen a washcloth with liquid fabric softener and toss in the dryer. It's cheaper than disposable fabric softener sheets and works just as well.

If you go to a Laundromat, set up a caddy with all the products you need, including a stain-treatment kit. Also keep a basic mending kit handy. If you do your laundry at a Laundromat, be sure you take your kit with you to do small mending jobs while you wait.

Kids mean more repairs and more laundry. Look for shortcuts: use fusible bonding fabric, iron-on patches, a button puncher, and anything else that'll save time and effort.

Sort ironing by the temperature required. Dampen as you go.

Simplewise _____

Take clothes out of the dryer immediately and fold or hang them up right away. You may hardly ever have to iron if you observe this simple rule, and you won't pile up laundry waiting to be ironed. If you forget to take your clothes out of the dryer, throw in a damp towel and dry 5 to 10 minutes to remove wrinkles.

If the laundry has really piled up, you can go to the Laundromat and get it all done at once, even if you have laundry facilities at home. If you have five loads to do, you can fill five washers and dryers and do all the loads in the time it takes to do one at home. Go at off-peak hours so you don't have to wait for a free appliance. You go home with everything washed and folded and only a few things to iron or mend. Then implement your system and keep up.

Limit the purchase of items that take special care, and be sure you really enjoy the extra work it takes to keep them.

Dry Cleaning Made Simple

Did you know a lot of the clothes labeled "dry clean only" don't have to be dry cleaned? It takes some confidence and maybe a few mistakes before you get the hang of it, but over time you'll find you can really save on the dry-cleaning bill with just a few pointers. Items with linings or inserts of a different fabric aren't good candidates, but simply constructed garments of all the same material can often be hand-washed rather than chemically dry cleaned.

Here are the basics to DIY dry cleaning:

- Before putting your clothes in the closet, air them out—outside or in a covered porch if possible. They may not even need cleaning, just some deodorizing.

- Use a mild liquid, flaked, or powdered *soap* (not detergent). Dissolve whatever you decide to use completely in a basin or sink before adding the garment.

- Wash one item at a time so if colors run you haven't ruined anything else. Clothes tend to wash better in plenty of water, anyway.

- Rinse thoroughly—several times if needed.

- Don't wring the garment—gently squeeze it. Roll in a towel or several towels until fairly dry, and lay flat or iron to dry. You won't have to dampen a second time when you iron.

If an item does need dry cleaning, don't wad it up or roll it in a ball until you take it to the cleaners. Hang or fold it neatly. Tell the dry cleaner about any stains you know of and what they're composed of. Check buttons and seams. Repair them or ask whether the dry cleaner has someone who can do it and what it will cost and arrange to have it done.

Finishing Touches

Survey your domain! Is it beginning to look more like the picture you created at the beginning of this chapter? As you look around, the floor should be free of clothes, shoes, and papers. The only accessories should be those that truly give you pleasure and create beauty for you in this important space. When you walk into your closet, only your favorite clothes should be hanging there, all ready to wear and organized to make putting together outfits each day a cinch. You now have a working system for handling all aspects of your laundry.

So reward yourself with some of the elements you envisioned in your dream bedroom. If you imagined a reading area, find a chair and a lamp and an ottoman. Add a comfortable throw and a small pillow and presto—instant comfort! Little things such as a small pitcher and glass to set on your night table for fresh water each night, a vase with some fresh flowers, or some artwork that evokes the mood you wanted to create can be added now. Continue to create your personal haven. This is one of the most vital rooms in your home!

Allow the other members of the family to create their own dream bedrooms as much as possible. Children need space for doing homework and studying, so take this into consideration, but it's also where they go for privacy and respite, and it should reflect their tastes as well.

If you have a guest bedroom, spend a night in it yourself and see how comfortable it really is. Pretending to be a guest in your own home can be an enlightening experience. Add whatever amenities you think would make it a cozier, more inviting place to stay.

The Least You Need to Know

- The bedroom is one of the most important rooms in your home. By unstuffing and organizing it, you can create a haven where you sleep better and renew your spirit.

- You can make dressing, shopping, and clothing care simpler by planning your wardrobe and weeding out what you have to conform to that plan.

◆ A professional closet consultation or a well-thought-out DIY plan can at least double your clothing storage space.

◆ A carefully planned laundry system keeps your clothes ready to wear and takes less time. Even a child can be taught a simple sorting system.

◆ Regular maintenance of your clothing saves time in the long run and keeps your wardrobe ready to wear.

◆ Spending a night in your guest bedroom gives you insight into how comfortable it actually is. You may need to make some improvements!

Rooms for Living

In This Chapter

- ◆ Strategies for unstuffing the living room, family room, and den
- ◆ Setting up family spaces for multitasking
- ◆ Storage problems and solutions for shared living spaces
- ◆ A word about the dining room
- ◆ The fine art of preventive maintenance

Whether you call it the living room, the family room, or the den, there's always a room in the house where the family congregates on a daily basis. There's usually one location where you watch TV, read, and maybe eat a snack or even most of your meals. Along with the dining room or eat-in area of the kitchen, these are the "common" rooms, the rooms shared by all the people living in the house and often are where visitors spend time, too.

If you have both a formal living room that's used mainly for company and a family room or den, the information covered in this chapter is geared toward the room where the real "living" takes place. The "other" living room should be covered by the basic unstuffing, organizing, cleaning, and maintenance routines outlined in other chapters. I want you to tackle the room you spend the most time in first, using this chapter as a guide, because it will have the biggest impact on how you feel and function.

The Real "Living" Room

Take a minute to analyze the layout of your living room. Is it a separate room that's closed off from the rest of the house, or is it part of a larger, more open great room? How does traffic generally flow into and out of that room? Survey the room. What clues are there to the activities taking place there?

Visualize It

Create a vision of what you want your living room to be and say about you and how you live. How should it feel? What would it take to make it more that way? How do you want your family and guests to feel here? Can you make your vision a reality with what you have now, or do you need to purchase some new things? Is the furniture shabby or in need of a good cleaning? Are you happy with the colors, textures, and style of the space? Let your imagination go, and write down your idea of the perfect room. Think about spaces you like to spend time in. Notice pictures in magazines that seem to suit your vision.

The living room is the true multitasking room in the house. We ask a great deal of these spaces. Which of these activities is your living room handling (either by design or by default):

- Media center
- Playroom (where the kids can play)
- Study/homework/computer room
- Home office
- Hobbies and crafts room
- Game room (for pool, cards, board games, computer games, etc.)
- Entertaining area
- Reading area

It's easy to see why this area can get cluttered and chaotic. Keeping it clean is a challenge, too, because it takes a beating from hard, everyday use.

Setting Up Activity Zones

One of the best ways to begin to get a handle on organizing the living room is to set up zones in different parts of the room determined by the various uses of the space. You need to be realistic about whether the room you have, given its size and configuration, can actually manage all the activities you have going on in this room or whether you need to rethink the space and move some of the activities elsewhere.

If the kids' rooms were more organized, would they be doing their homework there instead of in the living room? If you created your Life Management Center elsewhere in the house when you read Chapter 7, perhaps the papers and other items in the living room space should move to that area. Remove any obvious things that now make more sense relocated to newly organized spaces in other areas of the house. Do this *now*.

If you're doing crafts or hobbies in the living room, could you store the majority of your materials somewhere else and make a space for your current project only? I'm an avid beader, but most of my supplies are stored in the basement. I keep a basket and a tray for my current project so it's contained and can be put away, but I can grab it when others are watching a TV program I'm not particularly interested in. It's easy to transport to other spaces as well, like our screened porch in the warmer weather.

Your job right now is just to think about whether there's simply too much going on in your living room for it to function well and see whether you can relieve some of the burden by relocating stuff to a more logical place elsewhere in the house.

Next, remove any stuff you can immediately identify as trash or you can see at a glance just doesn't serve a purpose in your life anymore. Especially pay attention to the flat surfaces around the room—the coffee table, side tables, shelves, top of the television and entertainment center, the mantle, and of course, the floor! See whether you can fill a garbage bag with stuff that can go in the trash or to charity right away. Pay particular attention to knick-knacks and memorabilia and ask yourself if you really *love* them.

Now that you can breathe a little, let's consider those zones again. There could be a media area, a kids' area, a home office or computer area, a hobby or crafts area, or a place to read—although, after reading Chapter 12 you may have already created a cozy little nook in your new, relaxing, totally organized bedroom! Make a list of *your* zones and decide approximately where they most logically belong in the room.

Contain and Control: Furniture That Works

The furniture in this room is a key piece of the organizing puzzle. You need adequate storage space so you can put away the things you take out each time you use them. It needs to be easy not only for adults but also for kids sharing the space. Consider the height of shelves and cabinets as you rethink how you use this room. Generally, you want to have the kids' stuff on the lower shelves and the adult stuff at a higher level, unless you want more control over what kids have access to at any given time. Look at your current furniture that doesn't do double-duty as storage, such as ottomans, side tables, or seating, that might be replaced with some that does.

Now let's get more specific about the stuff you're likely to have in this space. Add to the following list anything unique to your life I might have overlooked. Subtract what isn't true of your living room.

- Media: CDs, DVDs, tapes, computer games
- TV, DVR, DVD player, VHS player
- Stereo equipment
- Computer gaming equipment and accessories
- Board games and puzzles
- Toys
- Computer, peripherals, and accessories
- Books, magazines, and newspapers
- Mail and other papers
- Photos
- Craft projects and supplies
- Entertainment center
- Shelving and cabinets
- Seating
- Ottoman or footstool
- Coffee table
- Toy box/storage

- End tables

- Lighting

- Table for playing games or doing crafts

- Computer furniture or desk

How well do the pieces of furniture you have in this room function? Do they allow for storage, or are they more decorative than functional? Are there enough shelves or storage units for the things you regularly use in this space? Is there a designated place to store electronic media and contain printed material?

I'm not asking you to go out and buy all new furniture, but do make a note of any pieces you feel could be replaced with items that would help you more in your efforts to get organized. After you've purged and sorted what you're keeping, you'll have a better idea of whether you really need to replace some furniture items in this room. Perhaps you even have pieces elsewhere in the house that could be repurposed for this room.

A Room of Another Sort

By now you know the routine. The first step to getting organized is as always to unstuff the room or area you want to bring order to. Get out your sorting boxes, grab your timer, and start your engines! Get the whole family into the act because the clutter likely belongs to everyone. Set aside a weekend day, and plan a reward for the whole family when you've finished.

After you've done the first purge of clutter, removed the stuff going to the trash and charity, and have put away what belongs in other rooms, go back to the pile of things you decided to keep initially and see if you can pare that down by a third or half. Do a more detailed sort by type of item keeping in mind the zones discussed earlier. How old are those magazines and newspapers you have stacked up? Do you really listen to all those CDs and tapes or watch those movies? You may be able to let go of a bunch of stuff right away!

As you create piles of stuff you want to keep, start envisioning some storage solutions. Do you have a "home" for everything, or do you need to add some organizational tools to your list? Let's look at some clutter traps for the living room and some solutions for keeping what stays neat and easy to use, then simple to put away when you're done.

High-Tech Horror Show: Wires and Cords

Whatever your electronic poison—a personal computer, stereo system, home theater, or just a TV and VCR or DVD player (or both)—you'll inevitably have a tangle of cords and shared electrical outlets to deal with.

The first step is to see if there are ways to cut down the number of cords from the get-go. Bluetooth and WiFi technology might be just the ticket for reducing the number of cords you need in the first place. Various hubs and docking stations are available to help centralize things, too. But eventually you'll have to deal with the cords you have left.

You'll find two types of products on the market for managing cords and wires. One type is a flexible tube, slit down one side. You open it up and insert each cord or wire individually, snaking it along shelves to catch each set from individual pieces of equipment, and guide down to where the electrical outlet is. The second type of cord and wire management system either gathers cords into bundles or catches them and sticks to various surfaces to hide them along baseboards, shelves, racks, or desks. Do your homework and see if one of these solutions will help corral your cable clutter.

Simplewise

Lots of ingenious products are available to help you manage the tangle of cables and cords in the living room. Many can be found online at www.hometech.com and www.amazon.com. One of my favorites is Cable Buddy, available at Amazon. Check out the space station for laptop cords and the cable box for power strip clutter at www.bluelounge.com. Or you can use inexpensive twist ties, toilet paper tubes, and Velcro strips to bundle cords. I have a friend who cuts plastic shower rod covering to size and slips her cords in. There's always a way!

Another decision to make is how you want to display your electronic equipment. Do you want it out in the open, or do you want it discreetly hidden behind closed doors? If your equipment is somewhat smaller in scale, you might be able to hide it in a sideboard, armoire, or cupboard. You can have a unit custom-made, or you can adapt an existing one. Check out unpainted furniture places and used furniture shops, and don't overlook yard sales and newspaper and online classifieds. Entertainment centers specifically designed for audio equipment, TVs, VCRs, and DVD players can work. The better ones are quite pricey, however, and the less expensive ones can be flimsy.

When shopping, don't forget to consider the weight of your components, size (take measurements and bring them with you), air circulation, and ease of access for use and cleaning. Also think about components you can mount on the wall, such as flat screen TVs and speakers.

Composing Your Music and Video Collection

Many options for camouflaging or completely hiding your musical and film media are available. You need to decide whether you want to store them so you can see them (some people feel it's part of their décor) or get them out of sight. But before we start organizing what you have, let's consider paring down even more! Are you watching, listening to, or playing what you own? When my husband and I went through our video and DVD collection, we realized there were only very few movies we rewatched periodically. The rest we could pass on, and if we really missed one, we could rent it or borrow it from the library.

Now that most music is available as MP3s or other digital files and you can convert hard audio media to digital quite easily, you may be able to pare down your audio collection to almost nothing. I find that I only really like a few tracks on an audiotape or CD anyway, so now with my subscription to Rhapsody (iTunes is another choice), I can listen to music I enjoy, and when I find something I really like, I can purchase an MP3 file of that track and eventually burn it to a CD. I even have a radio station customized to my tastes where I'm constantly discovering new and old artists at Pandora Radio (www.pandora.com). Best of all, it's free unless I want to purchase a track I really like so I can add it to my music library.

My music collection is much more selective now and easy to manage on my computer, and I expect I will be getting rid of a lot of tapes and CDs in the months to come as I covert them to digital files. Maybe you can, too. When you consider a typical iPod can hold 10,000 tracks and some can even store up to 40,000, it's easy to see the advantage of going digital when it comes to creating glorious space, not to mention the environmental aspect of creating less waste to go into our shrinking landfills.

Not there yet? That's okay. There are lots of racks and towers for storing these items. Some are intended to be out in plain sight, but if you opt for getting them behind closed doors or drawers, look for pieces of furniture originally intended for other uses and retrofit them for music and movie storage. For example, don't overlook the storage possibilities of drawers. If they're the right height, you can store your media so the spine is easily read. Drawers also keep your collection at a lower height, so they're easier to see and you don't have to reach up to get them.

Because tapes and CDs are fairly narrow, you can build custom shelving that makes use of shallow hidden spaces. Look behind doors or along walls. We made storage shelves that just fit the depth of our largest cases. They line the wall in the guest room. Often overnight guests appear from their room with a movie request in hand! If a piece of furniture doesn't fit the bill, consider stacking boxes. Narrow plastic shoe boxes are just about right for CDs. Larger ones might fit videos. Some sturdy, attractive file boxes are created just for CD, DVD, and video storage.

If you're really challenged for space, consider ditching the jewel cases CDs come in and moving to a scratchproof plastic sleeve system that holds both CD and liner notes. These come in flip-through album styles and individual sleeves designed for a file drawer unit. One caution on this design is to be careful of transporting CDs in these plastic sleeves where they're going to be exposed to heat or dirt. The plastic can melt more easily than the hard plastic of jewel cases and ruin your CDs.

Old-fashioned vinyl is fast becoming replaced by the new forms of digital media, but there are those who feel vinyl is still technically superior, or for sentimental reasons have a few LPs they want to hang on to. Always store vinyl albums vertically, never flat, because they're easy to warp. Keep them upright (use bookends, if needed). Acid-free and polyethylene sleeves are available to replace the inferior paper ones that often came with the original album.

Consider temperature and humidity when storing your electronic media. Ideally your air temperature will be constant, with a steady 40 to 60 percent humidity—which, by the way, is also ideal for musical instruments.

Black Hole _____

The enemies of all electronic media are dust, fingerprints, dirt, moisture, and extremes in temperature. Think carefully about where you choose to store CDs, DVDs, tapes, and LPs, and use the right cleaning systems to maintain them. Don't forget to keep your electronic equipment clean as well. Digital media also needs to be backed up "just in case." Burn CDs or back up to an external hard drive and you're covered.

You need a labeling and filing system for your music and movie collection, whether on shelves or in your computer. We have our movies organized by general categories and then alphabetically within those categories. This proves especially helpful if you have a large collection. DVDs take up less room, but you may not be up to replacing all your favorite videotapes with DVDs. Before you do that, consider whether you really watch them as often as you thought you would anyway.

Periodically purge your collection, and carefully consider how likely you are to watch them before you purchase more. Give away music you no longer listen to. Or make a CD of the few cuts on the albums, tapes, or CDs you truly enjoy, and let the individual volumes go.

Racks created just for the purpose of storing CDs are fine, but they do have some disadvantages, especially individually slotted racks. If you're trying to set up an alphabetic filing system, every time you get a new CD you have to move each CD and reinsert it into a new slot. If you have an especially large music or movie collection, you may need to go to a more complex filing system. You can use index cards if you want to go low tech, or check into some of the computer programs designed for this purpose. These are essentially databases, and their advantage is that they allow you to search for titles based on key words, artists, labels, or even individual song titles, if you want to get that detailed.

Consider replacing an older stereo system with a more compact newer model. These components have come down in size and price. You gain space immediately when you get rid of those gorilla-size speakers! Better yet, maybe you can go micro and create a music system around your iPod or other MP3 player. The footprint is amazingly small. If that's too micro for you, you can put together a media center with a limited amount of storage space and keep your collection confined to that space.

With new technology such as digital video recorders you can save a movie or show, watch it a couple of times, and then get rid of it. We have one of these, and I'm a big fan. There are very few television programs or movies we're likely to watch more than two or three times. If it's something we really love and are sure we will want to see again, we can purchase the DVD or record the movie or program to tape.

Another good thing about digital video recorders is that when they're full, you can't record any more! You have to dump some to keep recording. Think how much space (and time) you'd save if you just limited yourself to the 35 hours or so your DVR can hold. If you don't watch what's on it in a day or two, get in the habit of deleting it.

Toys in Tow

If your living room is also a playroom for younger children, start by paring down and getting rid of toys that are broken, toys they've outgrown, and items they've simply lost interest in. This may be the time to give serious thought to where all the toy clutter comes from in the first place and stop it at the source. Are you, Grandma, or Aunt Fanny guilty of showering the kids with toys and games when they don't even play with the ones they have? Would time spent outdoors be a better option? Maybe relatives could pay for karate lessons, nature workshops, or soccer camp instead of buying the kids more stuff to store and keep them sitting in the house.

So do that serious purge first, get down to the serious Keep items, and then sort into piles of large toys, smaller items, stuffed animals, games, art supplies, etc.

Black Hole

Be sure whatever device you use to contain toys is easy to reach and safe for small fingers.

If the children have other areas to store toys, like their rooms or a basement recreation area, you might want to get the bulk of them out of the living room and allow them to bring in one at a time—and put them away again before bed!—or create a cabinet or toy box for those items they're most interested in now. Toys can be rotated from storage to this limited space.

Divide toys into categories with smaller boxes, bins, or baskets and label them. If a child is too young to read, use color or pictures to help him or her remember what goes where. See whether some storage options on wheels might be appropriate. That way they can either be removed from the room to create an adult space after the little ones are in bed or when entertaining, or at least pushed out of the way.

Make it a fun daily routine to put a toy back in its place when a child is done playing with it and before another item comes out into the room. At the end of the day, the toys can be "put to bed" along with your little one as part of his or her bedtime routine. If permanent toy storage is in another part of the house, keep a bin or basket (a laundry basket works well) for your child to put things in to cart them to where they belong. Have toys sorted there in bins, and have your child put them in their proper "homes" before bed or before moving on to another activity.

Impose the "new one in, old one out" rule on toys, too. Kids will learn at an early age that space is finite and clutter destroys peace and tranquility. Let them experience the enjoyment of giving a no-longer-used toy to a child who can really use it by passing it on to charity.

Life's a Game (or a Puzzle)!

Sort through all the board games you have, and get rid of any you don't play or that have missing pieces. Pass on the ones you're bored with, and trash the incomplete ones (so you don't frustrate anyone else!).

Game and puzzle boxes tend to sit in a pile, and when one is removed the others fall down. Boxes can become crushed or worn. If the box is coming apart, replace it with a plastic box large enough to hold the board and all the pieces. Another solution is to get smaller boxes for each game's pieces and group all the boards together. Label both the boards and the boxes. (Don't forget to include the instructions and rules, too.)

Replace puzzle boxes with rigid plastic ones if needed. Photocopy the cover of the puzzle so you can see what it looks like finished. After you've done the puzzle, pass it on unless you truly think you will assemble it again.

If your coffee table, ottoman, or side tables don't allow for storage, you may want to think about purchasing ones that do. These are great places to store games and puzzles. If you make them easy to retrieve and put away, you may actually find the family will want a weekly game night!

Gaming Goes Digital

Pass on the electronic games no one plays anymore. Do the same with outdated equipment. Consolidate equipment and games in one place.

Consider renting rather than buying. Kids can also exchange games with their friends. Those games that are favorites need to have a consistent place for storage (see "Composing Your Music and Video Collection," earlier in this chapter). There are plastic systems that attach to conventional shelves and slide out for easy viewing of CDs and DVDs. These fit Sega, GameCube, XBox, and PlayStation games. Some Wii accessories are good size, so think about where you're going to store them before you purchase. The Wii Fit Balance Board, for example, is quite large. But if you want to make the most of this fitness tool, you'll need to store it in a way that makes it easy to take out and put away, such as under the sofa or entertainment center.

Computer Time

If your living room must double as a computer area for the family or a home office, think carefully about how much space to give it and how to keep it contained and clutter-free.

Give some thought to your computer equipment before you buy. If a laptop will do for your needs, maybe that's the best all-around choice. You can use a laptop for a main computer with just the addition of a printer and perhaps an extended keyboard and a more ergonomic mouse. A wireless keyboard and mouse help reduce the cord clutter as well. A laptop docking station is also a solution to investigate. It expands the connectivity of the laptop while keeping everything in one manageable place. Having a laptop as the family computer also allows the family members to move the computer to other places when working there makes the most sense. A wireless router provides access to the Internet from just about anywhere in the house.

Choose computer furniture that's space efficient and easy to keep organized. It helps to have storage for discs and accessories, paper, and manuals. Closed cabinets help keep things dust-free and look neater in the room.

Look for multipurpose peripheral equipment options, such as fax, scanner, copier, and printer combinations. Be sure you have adequate space to write as well. If you're going to be doing bills in this area or kids are going to be doing homework, set up a system for handling the paper. Use stacked boxes or upright slotted systems. Sort the mail when it comes in, and take bills directly to this area. If this is your Life Management Center, go back to Chapter 7 and reread how to organize that area.

If several people are going to be using this zone, be sure each one knows the rules and how things are organized so they can follow the system, too. You may need to set up individual cubbies nearby for each computer user.

Dealing With Books

To book lovers like my husband and me, a house is not a home without a substantial reading and reference library. When we married, between us we had thousands of books. We've pared down to old favorites and the most useful reference works, but we have a tendency to acquire new books on a regular basis. Some people have very few books, so organizing their library is not a major issue, but for us, it has been a major challenge as it is for lots of other avid readers and book aficionados.

Begin to categorize your own library and see what you have that you can pass on to new readers. Be honest about how likely you are to reread fiction books or refer to nonfiction ones. If you're not sure what you have or suspect you have quite a large number of books you could pass on, do a major overhaul and gather all your books together into categorized stacks for redistribution.

How do you organize your books once you've gotten your library down to size? The system that seems to work best for us is to organize our nonfiction books according to subjects and then alphabetize within each. Fiction has its own section. Like most people, we don't have the space for a separate library room, so our books are spread throughout the house in logical groupings. Books related to movies and TV, cooking, gardening, and travel live in the guestroom, where the videos, CDs, and DVDs are stored. Guests seem to enjoy perusing these volumes the most, and the shelf of local history and travel books makes a practical addition to this location.

Simplewise

Books can be a decorative feature, as long as they aren't crammed into tight spaces or left all over to become clutter. If you have an especially attractive leather-bound set, display it in a living room or study. A neat pile of splendid picture books looks attractive on a coffee table or occasional table. Small volumes of poetry can grace a small nook almost anywhere.

My husband's Civil War, World War II, and American Western history collection is downstairs where he spends a lot of time. Books related to my profession as a writer are on bookshelves in my office. Fiction, poetry, and craft-related books have their own home in a series of bookcases in my hobby area. We regularly purge our books as our interests change, better books come along, or books become outdated—at least I do!

If you sometimes have visitors who need to wait in a foyer or living room, or if you have a client waiting room for your home business, have a stack of interesting books and magazines available to keep them occupied, and change out these materials regularly. Don't put any special favorites there, though, just in case one decides to walk away!

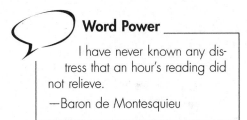

Word Power

I have never known any distress that an hour's reading did not relieve.

—Baron de Montesquieu

Keep a list of books you've borrowed from others and books you've lent. A bulletin board is a good place for this. I keep a list in my planner/organizer. I've lost many treasured volumes by loaning them to others. I'm sure they don't intend to keep them, but over time they forget, and so do I, so that's why I always keep up my list. Put your name inside your books, too, so borrowers have no excuse for not returning them, like forgetting who they borrowed them from!

Keep books borrowed from someone else's library in one place, so they don't somehow get absorbed into your own library and become lost forever. Put a sticky note on the inside front cover with the name of the person you borrowed it from, and you'll remember where to return it.

Dust books and bookshelves regularly. Once a year, take them all off the shelves, dust, and vacuum. Be sure wherever you're storing them is free of dampness. If there's any chance they might get mildewed, put a dehumidifier in the room and monitor it. Don't squash books into shelves—you'll damage them. Most books like to be stored upright, but very large books are best stored on their sides individually.

Once you have your library organized, you may decide you can get rid of even more of your movie or computer game collection because you'll be busy reading from now on!

Photo Finish

Photographs capture the past for future generations. But in piles with no rhyme or reason, they are simply clutter. Group all your photos together. This includes framed photos as well as snapshots and negatives. Maybe you have trays of slides as well. The living room is a likely place to display your favorite family photos, but have they taken over? Be selective and pare down to those you most treasure and what you have room for.

Black Hole

If you have photos in magnetic albums, boxes, or envelopes that are not acid-free or are in their original developing envelopes, take them out and put them in the appropriate (acid-free, archival) albums or boxes or else they'll be damaged over time. This is a great family project and can be done in small chunks of time, a little at a time.

Now sort through the photos you've gathered. Keep only the best shots. If you have duplicates, either pass them on or throw them away. Now group them chronologically or, at the very least, in general categories. You may want to do all your Christmas photos in one box or album or all your summer vacations, or you may want to group by person. You can probably ditch the negatives because digital technology will now allow you to scan photos and make as many copies as you desire. (Be sure to back up your digitals!) If you feel you must hold on to negatives, label them with the subject and date and put them in a safe place.

Photos are only valuable if they're put in some context and if they can be viewed easily. Get in the habit of trashing "out-takes" or poor-quality photos, be they prints or digital. Display a select few that have real meaning in quality frames, or consider one of those changing digital frames. If you keep every photograph, the really special ones will be lost in the clutter of junk photographs. Keep only those photos that inspire and "tickle" you, and let go of the rest.

Put what's left in photo albums (be sure to use archival quality albums or your prints will deteriorate) or in sectioned, labeled archival-quality photo boxes. Date everything, and note anything important about the event they commemorate that might be forgotten years from now.

If you have a lot of photos to organize, work backward so you don't get too overwhelmed. Start with the current year, move to the previous year, and so on. Label photos to the best of your memory using a photograph-safe pen or pencil. (Check your art-supply or photo store.) Even if you can't remember the exact date, a close approximation will be helpful years from now.

Simplewise _____

Looking for archival photo storage supplies? Log on to www.gaylord.com for the same ones library archivists use. Another good source is www. exposuresonline.com.

Unless scrapbooking is a bona-fide hobby of yours, skip the elaborate layouts, cute stickers, and add-ons. You can add captions later. If you have time to do something more with your photos in the future and you really want to, fine. At least this way, you'll be way ahead of the game when you do.

If you're working with digital photos, the organizing process is similar to what you'd do for print photos. Delete poor images, and set up labeled folders with event names and dates. Burn images to a backup CD when you have a few hundred. Be sure you label the disc with the dates and events it covers. If the photos are very important to you, make a copy of the CD and keep it in a safe place. Share photos with family and friends by sending them via e-mail, or mail the disc. And the key word here, of course, is backup, backup, _backup!_

Check out some of the several photo organization programs on the market appropriate for your operating system, and read reviews before you buy. Adobe Photoshop Album Starter is a popular one.

Another great way to share photos is online through a service such as Snapfish (www. snapfish.com), Picasa (picasa.google.com), or Webshots (www.webshots.com). Simply set up albums and e-mail folks to tell them photos are up for them to view. They can even order prints if they find one they really love. And remember to backup any photos you place online.

Consider having old family slides and photos scanned onto CDs or DVDs (or do it yourself) or directly onto your hard drive. They are far less likely to be damaged by moisture, light, or age, plus you can make up copies for other family members to use as they wish or create digital slide shows. Just be sure you label these as well. And again, be realistic about your photos and what ones are really worth keeping. Honor and preserve those you decide to keep for the future in a way that will take up the least amount of space but keep them safe.

Crafty Solutions

If your living room is a place where you do needlework, scrapbooking, beading, or other crafts, corral your equipment and supplies so you can make the most of your hobby time.

But there are hobbies and then, well, there are good intentions. Sometimes projects seem like something we'll enjoy and then we lose interest. Some hobbies become excuses for accumulating and cluttering. Make an honest assessment of your favorite pastimes—the ones you always turn to when you have some free time. Be honest, too, about the passing fancies you haven't touched in years. Pass on unfinished projects, supplies, and tools to someone who will really enjoy them (and finish them). Concentrate on the ones you truly enjoy.

> **Word Power** _____
>
> In our play we reveal what kind of people we are.
> —Ovid

One reason hobbies may not be completed is because they'd take too much trouble to dig out. Ferret out all those orphaned projects and gather them in one place. If finding them again piques your interest, put them where you'll be able to take them out at a moment's notice and see whether they strike your fancy again. If not, pass them on.

Because a craft or hobby isn't necessarily something you're likely to do every day, you may not want it lying out where it can get soiled, pieces can get lost, or where supplies might be chewed by the dog. Have a space in your living room for projects you're currently working on, and store the rest elsewhere. When it comes to storing projects, tools, and supplies, see whether there's a carry-all, case, or box that can house all you need to do your hobby. This can be grabbed any time and keeps everything together.

My main hobby, for example, is beading, and I have a rolling tool box with several compartments that holds just about everything I need in a very small space. I roll it out into the living room when I want to work on it and roll it back into a closet when we entertain or I'm busy with other things. Try a rolling cart with drawers in various sizes. These come in a variety of sizes and can be found in the closet department of your favorite department or art-supply store. Roll it away into a corner when it's not in use.

Black Hole

There's nothing worse than a space hog. I know one couple where the man dominates the whole house with his hobbies, and the woman, a seamstress, has to use the kitchen table and pack up her projects every time they eat. No fair! Be sure you check with the other residents of your abode before you appropriate space for your hobby. And share! Didn't they teach you *anything* in kindergarten?

Some projects lend themselves to a box or bin for storage. You'll usually want a lid to keep light, moisture, and inquisitive hands out and pieces in. This works well for hobbies such as embroidery and hand sewing. You may want a special keeper for threads and needles that fits neatly in the box. If your hobby involves many small pieces—such as beading!—you probably want compartmentalized storage boxes that close tightly.

Check hardware, marine supply, office supply, kitchen, closet organizing, and scientific supply catalogs and peruse them from a new vantage point—storage solutions! Also request catalogs for your particular hobby to find storage solutions specifically tailored to its tools and materials. Before you buy specialized boxes and chests from craft stores, check these other sources. Often the hardware store variety is less expensive and sometimes more sturdy. So what if it's battleship gray or military green instead of pink, mauve, or turquoise? If the color bothers you, an inexpensive can of spray paint can make it any color you want!

Use binders to keep instructions and printed directions for projects. Rip out what you want from craft magazines, three-hole punch, put it in the binder, and throw the rest away. Like recipes, there are only so many projects you can make, so be selective and realistic.

Sewing patterns never fit back in their envelopes after they've been unfolded. If you use patterns more than once, set aside space in a file cabinet; put patterns in manila folders, large resealable plastic bags, or large envelopes; label; and file. Be sure to include instructions and the original envelope in the file, plus any notes you'd like to add.

If your hobby is portable, keep your supplies in a living room drawer, next to your favorite chair, or beside the bed—wherever you're most likely to spend time and think to pick up the project. I have my beading in a tray and basket that sit in the family room under the coffee table. While the family watches TV (something I don't really do much of), I can grab my project and still be a part of the social scene.

Sometimes your choice of hobbies or the extent to which you can pursue them is decided by the space you have available. If you live in a two-room apartment, is it really practical to start model railroading as a hobby?

Use basic organizing principles once you get the containers, shelves, and carrying cases you need:

♦ Group like things together by type, subject, color, texture, or purpose—whatever makes sense.

♦ Consolidate and compress. Use smaller, compartmentalized containers if possible. Stack and layer, and keep things from spreading out.

♦ Label it! If the container isn't see-through, label your supplies so you don't have to go through a dozen boxes before you find the right one.

♦ Set limits on your crafts and hobbies. Let your containers or shelves be your limiting factor. Use the "new one in, old one out" rule.

Black Hole

Beware of collections becoming just another Acquisition Trap. You know you're in trouble when your collection starts taking over the house and pushing other activities out of the way. Be aware of changes in your interests, as well. When a collection no longer gives you any pleasure and just collects dust, it's time to let it go.

Collection or Clutter?

Whatever your favorite collecting hobby, be it baseball cards or art glass, find some sort of special container or cabinet to house it in and use that container as a limit-setting device. My Depression glass has its own cabinet, and when that's full, the size of my collection is determined. If I see something else I'd like to have, I need to make a decision to retire another piece to make room for it or hang on to what I already have and pass it by.

If you've got a really special or rare collection, why not donate it to a museum related to your particular interest so other collectors can enjoy it? There's a museum for almost anything. Check with your reference librarian if you're not sure where there is one.

Or why not use your collection? Although I wouldn't be pleased if I broke a piece of my Depression glass, I gain the greatest pleasure from setting a table with it, not from keeping it in my china cabinet.

Another suggestion is to simply pare down your collection. How about keeping only the rarest or most interesting examples? Narrow your collection to only one category or color. Or use the "trade up" principle. Keep only a certain number, and when you find something that's better than what you have, trade up—get rid of the lesser example and replace it with the better-quality or more special one. Display your collection and make it a part of your décor. Just be prepared to dust it!

Dining in (Organized) Style

Where does your family eat? In front of the TV? You might want to change that, but how can you when the dining room or kitchen table is always covered with piles of clutter? Wherever there's a flat horizontal surface, that's where clutter lands. Take a look now at the flat surfaces around you, and you'll see I'm telling the truth.

In many households, the dining room or kitchen table often doubles as a work table, homework table, or crafts table. With today's open floor plans, the kitchen, dining area, and living room are often all one large space. This is both a help and a problem because stuff tends to spread out all over the place.

Think of your dining area as having zones, just like your living room. You may need to store dishes and serving pieces there. Possibly linens need to live there as well. First consider function and then make an assessment of the furniture and existing storage in the room. Do you have room for a hutch, china cabinet, buffet, or sideboard? This can be both for typical items used in the dining room as well as for storage related to other activities regularly done there.

If the dining room table is a space for children to do homework or artwork, consider a rolling cart with drawers that can be put out of the way at meal times. This will encourage putting things away and make it easy to keep things contained. Look for places to add storage cabinets or shelves. (Look up!) Make them a part of preparing the table for the family meal.

Because the dining area is one that needs to be cleaned two or three times a day after each meal, keeping it as clutter-free as possible is a priority. The materials used in the construction of furniture and on other surfaces and their ease of cleaning are very important, so consider this when making any future purchases for this room.

Keeping Your Cool

Maintaining spaces where everyone spends so much time is a daily job. Let it go for a day, and pretty soon you have chaos! These rooms usually have particular areas prone to clutter. I call them "danger zones." Determine your danger zones, and police them regularly.

Get the family (and yourself) into the habit of picking up the living room each day before retiring and the dining room before and after every meal. Make it into a ritual, and everyone will be more likely to remember. Make it fun for children, and you'll be creating an important lifelong habit. Maybe you can come up with a "pickup" song! Maybe they'll put a spring in their step as they learn to "Whistle While You Work."

The Least You Need to Know

- The living room is a true multitasking room that sees hard use and lots of activities. Keeping it clean and organized will have a huge impact on how you feel and function.

- Unstuffing is the first step toward organizing your living area. Start by sorting and purging and then organize the rest.

- Be realistic about how many tasks your living space can be asked to perform. Try to relocate whatever you can and then organize the room into zones.

- Finding storage solutions for what you decide to keep in the living room helps keep it organized.

- If the dining room table has to do double duty for homework or other tasks, having a cart, caddy, or cabinet to contain supplies is a must.

- Making a daily ritual of picking up the common living spaces helps keep them orderly and teaches valuable lessons to children.

Part  5

Money and All That Stuff

Money isn't everything, but when your finances are coming unglued, it can certainly seem that way. And then there's the question of what's in store for the future, from as little as a year away when the IRS comes knocking, all the way to retirement.

The chapters in Part 5 guide you through an organization plan for the financial side of your life. First, you learn to take stock of where you are now and find out how to get control over your current finances. Then you prepare to meet the future with financial confidence.

Winning the Money Wars: Guerrilla Budgeting

In This Chapter

- Assessing your current financial condition and preparing a realistic budget
- Repairing damaged credit and staying out of debt
- Getting help out of financial chaos
- Surviving the holidays without plunging into debt
- Avoiding credit card fraud
- Discovering the benefits of frugal living

Organizing your financial life is worthwhile both from a cost/benefit standpoint and as a major contributor to your sense of well-being and control. I mean, how can you feel (or truly be) organized if your finances are spiraling out of control? In fact, after you get your finances organized, many other areas of your life will seem to skyrocket to new heights overnight. I can't emphasize enough how important this is.

In this chapter, I guide you through the first steps: taking stock, setting up a budget, cutting costs, and repairing your credit. You may not need to do all of these, but if you're like many Americans, you need help with most of them. Afraid to find out the truth? Don't worry, there's help even if you're in serious debt or suspect you may have a compulsive spending problem.

Facing Facts About Finances

Let me ask you a question. What are your financial goals, and are you meeting them right now? If your answer is something like, "To be able to find the checkbook," then it's time to take serious action.

Whether you're dodging creditors, trying to stretch a paycheck, or wondering how you're going to put the kids through college, the first step is to find out where you are now and make a plan for where you want to be.

Simplewise _____

If you're looking for a step-by-step financial management system that's integrated into your overall life organization plan, I highly recommend you read *Your Money or Your Life: Transforming Your Relationship with Money and Achieving Financial Independence* by Joe Dominguez and Vicki Robin. This book can change your life!

Budgeting Baby Steps

It's pretty easy to set up a budget. First, gather your monthly bills—*all* of them—and put them in a pile. Be sure you have the very latest statements, and weed out any duplicates.

On a piece of paper, write down each payee on a separate line with the amount owed next to it. Add your total amount of debt. Don't just include minimum payments on your credit cards, but the entire balance. Include the entire balance of any loan you have as well, including a mortgage. If you're not sure of the balances on your loans, call the lender and find out. Then write down any other debts not represented by your monthly bills (for example, a loan from a friend or family member).

In another column, write down the amounts of the fixed bills again, but this time, only include the minimum payments on your credit cards and your regular monthly loan and mortgage payments. Add this column. You should have two figures now, one representing your total debt and the other representing your debt for the current month. If you're behind on any payments, add those back payments to the second figure.

Now create a third column and add up all your assets, with one line for each item and the amount written next to it. Include bank account balances, cash, and any paychecks or other payments that haven't yet been deposited, plus any investments, CDs, savings bonds, IRAs, 401(k) plans, life insurance policies, and the like. Add to this the estimated current value of your home, cars, and any other major asset, such as a boat, second home, or valuables. Do *not* include any future payments, such as bonuses or commissions that are not definite or that have not yet been earned.

Do a second calculation of only your liquid assets—all the cash you could easily lay your hands on without any penalties or fees.

Do a third calculation, this time of your total yearly income. You can do a gross income statement or a net income statement. I prefer to use a gross figure and include in the budget all deductions that might come out of a paycheck (401[k], automatic savings, FICA [Federal Insurance Contributions Act], Social Security, etc.) in a budget. That way you see where all your money is coming from and where it's going. The gross income system would also work best if you're self-employed. Also include in your year's income statement any anticipated bonuses or commissions.

Arrange to get a copy of your credit reports. The Fair and Accurate Credit Transactions Act of 2003 gives you the right to obtain a free copy of your credit reports from the three credit bureaus once a year. The three major credit bureaus are Equifax, Experian, and TransUnion. You can get all three at AnnualCreditReport.com or by calling 1-877-322-8228.

Check for any mistakes and then find out your credit or FICO (Fair Isaac Corporation) score. You can get your score from each of the three bureaus directly on their websites. Their sites also have information on how to dispute any information on your report and how to improve your credit score.

> **Black Hole**
>
> While you are preparing a profile of your financial status, it's absolutely key not to withdraw and try to ignore the situation if it's not looking good. As difficult as it may be to face reality, this is your chance to get valuable information and use it to improve your financial outlook. To improve your situation you need to know the truth.

Looking at your cash on hand and immediate monthly debt, you obviously need to have more in the plus column than the minus column. If that's not the case, you need to look at some of your other assets and see what you can access to pay your bills for this month. If that's not possible, you somehow have to generate enough cash to cover your bills.

Difficult Decisions

You *must* make an honest assessment of exactly where you are and find a way to work your way out of your immediate debt. If you're not standing on the financial precipice, you can skip this section and move on to the budgeting section. But if you're in a financial crisis, can you …

◆ Work a second job for a short time to get yourself on a more even keel, while at the same time reducing spending (with a clear budget you can follow)? Do you have a skill you can temporarily use to create some income?

◆ Sell something of value that will take care of the immediate crisis?

◆ Consolidate your debt into one payment at a lower interest rate? Be sure you can afford one lump payment a month as opposed to making smaller payments spread throughout the month.

◆ Declare a moratorium on spending (other than fixed expenses) until you get yourself on track? Try using the food you have in the house, cutting out all entertainment (read a book), packing a lunch instead of eating out, and walking to work. Challenge yourself to be a tightwad.

◆ Qualify for temporary assistance? You know what has to be done if you have more bills than income. It's really pretty simple. You either need to increase your income or reduce your spending.

Simplewise

While you're getting your finances in order, separate essential from nonessential expenses and see how many nonessentials you can do completely without—at least until you get yourself out of the woods.

And while we're on the subject of spending, what kind of spender are you? Here are some additional questions to ask:

◆ Do you continue spending on credit, even though you're unable to pay off your current credit card debt?

◆ Do you spend inordinate amounts of time shopping or thinking about shopping?

◆ Do you shop to avoid pressure, to escape or fantasize, to increase your self-esteem, or to feel more secure?

◆ Do others regularly make comments about your excessive spending, or do you spend money you don't have on things you don't need?

If you answered yes to any of these last four questions, you may need some extra help. Go back to Chapter 4 for resources to help get control of your spending.

Back on Track: Creating a Household Budget

After you're out of the fire and back in the frying pan, you need to figure out how you heated up in the first place. Go through your checkbook, your credit card statements, and any receipts you have to gather a picture of what you've spent over the last few months. Include no fewer than 3 months; 6 is even better.

Simplewise _____

Keeping your finances simple cuts down on clutter and paperwork. Set up a financial center where you manage your other household affairs (your Life Management Center would be a good place—see Chapter 7), keep bill-paying supplies and financial files handy, give yourself a comfortable chair, and turn on some soothing music. Make your weekly financial chores as pleasant as possible!

What Are the Details?

Down the left side of a piece of lined paper, write out the following categories:

◆ *Housing,* which should be broken down into mortgage (or rent), maintenance, homeowner's insurance, and utilities.

◆ *Auto,* which should be broken down into car payments, maintenance, fuel, and auto insurance.

◆ *Medical and dental* (include each member of the family), with a separate category for medical insurance.

◆ *Clothing,* broken down for each member of the family, including dry cleaning.

◆ *Food,* which includes both groceries and meals out (broken down separately).

◆ *Child care,* if applicable.

- *Education*, if applicable.

- *Interest* on credit cards and other debt, as well as regular monthly credit card (when you pay off the balance each month) and loan payments.

- *Life and disability insurance payments.* If these are already deducted from your paycheck, look at your pay stubs for the correct amounts and put them in the appropriate category.

- *Taxes*, including federal withholding, Social Security, and state income taxes. Make a separate category for real estate taxes.

- *Entertainment*, including cable or satellite TV bills and video rentals.

- *Gifts*, including holidays.

- *Miscellaneous*, which might include cash expenditures such as newspapers, cigarettes, and so on.

- *Charitable contributions.* Keep thorough records of your charitable giving. You just might find yourself eligible for a tax break based on your generosity.

- *Savings*, including any automatically deducted 401(k) savings plans.

Across the top of the paper, put each month you're going to be calculating and draw lines down to make a grid. Now write down the total you spent in each category during each month. Be consistent about putting expenses in the same category each time.

Now calculate the monthly average for these categories. In some categories, you can make projections for the year just by multiplying the average by the number of months left in the year. Some categories may need to be adjusted, however, for seasonal variations. For instance, you may find most of your gift category spending is concentrated in the months before Christmas. So if you've calculated a 6-month picture that includes the holiday months, you probably don't need to double that amount to get a 12-month projection. You might only need to add another third or less of that figure for the remaining 6 months of the year.

Add all your expenses for a grand total, and as a final part of the process, compare your expenditures with your total income.

What Do the Details Tell You?

Where do you stand? Are some areas, such as food or entertainment, way out of whack? Are you paying higher mortgage or rent payments than you can afford? Are utility bills, especially phone bills, too high?

If facing the facts means you can see that you're living too high on the hog for your income, you have some decisions to make. Again, it's a matter of "stuff" versus "time." Some people would rather work more hours or find a better job so they can make more money and enjoy a more materialistic way of life. Others would rather have more time for themselves and choose voluntary simplicity, either saving money for the things they want or simply doing without. No judgment here, just a different approach to time, stuff, and money. But the facts are clear—you need to either cut expenses or increase income. Otherwise, you're headed for disaster.

Black Hole _____

Don't get caught short! Overestimate your expenses and underestimate your income. If you make more or spend less than you figured, rejoice and use it to pay off debt or deposit the windfall into savings.

In addition to the obvious areas where expenditures are too high, take a look at the less-obvious areas where you can save money. Have you done some comparison shopping for insurance rates lately? Perhaps you can lower your monthly payments. Have you looked at mortgage or car loan rates lately? Would a refinance at a lower rate help your situation?

If you've done your assessment and realize you should have more money than you do, you probably have a spending leak you're not aware of. The cure for this problem is to keep a spending diary for a few weeks. In your planner/organizer, write down every penny you spend, recording the date, what was bought, and how much was spent. Look for patterns and categories you may have missed.

Simplewise _____

If you're looking for ways to cut costs and simplify your life at the same time, join the ranks of the tightwads and simple-living advocates. Check out the Simple Living Network at www.simpleliving.net and Trent Hamm's The Simple Dollar blog at www.thesimpledollar.com for all kinds of resources, ideas, and inspirational stories.

From this exercise, you can now develop a budget. Transfer your categories to another sheet and then transfer the fixed expenses. Next, decide on cost-control measures and come up with realistic figures you can adhere to each month for variable expenses, and put down those amounts on your budget sheet.

If after a couple of months you still can't seem to control your budget, make yourself stick to a cash system. If you haven't done so already, do away with all credit cards (you may want to consider a debit card, however, only for emergencies), and even stop using your checking account for a while. Put all money into a savings account and pay all your fixed expenses with cash or money orders. Whatever's left is what you have to live on. This takes discipline, but it can really help get you on the right track. If a cash system is the only way you can make ends meet, stick to it for a while. In the meantime, you may want to take emotional stock, too. What is it about you and money, anyway?

This is your chance to figure out your relationship with money and get it right. You may find that when you begin organizing your life you end up changing your life in deeper, more meaningful ways than you ever imagined. Who ever thought that getting organized could help get you out of debt and raise your standard of living?

Budget Review

In the beginning, it's probably a good idea to review your budget each month after you pay your bills (more often, if necessary). This holds you to a monthly standard, and you'll know immediately whether you're going over or under what you estimated. If you decided you needed to cut costs in certain areas, you'll see how your efforts have panned out—and if you succeeded, you'll be motivated to continue the trend.

When you achieve some monthly financial discipline, I recommend building a quarterly review into your schedule. Put the date in your planner/organizer so you don't forget. It's a good idea to hold yourself accountable on a regular basis. You can correct any problems before they turn into disasters, and if you're ahead of the game, you can channel resources into savings and investments.

When you get out of debt and tame your financial tigers, you'll be amazed at the energy you'll regain and the extra time you'll have. The more you owe, the more enslaved you are, and the more time you spend trying to catch up. Free yourself of the burden and worry of debt.

Computer Finance Tactics

Several good computer software programs can help you manage your finances. For 15 years, I have used Quicken from Intuit, which is one of the most popular. The best packages are set up in checkbook format, and you can hand-write checks and manually record deposits and withdrawals in your computer, print checks directly from the program, or pay bills electronically online.

There are many benefits of using a computer program for managing your finances:

◆ Balancing the checkbook takes less time.

◆ All accounts are searchable and integrated so you can find things faster when you need to track down something.

◆ Paying bills online is cheaper per transaction than the cost of a stamp and envelope, and it eliminates having to write a check. You can save even more by using your bank's online bill paying service and then downloading the information into your money management software.

◆ You can set up, modify, and monitor your budget, right in your computer program.

◆ Tracking investments is easier.

◆ When tax time rolls around, you can pull things together faster by assigning categories to all your transactions as you enter them.

Depending on the program, you might have the ability to set up a debt-reduction program, do mortgage comparisons, develop overall family financial plans, keep a home inventory, and get online stock quotes.

The initial setup, where you enter all your financial information to get started, can take some time, but the benefits in terms of knowing where your money goes and saving time in the long run make the effort worth it. Much of the data can be downloaded from various sources to save you from having to enter it manually.

It's a good idea to choose one day a week every week to do your financial record keeping. Fridays are my time in the office to do paperwork, file, catch up on correspondence, and handle various odds and ends. I add to that paying the week's bills online and downloading data into Quicken. My son-in-law (the one who travels all over the world) does his every day after work. He pays bills as they come in and enters the day's checks and statements. This way he's on top of his finances all the time, including his investments. He's my Quicken idol!

 Black Hole

A computer program can do certain things efficiently—for example, it will catch mathematical mistakes you might otherwise miss. But remember that it is only as good as the information you give it. Take care that the information you type in is accurate and complete.

Don't forget to back up your computer data periodically. I do this on Fridays, along with all my other maintenance chores; but whenever you do it, do it *regularly*. See Chapter 9 for more information on computer file backups.

You'll need to decide whether using personal finance software is for you. Ask someone to give you a demonstration, or download the free trial program. Talk to people who use it and get their feedback. If you decide to use a manual system, do just that—use a *system* and use it faithfully. The important thing is to keep track of where your money goes and stick to your budget. Whatever tools help you do that best are the ones to use.

Don't Let Santa Blow Your Budget!

Every year when the holidays roll around, families brace themselves for the ensuing debt. And they often spend much of the following year climbing out. This doesn't have to be the case ever again, if you make a pact with yourself and your family *right now!*

The vast majority of families don't make a holiday budget. Without a plan, disaster is far more likely. When you make up your overall family budget, don't forget to include holiday spending.

Black Hole

Beware of "pay later" or "skip a payment" offers from credit card companies. These are *loans*, folks! The interest still accumulates, so read the fine print. The same warning applies to "checks" you may be sent in the mail. These are actually loan applications, often with very high interest rates.

There are at least two good strategies for handling holiday spending so it doesn't put you into debt. One is to put a portion in savings just for the holidays each month, and use only that money when shopping time comes. This means *no* credit. What you've saved is what you can spend.

A second strategy is to budget a small amount for gift buying throughout the year and do your shopping a little at a time, taking advantage of sales and the less-frenzied shopping environment. Catalogs and online stores can also help, and although shipping can add to the overall cost of the item, keeping you out of the stores may mean less money spent in the end.

Some families set up a gift exchange early in the year, drawing names so each family member only needs to shop for one person. The benefits are obvious—there's only one person to shop for, so you can get just the right gift and the financial pressure is removed. Or you can set a cap on spending for each gift—not to exceed, say, $25. This can present a fun challenge, as each person tries to outdo the other for less. It also makes it easy to budget.

Or consider alternatives to traditional store-bought gifts. Make something instead. I like to make what I call "consumables"—items that are used up and don't remain as clutter after the holidays. Food items, bath salts, potpourri, and homemade toiletries are a few suggestions. We also give holiday coupons, that entitle the bearer to any one of a number of services to be redeemed at a later date. These could be for baby-sitting, a massage, a car wash, a day running errands, preparing a meal, cleaning—use your imagination! Or how about a pair of tickets and your time? One year we gave contributions to a worthy cause in each relative's name. This works well for the people on your list who have *everything*. Throughout the year, they usually received a newsletter or regular updates, and nothing had to be returned because it was the wrong size or a duplicate!

Credit CPR

Even though you may now have a handle on your budget and you've got your expenses down, what do you do if you've ruined your credit? You can take some definite steps to repair damaged credit. You've already taken the most important one—you've done an honest inventory of your financial situation, set up a budget, and begun to get yourself out of debt.

Before you do anything else, find out how bad it is. (You should have already requested your credit reports from the major credit bureaus mentioned earlier in this chapter. If you haven't, do it now. You can't see what has to be done until you know where you stand.) Contact your local credit bureau, which is basically a credit-reporting agency that may cover only a single state or county. If you're not sure whom to call, check your local Yellow Pages under "Credit-Reporting Agencies." Call them all.

 Simplewise

You are entitled by law to one free credit report from each credit agency each year. But if you have recently been turned down for a loan or credit card, you can get a free copy from the agency that reported your credit, as long as you act quickly. Send the agency a copy of the credit denial letter with your written request to see your report.

When you receive your report, look for any inaccuracies or missing accounts on it. You may request an investigation of anything that's incorrect or incomplete. You can also have out-of-date information removed by writing a letter to the credit bureau. You are also entitled to tell your side of the story in any credit dispute that's on your record by sending a letter to be added to your file. Follow up on any changes and request a copy of your updated file to ensure the changes were made.

Reduce the number of credit cards you carry. One is usually enough. Two might be helpful if you own your own business, to keep expenses separate. Or leave credit cards at home altogether unless you're making a planned and budgeted purchase. Only charge items you're able to pay cash for. Remember to calculate into the cost the interest charges if you don't pay your credit card bill right away. Imagine what that interest money would earn you if it were invested at an 8 percent return. Investing $250 a month at that rate would grow to almost $600,000 in 35 years!

Return all unwanted credit cards to the issuing company. Just cutting them up means they're still on your credit file. Ask the company to close the account and send you a letter of verification stating you requested the account to be closed.

Buy or borrow a copy of Deanne Lonnin's *Guide to Surviving Debt* and read it! There are probably things you can do to help yourself you didn't even know were possible.

Be sure your credit file includes any positive account histories that might be missing. Try to build a positive credit history when you're financially healthy by borrowing small amounts using a secured credit card or bank passbook as collateral, or by finding a co-signer. Be diligent about making payments in full and on time.

Avoiding Credit Fraud and Identity Theft

Credit fraud costs everybody money, even if it never happens to you. Credit card companies cover the cost of fraud through higher fees and interest rates, and it's a growing problem. Identity theft is the fastest-growing crime in America today, with more than 12.7 percent of Americans reporting they were victims of identity theft in the past 5 years.

Types of Credit Fraud

There are different kinds of credit fraud, some more easily detected than others. The most common is the lost or stolen credit card, which can be stopped simply by reporting the loss or theft to the issuing company. But some fraud can occur even when you have possession of your card. Criminals steal account numbers through a variety of methods, including telephone or Internet scams, looking over your shoulder and copying the information from your card when you're not looking, or "dumpster diving"—taking information from receipts or account statements you've thrown in the trash.

A more serious form of fraud is identity theft, where a criminal uses your name and Social Security number to take over existing credit accounts or start new ones in your name.

Ways to Avoid Fraud

How do you prevent this kind of fraud? Well, getting yourself organized as you have, following the steps in this chapter, goes a long way toward keeping you out of harm's way. You're more aware of what's happening with your accounts, you've gotten your credit reports, and you've cut down the number of credit cards you have. These are all steps to preventing credit fraud.

> **Word Power**
>
> Through want of enterprise and faith men are where they are, buying and selling, and spending their lives like serfs.
> —Henry David Thoreau

Here are some other tips:

- Treat your credit cards the same way you would cash.

- Don't carry your Social Security card, birth certificate, or passport with you on a regular basis. That way, if your purse or wallet is stolen, you minimize the information a criminal has.

- Sign your credit cards as soon as you get them. (As an added safeguard, next to your signature on your credit card write with a permanent maker "Ask for photo ID.")

- Know the billing dates of your credit cards and call the issuing company if the bill is late. It may mean someone has diverted your bill to a different address.

- Read your statements carefully each month, and check for charges you didn't make. Report any suspicious charges immediately. Each month I download my credit card purchases and code them under individual categories in my finance software for tax purposes, so I'm on top of my statements and can detect any irregularities.

- Don't give anyone credit card or any other personal information over the phone or online unless you initiated the communication.

- Get a shredder and use it. Shred all preapproved credit card offers, receipts, and any other documents that indicate your credit card number.

- Get a credit report once a year, and check it for errors.

Another credit ploy to avoid is so-called "credit doctors" or "credit-repair" companies. These agencies charge a fee for something you can easily do yourself, and some are actually conducting scams, promising to expunge negative but accurate credit information from your record. (This is not legally possible.) Instead, contact the National Foundation for Credit Counseling at 1-800-388-2227 or at their website at www.nfcc. org and get the name of the local member agency near you.

If you suspect identity theft, contact the fraud departments of all three credit bureaus and log on to the Federal Trade Commission's Identity Theft Resource Center at www.consumer.gov/idtheft for step-by-step instructions and to file a complaint.

Frugal Living Is Fun!

Getting your financial life in order is crucial to organizing the rest of your life. You now know where you stand, you know where you're going, and you have a plan. One benefit to having a financial reckoning may be less noticeable: you may actually have embarked on a lifestyle change, a simpler more frugal way of living, and you may find you like it much better that way!

The frugal living/simple living movement (yes, I think we can call it a movement— just look at the number of websites and books on the subject!) is here to stay and is a logical reaction to the "buy-more, do-more, enjoy-less" direction of much of today's consumerist society. As Joe Dominguez and Vicki Robin put it so well in their book *Your Money or Your Life:* "If you live for having it all, what you have is never enough. In an environment of more is better, 'enough' is like the horizon, always receding." Create financial freedom by living within your means and wanting what you have.

The Least You Need to Know

- To organize your finances, start by determining exactly what your assets and liabilities are.

- Designing a realistic budget keeps you on track.

- If your credit is damaged, you can take some simple steps to repair it on your own.

◆ Nonprofit agencies can help you with debt counseling or financial planning, but beware of quick-fix "credit doctors."

◆ Debt elimination can be the beginning of a healthier (and happier) financial lifestyle.

Chapter 15

Tax Tactics and Advanced Money Maneuvers

In This Chapter

- Getting a head start on April 15
- What records to keep and for how long
- Organizing your insurance
- Preparing your will
- Tricks to organize yourself into saving
- Choosing a financial planner and accountant

If your tax, insurance, will, and investment records are in a jumble, you're playing a high-stakes procrastination game. As you saw in the preceding chapter, a little sober reflection and a solid plan can get your household budget straightened out. In this chapter, you're going for the longer view and looking at your future. How well you prepare for it will determine whether it's rosy or not. You'll also put your affairs in order so if anything happens to you, the people you care about won't be burdened by any lack of preparation or disorganization on your part. Think of it as a gift, both to yourself and to those who survive you.

There are benefits to financial planning in the here and now. Because you're on top of things, you'll be able to sleep well at night. Moreover, you'll have the information you need to take advantage of financial opportunities and adjust your plan if the winds of change dictate. As recent history shows, those winds can sure change in a hurry! The disorganized person doesn't know what's happening and leaves everything to luck or providence. You, of course, know better than that!

The Tax Man Cometh

Are you one of those people who file for an extension every year because you just can't get your records together or even face preparing your tax return? Do you always have that nagging feeling you might have been able to pay less or get back more if you'd been more together?

Well, you're going to fix that right now. First of all, let's review a bit. In Chapter 6, we organized your household financial records. If you haven't done that already, go back to Chapter 6, reread that section, and *do it now!* This is the first step in getting ready for tax time, this year and in years to come. If you're thinking of buying a personal finance software program, do it now and take the time to enter your information.

Simplewise

Need more help getting started organizing your tax and other records? Consider purchasing or downloading (you save shipping this way) a copy of Melanie Cullen's *Get It Together: Organize Your Records So Your Family Won't Have To* from Nolo Press at www.nolo.com. A CD accompanies the book so you can work in your computer, print it out, and put it in a binder so anyone can find what they need.

It will take longer to prepare your tax return if your financial records are incomplete or scattered hither and yon. If you have a professional prepare your taxes, the more he or she has to pull together, the more it'll cost you. So I'll say it again: get your regular financial files complete wherever your Life Management Center is set up, and keep them up-to-date. Doing a little bit each week or month (however often you pay bills) will make tax preparation relatively simple.

Now that you're on a budget (you're not yet? review Chapter 14!), you should have an idea of what's ahead. When tax time arrives, that's a good time to evaluate your budget and see whether you're on target.

The Not-So-Tender Tax Traps

There are some common mistakes taxpayers make that can be the indirect result of keeping poor records. For example, forgetting or not budgeting for a tax-deferred retirement plan contribution. In the current economic climate, retirement planning is fraught with pitfalls and challenges. Company 401(k) plans haven't kept up their earnings, and all investment choices need to be reevaluated. Just remember that economic conditions change, and what you need is a long-term plan. If you're self-employed, you need to take another look at your individual retirement account (IRA) or a simplified employee pension (SEP) plan and see whether you should make a contribution to one of these. If you're not sure, you may need to talk to a financial planner or accountant.

> **Black Hole** _____
>
> Don't forget to claim deductions carried over from previous years. Have your previous years' tax returns handy, and be sure you've included all losses, depreciations, and so on.

Having too much withholding deducted from your paycheck is another common mistake. Why make a tax-free loan to the government when you could be saving or investing that money—or paying off your debt? If you get a large refund each year, go to your employer and fill out a new W-4.

Overlooking deductions is a biggie, too. Again, this is where good records can save you money. Did you take all your medical deductions? How about mileage, phone calls, parking, and postage relating to charitable activities? The best way to find these hidden deductions is by going over your planner/organizer. If it's well kept, it will be a record of your day-to-day life over the past year and will tell you where you went, whom you saw, and what phone calls you made. You can record mileage and expenses there as well.

Tax Records Demystified

After you've filed your return, what do you keep and what do you toss? Good question. Here's a simple list of what you should keep:

♦ Receipts for deductible expenses

♦ Bank statements with deductible expenses and estimated payments highlighted

♦ Automobile mileage logs

◆ Any other proof of deductible expenses such as your daily planner/organizer sheets with notations of business appointments, and so on

◆ W-2 forms

◆ Interest income statements

◆ Investment income statements

◆ 1099 statements

◆ Records of charitable contributions

◆ Records of all medical expenses, as well as any medical insurance payments you made or may have received

◆ Records of any other deductions, such as mortgage interest, real estate taxes, or tax preparation fees

◆ A copy of your annual tax-return form

Simplewise

Know your bank's policy for getting copies of canceled checks. Few banks return canceled checks these days, and most don't even send photocopies with their statements. Be sure you can get a hard copy by printing it out online or requesting one by phone or mail.

Keep your planner/organizer pages for the year with that year's tax information. They can help you re-create events in case of an audit. The only time I was audited, my detailed daily records proved my case. The IRS auditor, after seeing how thorough I was, told me to "just go home."

These items all go in whatever container you use to store each year's tax information. Corrugated cardboard boxes are available from local office-supply stores such as Staples or Office Depot or from mail-order and online office-supply houses such as Quill (www.quillcorp.com), which is where I got mine. The ones made for checks and vouchers are just the right size to keep a year's worth of tax information, but you may need something bigger, or perhaps you can manage with something more compact. Whatever you use, be sure the containers are uniform so they can be stacked easily. If you store your tax records in a location that's prone to dampness, use plastic containers that are tightly sealed. And of course, *label them!*

Black Hole

Don't rely on your memory! If you had anything unusual on a return, such as a discrepancy between your declared income and the sum of your 1099 forms, write a note to include in that year's file box about how you came up with your calculations. You'll never remember 3 years down the road.

Remember, tax time isn't just another excuse to start piling up all that *stuff* again! Use the same criteria you used for all your paper in Chapter 6. If it's a duplicate of information you have or could easily obtain elsewhere, if it isn't truly related to taxes and you wouldn't need it in an audit, toss it!

Tossable items include the following:

◆ Loan books for loans you've already repaid

◆ Tax-related receipts more than 7 years old

◆ Receipts for non-tax-related items such as food, spare cash, dry cleaning, or haircuts

Keep all your statements, receipts, and paid bills until you've had a chance to tally them for the month and check the totals against your budget. If you do this each month, you'll have a handle on where the money's going and be able to decide quickly if you need to adjust your spending habits, bring in some more cash, or can put some money in savings or investments.

How Long Is Long Enough?

How long do you keep your boxes full of tax information? The common wisdom is that you should keep your current year's return plus those from the 6 previous years. Generally speaking, the IRS can audit up to 3 years from your due date or the date you finally filed if you were late. However, if auditors suspect a problem with a return, they can go back 6 years.

Laws on tax audits vary from state to state, so you must also check with your local tax authorities. And by the way, the "records" you keep include electronic records, if you do your cash management or taxes on computer. I recommend keeping a backup and updating it regularly. (See Chapter 9 on backing up computer files.)

After you're clear on both federal and state requirements, go back and weed out the previous year's records so you have the essentials, transfer them all to uniform boxes, and label them. Get rid of anything older than 6 years, except the documents you should keep longer, which are listed next.

 Simplewise

Toss the oldest year's records when you store the newest ones. Just empty the oldest box, relabel (use pencil, so you can erase), and put in the newest information. Hang on to just the tax forms, and shred the rest.

While You're at It: More Records to Keep

Besides backup information for taxes, you should keep files for additional financial records. Store these in your regular file cabinet, the one you have at your Life Management Center, or at least somewhere you can easily get at them.

Simplewise _____

To get the skinny on what federal tax information to keep and how long, log on to www.irs.gov and download the PDF file for IRS Publication 552, "Recordkeeping for Individuals."

First, there are medical records. Keep a file for each person for each year and put in receipts for treatment and prescriptions chronologically, as well as statements from the insurance company. At the very least, keep indefinitely a record of illnesses and injuries and the doctors who treated them, as well as drugs prescribed.

In files you store separate from your individual year's tax returns, you should keep the following:

♦ *Profit-and-loss statements*, if you own your own business. Keep these indefinitely. You may need them to apply for a loan, analyze your business direction, or appraise the market value of your business should you decide to sell.

♦ *Personnel records.* Again, this one's for business owners. You need to keep employee records for 7 years after an individual has left the company.

♦ *Payment records* for all equipment you depreciate on your return. Keep these for 7 years after the last return on which the equipment (such as a computer or fax machine) is listed.

♦ *Pension records.* Keep your 401(k), IRA, or SEP records in a separate file and hang on to them until you retire and are happily spending the money. Keep both the plan documents and the statements, at least the annual ones.

♦ *Investment records.* If you're investing money that's not tax deferred in stocks or mutual funds, keep records of all your transactions so you can create a basis for those assets when you sell them. If your annual statement shows all your transactions for the past 12 months, you can keep that and toss the monthly or quarterly statements. If not, you need to keep them all.

♦ *Data about your home* if you own one. This includes bills, receipts, and information for any improvements you make. When you sell, you can reduce the tax due on your profit by deducting the cost of permanent home improvements.

♦ *Receipts for high-ticket purchases* such as expensive jewelry, antiques, and artwork. You may need these as proof of value in case they're lost or stolen and you need to file a claim. The best place for these might be with your Home Inventory file (I discuss this in the following section on insurance), in a separate Valuables file or, if you have a lot of valuables, in separate files by category.

Hard-to-replace original documents such as birth certificates, cemetery deeds, marriage papers, and the like should be kept in a safe-deposit box, but only if your state law doesn't require the box to be sealed upon the owner's death. In that case, you may want to consider keeping a fireproof safe on your own premises or having your lawyer keep them.

Get the Most from Your Insurance

Being disorganized can cost you money when you need to file insurance claims. When you did your budget, you may have found you were short on cash. Did you overlook medical insurance claims you failed to file? If someone broke into your house, could you document what was taken and its value? Do you know whether your auto insurance covers a cracked windshield?

Setting Up

If you haven't already done it, set up files for each of the different types of insurance you have. For most people that'll be four files: Health, Auto, Life, and Homeowner's or Renter's insurance. If you're self-employed, you might need to add a file for business disability income or liability insurance.

Some people recommend storing life insurance policies in a safe-deposit box. I think, however, that if they aren't stored in the home, they can easily be forgotten in case of emergency—out of sight, out of mind. Besides, you can get replacement copies of your policy from your insurance company, and if you have an emergency, you'll probably need it to refer to right away. If you have a fireproof box or safe, keep your policies there rather than in your safe-deposit box.

I suggest putting basic policy information for all types of insurance you carry in your planner/organizer on one sheet. Include the type of insurance, the insurer, the policy number, deductible amount, agent information or number to call to make a claim, the dates the policy is in force, the key provisions of the policy, and anything you might find useful in an emergency.

Always Read the Fine Print

Now gather your policies and *read* them. I don't want to hear all that moaning and groaning! This is for your own good. Just go through each policy and make some quick notes on what your coverage includes, plus any exceptions. How big a deductible do you have? Does your homeowner's policy cover water or wind damage?

Simplewise

For a comprehensive glossary of insurance terms, check out the list at the National Association of Insurance Commissioners website, www.naic.org/consumer_glossary.htm.

How about vandalism? If your home is completely destroyed, does your coverage provide for guaranteed replacement cost? Ask similar questions for your auto, health, and other insurance policies.

Ask questions about what the policy says and means. Imagine different scenarios that could occur and whether you'd be covered. If you're confused and need something explained, call your insurance agent and go over the information until you're satisfied you understand it. You need to know what you have before you can evaluate it. Even if you decide you can't afford better coverage, at least you know where you stand, and you may want to plan on upgrading in the future. An annual insurance review with your agent is a good idea in any event.

If you haven't evaluated your insurance coverage lately, you want to be sure it meets your current needs. If there have been any substantial changes, such as the birth of a child or a marriage, you need to revamp your coverage. Now that you know what you have, make a few phone calls and see whether you can get better rates or increased coverage for the same rate. Be sure to ask whether you're entitled to any discounts. Some homeowner's policies have discounts for nonsmokers and seniors. Health insurance discounts vary from company to company. Auto policies have discounts for safe drivers with no accidents or tickets over an extended period of time.

Opinions vary on how much and what kind of life insurance you should buy. I'm not an insurance specialist, so I can't advise you. When you go over your total insurance situation, inform yourself about life insurance and assess whether you ought to carry it, how much, and what type.

Stake Your Claim!

The next thing you need to review is the claims procedure. Do you have all the forms you need? Do you have all the information you might need to make a claim? For homeowner's insurance claims, this means knowing what you have (or had before it was stolen or damaged). Do a home inventory as soon as you're able. Put it on your Master List in your planner/organizer and schedule a time to start working on it. The Insurance Information Institute has free software to help you available at www. knowyourstuff.org. There's even a video to give you some additional motivation by explaining the benefits of creating a home inventory.

Pull out your medical bills and see whether you've neglected to file any claims. Find in your policy (or ask your agent) how far back you can make claims, and submit as far back as you're allowed. Even if you don't get any money back, you at least have everything applied toward your deductible for future medical expenses you're entitled to. If your doctor or hospital doesn't file claims for you, be sure from now on that you place claims to be made in your Action file, kept in your Life Management Center, so you won't forget.

Black Hole _____

If you're self-employed, don't overlook disability income coverage, business insurance, and liability coverage. If you have a home office, you may be able to extend your homeowner's or renter's insurance to cover your business equipment and inventory, but more often than not, you need a separate business policy.

The basic message I'm trying to get across is this: know where you stand, take advantage of everything you're entitled to, and be prepared to document any future claims you could conceivably have to make. By having your insurance materials filed so you can find them, reading your policies, making any claims you've failed to make, and completing your home inventory, you have taken the most important steps toward getting that part of your life organized.

Having a Will Gives You a Way

Experts estimate that 70 percent of Americans die with no will. Do you have one? If your answer is no, chances are you have your reasons. Which one of these has the ring of truth for you?

- ◆ I'm too young.

- ◆ I don't own enough.

- ◆ Everyone knows who gets what.

- ◆ It costs too much.

- ◆ I don't have the time.

- ◆ It's hard to find a good lawyer.

- ◆ I don't like making these kinds of decisions.

Guess what? None of these excuses cuts it. As long as you're an adult and have some assets that would need to be divided up if you died, you need a will.

Simplewise

Good books and software programs are available for writing your own will. Nolo's Will (www.nolo.com) is an online interactive form you fill out. Nolo also has Quicken WillMaker Plus software on CD or for download. LegalZoom.com has a variety of will-making products to choose from as well. Will-writing software, books, or kits may be adequate if your needs are simple, but if you have considerable assets, children under 18, or other special conditions, seek the advice of a lawyer who specializes in estate planning. It couldn't hurt to do a draft first, though.

Be advised that if you don't have a will, the state decides what happens to your assets and belongings, and it may decide in a way you wouldn't want. By the way, if you're married, don't assume everything goes to your spouse. It may end up being divided equally among your spouse and your children, and maybe even your parents!

Initial Considerations

In organizing your thoughts to write your will, you need to ask yourself some questions beforehand, starting with what specific property do you have that you would like to go to certain individuals, and who are they? If those people die before you do, would you like your bequest to go to their heirs, to someone else, or to an organization or charity? This is another good reason to do your home inventory, as recommended earlier in this chapter. You can refer to it now and select those items of value, monetary or sentimental, that you'd like specific people to have.

Do you need to name a guardian to care for your children? If you have someone in mind, have you discussed it with him or her? Would that person also manage your children's money and property? If not, who would?

Who will be the personal representative (called an executor in some states) for your estate? Have you discussed it with them?

Do you have any debts that would need to be paid off? Are there specific assets you'd like used to make those payments? Are there assets your personal representative should use to pay off estate and inheritance taxes and probate expenses?

Is there anyone (person or organization) you'd like to have whatever's left from your estate after specific instructions have been carried out?

These are just a few things you should think over (and discuss with your spouse, if you're married) before meeting with an estate lawyer or sitting down to write your own will. To save on probate fees and taxes, you may want to consider transferring property by means other than a will, such as the following:

◆ Gifts

◆ Living trusts

◆ Joint tenancy

◆ Pay-on-death bank accounts

◆ Marital trusts

◆ Life insurance

Discuss these options with a knowledgeable estate planner, and find out whether any of them would benefit you in your current situation. And be sure your will meets the requirements of the state where you live.

A word about where to store the original copy of your will: some people recommend storing it in your safe-deposit box, but that may be a problem if, as mentioned earlier, your state law requires your box to be sealed upon your death. Find out, and if your state does seal upon death, have your lawyer or a close member of the family or your executor keep it.

Other Issues

While we're on the subject of wills, you might want to consider preparing a living will. This document explains what you want done about life-prolonging medical care in the event you have a terminal illness and you can't speak for yourself. This can be coupled with a durable health-care power of attorney, also known as a health-care proxy, which gives someone you choose the ability to make all health-care decisions for you. Together, these are called your advance directives. Laws concerning living wills vary from state to state, especially with regard to state proxy requirements, health care during pregnancy, and witnessing and notarizing requirements.

Another document you may want to prepare is a durable power of attorney, which gives someone you choose the power to make financial decisions for you in case you become mentally incapacitated. You can make this power fairly limited or very broad in scope. That's up to you.

Simplewise

You can get help writing many of the documents referred to here by using your favorite search engine to locate sample documents and regulations from your state. You can also order prepared forms online at a fairly low cost. Check out LegalZoom. com and FindLegalForms.com for some choices.

When preparing your will, either by yourself or with an attorney, the question that should be uppermost in your mind is "What if?" When dealing with money, be careful of giving fixed amounts. Rather, work with percentages. Who knows how much you'll be worth when you die.

Figure on reviewing your will every 3 years after you work it out. It probably wouldn't hurt to read it over once a year, when you do all your other year-end tasks such as taxes. You're less likely to forget if you make it part of a yearly ritual. Other times you want to review your will include the following:

- If you get married or remarried

- If you have a child

- Whenever your financial situation changes markedly, as in the case of an inheritance or winning the lottery (lucky you!)

- If you get a divorce

- If you retire

- If your spouse dies

Saving for a Rainy Day

Besides a will, you should give some thought to developing a general financial plan. You may feel you don't have enough assets right now to even think about such a thing, but as soon as you start to accumulate even a little in savings, you want to put those funds where they'll earn the highest returns. That immediately puts you in need of some financial planning.

Plenty of reputable firms can help you set up a plan, and you can start with a simple stock investment plan. There are even investment clubs around the country (or online, for that matter) through which you can invest small amounts each month and learn about investing together. You can also join the National Association of Investors Corporation (NAIC) as an individual (most investment clubs belong to this organization as well) and learn all about investing in stocks on your own. Just call the NAIC at 1-877-275-6242 for more information or check out their website at www. better-investing.org.

Whether you're working with a financial adviser or making investments on your own, you need to have both short-term and long-term goals clearly in mind. A short-term goal might be a vacation or a new car; more long-term goals are children's education and your retirement. After you determine these, you can better choose investments that will help you achieve your goals.

Another factor to consider is your tolerance for risk. If you tend to be very conservative and tolerate very little risk, it may take you longer to reach your goals. This takes some soul searching and an honest evaluation of your temperament. Usually a mixture of conservative and more aggressive investments is recommended.

Because you did a household budget in Chapter 14, you know where your money's going and how much you can realistically set aside for saving and investment. This should be done before you pay bills. Either have your savings automatically deducted from your paycheck or pay yourself first—meaning write a check to yourself and deposit it in your savings or investment account the very first thing. This becomes your "do-not-touch" fund and can either help you make a major purchase down the road or protect you from a disaster.

The next step is making sure what you put away is earning money for you, not merely keeping pace with inflation or, worse, losing value over time. If you have an investment plan at work, go over it with your financial adviser and compare it with what you can do on your own. You may be able to get a better rate of return on something other than what your company offers. Sometimes 401(k) or 403(b) savings plans allow (or require) you to make one or more investment choices within your account. You want to base these choices on sound fundamental principles and be sure they're compatible with your financial goals.

Do You Need a Financial Planner?

How do you know whether you need a financial planner? Well, if you're achieving your financial goals, have no money worries, are rarely confused about investing, and have plenty of time to manage your investments, you probably don't need one! Most of us don't fall into that category, however, including me. I tried planning my own finances for a while, but I decided later to hire Mike, a professional planner, and this was a good decision. Even if you *do* have time to manage your own investments, you still might want to consider a financial planner, if only to do a "tune-up" now and then and to provide you with a second opinion on key decisions.

Studies show that, on average, people who work with a financial planner do considerably better than people who don't. I'm convinced! Since we started working with Mike 13 years ago, we've been able to move to a nicer home and manage our investment portfolio successfully in good times and bad.

There are independent financial planners and those who work for financial services companies, and there are pros and cons to each. The independent isn't selling any particular product, so he or she might be more objective in choosing investment vehicles for you. On the other hand, the planner who works for a financial services company has a lot of resources available that the independent might not. Mike works for one of the large corporations, but he frequently recommends investments outside his company's offerings. He wants us to make money. If *we* make money, *he* makes money.

A good financial planner analyzes how changes in financial conditions affect you personally. He or she understands your goals and knows how to diversify your investments to protect you from changing market conditions.

But how do you choose a financial planner? Here are some things to look for and ask about:

- Is the planner with a reputable company?
- Have you heard recommendations from others concerning his or her performance?
- What kind of background and credentials does the planner have? How long has he or she been in the business?
- What degrees, licenses, certificates, and registrations does the planner have?
- What services does the company provide?
- What is the overall financial management philosophy?
- What fees can you expect, and what do you get for them?
- How often will your portfolio be reviewed?

Interview several financial planners and make your decision based on how they answer these questions and whether you feel comfortable with them. Mike is like a partner; he's someone we share our hopes, dreams, and fears with. We feel free to ask questions of him when we're confused. He listens and has answers that make sense to us.

We liked the services Mike performed for us so much that we got referrals for planners from the same company for our children where they lived. The financial plan included helping them each put together a budget and evaluate their current job benefits. Some began while they were in debt and had no savings. Happily, none of them are still in that position today, and we believe working with a financial planner got them on the road to getting out of debt and starting to save and invest.

Simplewise

If you decide to work with a professional planner, use his or her time to your best advantage. Having your financial records in order and your budget in place, as you've done in previous chapters, will help you do that. A good financial planner will help you put all this into an overall plan for the future and review it with you annually.

Do You Need an Accountant?

Whether you need an accountant is based on a different set of factors. If your tax returns are simple and you don't own your own business, you may be able to handle things yourself or simply use a tax preparer. But if you feel your tax-related tasks are too complicated to handle on your own, hiring an accountant is probably the solution.

Don't think of an accountant simply as a glorified tax preparer. Think of him or her as a tax planner as well, part of your financial-planning team. And don't wait until just before taxes are due to hire an accountant. You need time to get to know each other and devise a tax strategy for the future.

Besides tax planning and preparation, an accountant can help you evaluate and install accounting systems for a new business, decide on a structure for a new business, help improve profitability of an existing business, help get financing or restructure existing financing, give advice on mergers and acquisitions, design employee compensation and benefits plans, and make sure your business is in compliance with government regulations.

How do you choose an accountant? If you know little about accounting, you need someone who can get down to basics and explain things so you understand. Be aware that the more you learn on your own and the more organized you are, the more money you save. Here are some things you want to know:

- How much experience does he or she have? How about experience in your particular type of business? In your initial conversation, does this person seem to understand *your* business? If you have a home-based business, how well does he or she understand the home-office deduction?

- What billing procedures are used? Can you get an estimate?

- Will the accountant you're interviewing be doing the work, or will a staff member be doing it instead?

- Can you get a list of references? Are any of those references for businesses such as yours or related to yours?

- Is the accountant willing to seek outside expert services if necessary?

Even if you're not in your own business, you may want to consider an accountant, especially if you're managing an estate, own rental properties, or simply have fairly complicated finances. Your financial planner can also help you decide whether you need an accountant.

The Least You Need to Know

- You'll save time and money by keeping accurate and complete financial records.

- Save most tax-related documents for 6 years; keep some indefinitely.

- A thorough review of your insurance policies may mean found money, either in unfiled claims or by finding better coverage for less money.

- Keeping a summary of your insurance policies in your planner/organizer can prove invaluable in an emergency.

- Everyone needs a will, even if it's a simple one you prepare yourself using will-preparation software or a published kit.

- It's never too early to think about financial planning and investing. Many resources for investing intelligently on your own are available, but hiring a professional financial planner is also worth looking into.

Part 6

Getting People Involved

By now you might be experiencing some resistance or downright hostility from the people around you. After all, you've been a lovable slob all this time and people have gotten used to you that way. All of a sudden you're on this organization kick, and your family and co-workers might not know what to make of it.

Be patient. Help is on the way. In Part 6, you learn how to make your transition from messy to marvelous easier for the people around you—and even get them to be part of the team! You also learn when and how to call in the cavalry and get some outside help.

Chapter 16

Nobody Promised This Would Be Easy

In This Chapter

- ◆ Listening to what other people want and need
- ◆ Communicating your organization systems to others
- ◆ Identifying problem areas and negotiating solutions
- ◆ Accepting limitations and resolving control issues

What kind of reaction are you getting at home to the organizational changes you've been making? At work? How have you been behaving? Have you become an evangelical organizer, pointing out other people's lack of order? Are you keeping these changes to yourself, leaving everyone unable to figure out where you put things that aren't where they used to be? Are you beginning to see some chronic problems in your household or workplace that you didn't see before? Is there someone at home or at work whose habits conflict with your desire to get organized? Or now that you're getting organized, do people suddenly want you to organize *them*?

If some of these challenges are cropping up, believe me, you're on the right track. It means you're making progress. Any time you move out of your comfort zone and start taking action, challenges will appear. You may even meet serious resistance. All that's as it should be. Just stand back and take a longer view of your behavior right now. Look for some ways you can make some minor adjustments to smooth things along. Maybe you need to take some time to communicate, negotiate, and enlist the people in your life in your mission.

If They Don't Know, They Can't Do It

The most common mistake newly converted unstuffers and organizers make is to fail to explain to people what they're doing. In your enthusiasm, you may simply have overlooked this. Maybe you weren't sure you'd succeed. Or maybe you thought your family or friends would laugh at you because you've tried this so many times before and your efforts never got off the ground before now.

In the very beginning, it may not be a bad idea to keep things to yourself. If you've attempted this many times before and failed, people just may not have the confidence that *this* time you mean it! No need to set yourself up to be undermined or criticized. Besides, you needed to prove to yourself that you could do it. But chances are, people have already noticed a change. They've watched you get on top of your paperwork, organize your time better, and keep your work flowing when it used to pile up. They see you managing things at home, getting control of your finances, and making plans for the future. Heck, your whole attitude has changed, and nothing succeeds like success!

Black Hole

Just because your new orderly, more goal-centered life brings you happiness doesn't mean everyone gets it. Pay attention to others' reactions, keep the lines of communication open, and beware of the zealot syndrome. Besides, other people learn best by example, not from hearing others preaching the gospel.

But they may not know *why* things have changed. They may not even trust the changes. They don't realize you've experienced a major shift in the way you see the world and are committed to having your life be more directed, more effective, and more satisfying.

I hope you involved other people as you tackled individual organization projects outlined in this book. When you revamped the finances, for example, you talked it over with your partner and your kids. If you found while taking stock that your financial picture was truly bleak, you called your creditors, explained that you intended to pay, and asked them to work with you. If you reorganized your filing system at work or changed the way you sorted your mail, you let your secretary or your boss know. These are just basic courtesies, fundamental communication that goes a long way to having people in your court. If you haven't been communicating in these ways, start now.

For some, the change in you will be welcome. For others, it may not be. At one time I was a temporary office worker at an international corporation. As a long-term temp, I had no axe to grind, no promotion or raise to seek; I was simply trying to make things work efficiently for my often-traveling boss, an executive vice president. I streamlined files, set up a better telephone-message system, and found that by computerizing some operations I could get through the work he left me in half the time it took the former secretary. Other secretaries in the department began to sabotage my efforts and even pointedly told me to "cool it." After I convinced them I wasn't angling for a full-time job and would keep the improvements to myself, I got a lot less flack and learned a lesson in team building.

Change causes all sorts of discomfort for people, for a variety of reasons in a variety of ways. Some may resent change because they feel it points out their own failings. It may mean they have to learn something new or adjust to a new system, and they may resist. Don't worry about the reactions in other people too much. Expect them and accept them. Be compassionate, and know that consistent behavior on your part can eventually change attitudes.

Listen Up!

When you explain what you're trying to do, allow a lot of room for feedback. Hear what other people have to say. Be conscious of other people's needs. When I started to get serious about organizing our home and home businesses, my husband stood in the doorway of his home shop/office with arms outstretched and said, "You're not getting in here!" I heard him, and to this day I don't touch that room. That's his inner sanctum, and he arranges it however he wants. (But I don't dust or vacuum in there either. That's his job!) He was perfectly willing to make changes in the common areas of the house, and of course I could arrange my own office and affairs the way I wanted, but he needed some turf all his own that could be however he wanted it to be.

> **Simplewise**
>
> At first, you might feel that making concessions to the needs of those around you reduces your efficiency. With more experience, however, you'll discover that by finding ways to integrate your needs with the needs of others, you're actually creating an environment that will sustain your unstuffed life.

Listening doesn't mean patronizing. It means listening until you understand. It means giving someone your full attention. It means putting aside your point of view and fully experiencing another's. It means checking periodically to see whether you understand what the person is saying and not injecting your own insights and information. It's so easy to say something like "I know exactly what you mean! Why, when I …." That's not listening—it's using what another person is trying to share with you as a springboard for talking about yourself. Instead, after the person stops speaking, rephrase what you think you heard and ask whether you understand correctly.

Some people talk about learning to compromise, but I prefer learning to *synergize*. This is a process where the sum of the parts is always greater than the whole. If you have worked it out that the laundry gets done on Tuesday and Friday nights but the family just wants to collapse and watch TV on Friday night, then be with them Friday night and agree to do the laundry in the morning.

Work Within Your Sphere

Stephen Covey tells us to concentrate on our "circle of influence." The well-known Serenity Prayer suggests we ask for the wisdom to know the difference between what we can change and what we can't. The Beatles simply said, "Let it be."

The first place you can effect change is within yourself. Work with yourself and the things you have control over. Perhaps you were always late, unprepared, and constantly in an uproar, but now things have changed for the better. If you maintain these changes, making them habits, people will eventually come to trust them. Continue to work in the areas where you've begun to make strides. Remind yourself of your goals, and work on your plan. Stick to the basic principles we've covered so far. Continue to take small, regular steps toward fulfilling your mission in life. Use your new skills to improve your life and the lives of the people around you. People will most likely come around!

What About the Kids?

One of the greatest gifts you can give your kids is to teach them organization and time-management skills. You'll help them excel in school, accomplish their career goals, manage their own households, flourish financially, and even get the most out of their relationships. The fact that you're taking steps to get your own life in order means you're developing the greatest teaching tool of all: your own example.

You didn't descend into chaos overnight, and neither did they. You can't expect them to change overnight either, so be patient. Have an honest talk about the way things have been for you, how you're trying to change them for yourself and the rest of the family, why it's important to you, and how they can help. Explain what you want for them and how keeping the junk out of their lives and honoring what they have by keeping it organized will make their lives easier, too.

Too much stuff in a kid's daily environment is overstimulating and stressful. Things get lost in the chaos and become difficult to see or distinguish. If your child tends to be a little overactive, you may find that helping him or her get organized may make a huge difference.

Don't try to do too much at once. Gear your organizing sessions to a child's age and attention span. Work on teaching organization skills as you go along. You might want to play the "Clean Sweep" game with your kids (after the television show of the same name). Clear out their entire room except for a few things they'll need for the week, and start sorting with them a little at a time from an outside "staging area." Leave only the essentials, and work through one category at a time.

Seeing the room empty can help everyone spot opportunities for storage and organization solutions they might not have been able to see amidst the clutter. You can begin to do a broad sort as you remove the debris, putting all the clothes in one box or area, all the toys in another, and so on. The breath of fresh air your child will experience by removing the clutter in one fell swoop may just have an immediate effect. Or work more slowly and use the box system you've already learned on one area at a time. Trash, Pass On, Put Away, and Keep are easy for a child to understand.

If your children are young, you're way ahead of the game. Sometimes all it takes is providing the tools and creating a routine together. By setting up their environment so it's easy to put things away and find what they need when they want it, they'll naturally gravitate toward doing the right thing.

If you're dealing with teenagers, you may meet with a little more resistance. You need to be even more patient (just like you've had to be patient with yourself), take a little more time, and think of rewards that will provide motivation.

When your children are ready to go off to college, think of what they'll be taking with them (besides your hard-earned cash). They'll know how to clean a house, fix a meal, look good at a job interview, organize their schoolwork, and make friends and influence people. Those things may prove just as valuable as a college education.

By teaching kids how to organize themselves and getting them in the habit of helping around the house, they will appreciate the things others do for them much more. Besides, while they're learning and you're teaching, you get to spend some great times together. When your children begin to help and become more independent, everyone will have more time to have fun.

The skills you'll be teaching them now and the self-confidence having these skills will engender can be powerful tools for success in adulthood. These are the building blocks for acquiring habits that will serve them for the rest of their lives and help them have the life they really want and deserve. We're doing noble work, my friend!

Your Spouse Is Not Your Child—Really!

Beware of treating your spouse like one of your kids. He or she is your adult partner and deserves to be treated as such. If your partner seems to be sabotaging your efforts to get organized, you need to work out some control issues. Does he or she understand what you're trying to do? Have you consulted your partner before making changes? Was he or she a part of the important decisions?

Black Hole

Your partner may be threatened by the changes you're making. He or she may be afraid of losing you or fear the relationship will change. Reassure your partner by doing special things to remind him or her how much you care. Remember, you're partners, not adversaries!

You could say mine is a fairly traditional household. Most of running the household falls to me. My husband is perfectly willing to help, but he just likes to be told what to do. He's not one to take it upon himself to see something that needs doing and just do it. There are good and bad parts to that. The bad part is that I'm responsible for seeing that everything gets done. That's also the good part. By being responsible, I'm also in control. It gets done my way, and I can organize things the way I want. I just need to remember to ask for help and I get it.

What's the situation in your household? Does your spouse like to be the organizer? Does he or she prefer to leave that to you? Is it more of a team effort? Can you split tasks by preference? Can you focus together on certain problem areas? What changes would have the most immediate impact for both of you? Don't forget to communicate clearly what's important to you. Be sure your spouse gets your commitment and understands your goals. Ask for cooperation and input.

What if your spouse is simply messy and wants to stay that way? Perhaps you can give the "offending" partner a place where he or she can be just that—messy! The deal is, the mess must stay confined to one area—preferably somewhere out of the way. Messy spouses aren't going to change their ways unless and until they see the value and they want to!

If you live with a packrat, the important thing is not to nag or take it personally. It's about him or her, not you. Recognize there's a deep psychological need at play here. It may be a need to feel thrifty and smart, or a need for security spawned by an emotionally or financially deprived childhood. It may be a sentimental attachment to the past due to events you may not know about.

Don't attack; just be an example and express the good feelings you experience as you make your way toward order and simplicity in your own life. Try to help your partner fulfill these needs in other ways. And most of all, be patient.

Caution: Work Zone!

Handling challenges at work isn't so different from handling those at home. Sure, you can't tell colleagues to clean up their room or brush their teeth (too bad!), but the basic principles of delegating (that's what you were doing at home, didn't you know?) are the same. Many people think of delegating as sloughing off or passing the buck. But if it's done right, it's more like building a team. At work, as at home, you have to work with the people around you, gain their cooperation, and depend on their input.

Here are some basic steps to follow to delegate effectively:

◆ Meet regularly with the people you want as part of your team.

◆ Pay attention to the people you're working with. Be sure they hear you and understand what you expect from them. Leave *how* something gets done up to the individual. The more freedom they have to choose the method, the more they'll take ownership of the task.

◆ Identify resources. Make yourself one of them.

◆ Give a minimum of guidelines, but give advance warning of pitfalls.

◆ Agree on realistic deadlines and standards of performance. Have people evaluate *themselves* at the agreed-upon time.

◆ Be clear about what the rewards will be when the job is accomplished—and the consequences if it's not.

◆ Say "please" and "thank you." Pay attention to simple courtesy and manners.

Simplewise

Collect in a folder all the things you need to talk to a team member about. Add a sheet of paper to jot down ideas and share them on a regular basis, whether at meetings; through phone calls, e-mails, or memos; or whenever you're in contact. This keeps you from forgetting to discuss important points or just reminds you to say, "Well done!"

Roommates and Other Strangers

When you decide to organize your life, sharing your space with someone who's not a family member or partner can pose some challenges. I mean, when the two of you moved in together you were a slob, so what happened? Well, maybe the change hasn't been that dramatic, but still, it's a change you decided you wanted to make, and your roommate may be happy with things the way they were!

Again, communication is the key. Hopefully, you and your roommate respect each other's values, goals, and desires and can talk about your feelings. That's the best place to start. Just as you worked out how to handle visitors to the dorm room or apartment, who takes out the garbage, and how loud the music can be, you need to discuss your excitement about getting organized. Recognize that this is a personal decision, something you've decided to do for yourself, and that your roommate may feel his or her level of organization is just fine.

Your roommate may want to work on this, too. But then again, maybe not. If that's the case, work on your own space, change your own habits, and work on improving your own life. Refrain from being critical or acting superior as you make strides toward your goals. Things will go more smoothly if you respect differences and let your progress speak for itself.

There will probably be areas where you need to make compromises, especially where you share space. Concentrate first on the areas that are yours exclusively, and slowly work on enlisting your roommate's help and enthusiasm about unstuffing and organizing common areas. You may also find that, although the other person doesn't want to get involved directly, he or she doesn't mind if you want to do all the work! If it will make things better for you, then why not just do it?

Don't Take Yourself Too Seriously

Lighten up! Admit you've been a slob or a ditz or both in the past, but you're committed to doing better. Don't become an ogre or a taskmaster. Whether someone is a professional organizer or just someone like me who works hard at being organized, none of us is perfect. The idea is not to become a machine enforcing a completely orderly world where every spill is eradicated immediately, there's never a dirty dish in the sink, no piece of paper ever lands on any surface for longer than half a second, and no hair is ever out of place. If that's being organized, I wouldn't want it either!

What you're aiming for is more time, less stress, streamlined methods for the must-do tasks, and doing more of the things you really want to do in life. If you get the basics handled, you can concentrate on the really good stuff! *Organized* does not necessarily mean "neat." Organized is not always pretty. And organized is not spotless. Organized is a level of order that allows you to function efficiently and be in control. That level of order is different for each of us. The object is to notice what's going on, change what's not working, make and implement a plan, and reevaluate it periodically, adjusting it according to what you've learned.

Visualize It

Go back and revisit the ideal day picture you created in Chapter 1. Knowing what you know now, imagine getting up in the morning in your restful, orderly bedroom; walking into your pared-down, fully functioning closet where everything inside is ready to wear; eating a leisurely nutritious breakfast with a quick cleanup in your newly organized kitchen; and climbing into your clean car. Be more specific than you were the first time. Allow yourself to feel pleasure about the things you've accomplished. Make a mental note of things you'd still like to attend to. Pat yourself on the back! How does this picture differ from the first one?

I've made lots of suggestions as we've taken this journey together. Some of them come from my own experience. Some of them were offered by others that I tried and found they worked. Others I mentioned because I know they work for other people, although they've never been particularly useful to me or I've simply found another way. It's up to you to find the formula that works best for you. Muster up your creativity, and come up with new ideas of your own. Remember, it's *your* starship, and you're the captain! Make it so.

Keep in mind that what works at one stage of your life may need some major adjustments at others (see Chapter 19 for a more in-depth discussion on this topic). When I was a single parent with two growing daughters, my life looked a lot different from what it does now that I'm remarried, my children are grown, and my husband and I both have home-based businesses. Sticking to the old ways wouldn't make sense. The principles don't change, but the methods and practice do. If you remember this and apply the basic principles, you can't go wrong. Getting and staying organized isn't "once and for all"—it's part of your life's work!

One final thing to remember: when it all comes out in the wash (as my mother and grandmother used to say), the only person's behavior you can control is your own. You're the one who wanted to get organized! Just because you made this decision and are taking action doesn't mean anyone else has to. You can have many areas of your life the way you want them, even if other people aren't very cooperative. You're responsible for yourself. Don't use other people as an excuse for not following through.

Amazingly, if you just go along doing your thing, making the improvements you want to make for yourself, other people may start to make changes, too. They may see how much happier you seem—how you seem to be getting more done and enjoying life more. They may actually be reaping the benefits of your newfound organization. Maybe you have more time for things they've wanted to do with you. As with so many things, the key ingredient is *time*. Give yourself time for this new way of life to become a part of you. Give other people time to adjust to the changes you're making. Just don't look back, and keep on keepin' on.

The Least You Need to Know

- If you want to gain cooperation and useful ideas from others, you need to communicate.

- Listening is an important part of communication, especially when you're implementing changes and getting organized. Give people your undivided attention when you listen to them, and maybe they'll do the same for you.

- Children need to be taught basic organization skills to succeed in life. You can play an important role in giving them the gift of these skills.

- Delegating well means you're building a team and getting things done, not just someone passing the buck.

- People don't appreciate a preacher or taskmaster. Having a sense of humor is extremely important, especially being able to laugh at yourself.

- In the end, the only person you can change is yourself. Accept people for what they are, and go forward with your plan.

Chapter 17

Calling In the Cavalry: Hiring Help

In This Chapter

 ◆ When hiring someone else makes sense

 ◆ Hire the right people and help them do their best for you

 ◆ Pitfalls to avoid when hiring professional help

 ◆ Getting the most from a professional organizer

There may come a time when you throw up your hands and say, "I quit!" Maybe you've worked your plan diligently and still can't get caught up with everything you need or want to do. Perhaps you've tried to get cooperation from others but somehow ended up doing everything yourself. There may be some special circumstance or maybe just some tasks no one wants to do, ever!

Solving the problem may be as simple as picking up the phone and dialing Dirtbusters, but before you do, there are a few things you need to consider.

When Should You Hire a Pro?

The goal is to get your life so you have systems in place that keep you on top of things. But sometimes, calling in a professional is simply the wise thing to do or something that can boost your organization efforts in a big way. So when might you consider hiring a pro?

When There's a Disaster

We once had a torrential rainstorm that separated a gutter pipe and caused water to wash into a window frame and behind the wall in our living room. It stained the wall and soaked the rug. This is an obvious instance when it's a bright idea to call a professional. Even though the damage didn't exceed the deductible on our homeowner's insurance, we didn't have the equipment or the expertise to do the job right.

In the case of a disaster such as this, time is of the essence. You have to drop everything and tend to it, or further damage could occur. If you happen to be a professional carpet cleaner, plumber, or carpenter, by all means feel free to handle the disaster cleanup yourself. But if you're not, this kind of work is best left to the experienced professional. Get a few estimates and get the job done quickly.

When You Get Behind

I'm all in favor of sending out the laundry or having a cleaning company come in occasionally to get caught up when there are extenuating circumstances or to speed you along on your organizing journey. The boon to your psyche is immediate. You're suddenly on track and can start working your plan again. Seasonal shifts might also make hiring help a good idea. Some years I've had an outside cleaning service come in and help with seasonal cleaning jobs that are becoming more difficult for me to do as I reach my senior years. There are also areas to clean that are somewhat dangerous or especially difficult and are best left to a professional, such as high areas requiring a ladder.

If I've kept up with washing windows and cleaning carpets, grand! But sometimes I don't get to those jobs as quickly as I'd like, and bringing someone in to handle them makes me feel (and the house look) like a million bucks. If you own your own business and generally handle most of the paperwork yourself, fine. But if it starts to pile up, consider hiring someone to get you back on solid ground again. Be sure to examine how you got behind though, and work to correct the flaws in your system.

Other chores you may want to consider hiring out are yard work, running errands, dog grooming, and home-maintenance chores such as cleaning gutters or raking leaves. Go over your Master List of things to do, and decide which ones would have the greatest impact on your life if you paid someone else to do them either on a one-time basis or regularly. Then go back and see what your budget allows.

Black Hole

If you're behind on a regular basis, something's wrong. Look at how you spend your time, whether your methods are efficient, if you have the proper tools, or you're expecting too much. Analyze the situation, and be honest about what's really going on.

When You Don't Know How to Do It

I'm not a plumber—never was, never will be. I could probably learn to do some basic jobs like change water filters and fix a leaking faucet, but I have lots of better things to do and you probably do, too. Leave things you don't know how to do to the people who have the expertise, the tools, and the training. Measure, too, the time, effort, and money (tools are expensive!) it would take to learn how to do something yourself versus the cost of paying a professional. Getting sidetracked with these jobs can also get you off track with your organizing mission.

There are also times when hiring a consultant makes sense. If you're not particularly talented in the home decorating department, it may be worth it to hire an interior decorator to guide you on a major redecorating job. This can save you considerable money and time in the long run, as well as save you from decorating mistakes. A computer consultant can be another worthwhile investment. Paying an expert for a few hours of time can save you many hours of frustration and trial and error when learning a new program or installing new hardware. Look again at your Master List and decide whether there are areas where professional consulting help might move things along.

When You Don't Have Time

Work schedules coupled with long commutes may make hiring someone to do regular cleaning and other chores a must if you're going to have time for family, friends, or other things you've prioritized over cleaning. It's a matter of time versus money: the time created for the important things is worth the money spent.

Some possible tasks to hire out include cleaning, laundry, landscaping and yard work, errands, gift-buying services, business paperwork, and household paperwork such as filling out insurance forms. Figure out what you make an hour, and compare that with the cost of having a task done by someone else. It may make economic sense to hire out the job. If this isn't an option, you need to streamline these tasks even more.

If you decide to hire a cleaning service, find one that will let you work along with them. While they do the heavy jobs, you can do your weekly chores. At least use the opportunity to get some things put away so you can get the most from your cleaning service while they're there.

When You're at an Impasse

My friend Marcia's husband, John, fancies himself a "do-it-yourselfer." He means well, but somehow things around the house just never get done. Secretly, I believe John wants to be rescued from himself, but he just won't call someone else to come in and do the job. His procrastination was driving Marcia up the wall until a wise friend said, "Why don't you just hire somebody to do it and see what happens?" It wasn't a matter of money in Marcia and John's case. It seemed to be more a matter of pride.

Simplewise

Look for free services to help you save time and get organized. For example, many large department stores have free wardrobe consultants who can help you find clothes in your size and color and style preferences. Ask about free home decorating and closet consulting at furniture and home stores, too.

Well, Marcia called a handyman and got all those neglected or unfinished jobs done. John secretly heaved a sigh of relief. Now when John suggests he'll do it himself, Marcia simply says, "Why don't I have someone come in and do it this time, and next time you can do it if you want to." John doesn't protest. It's a funny little game they play, but things get done and John still has his pride.

When You Need Backup

It's amazing how someone can come in from outside the household or the office and say the same thing you've said for years ... and suddenly it's a "great idea!" Don't throw a fit; just be glad it's finally sunk in—even if you don't get the credit. Professional organizers repeatedly relate this phenomenon to me. They may say something their client has heard a thousand times; somehow, though, because it comes from the expert, it holds more weight. So what? Results are what we're after, right?

A professional cleaning service can get away with things you'd never be able to. Try touching the stuff on top of your teenager's dresser and you'd get your head handed to you. When "the cleaning lady" does it, nobody complains; in fact, the kids may even put the stuff away *before* she comes!

When It's a Job You Hate to Do

Let's face it. There are some things you just don't like doing. That's why you procrastinate. You know they need to be done, but you just can't find a way to make them palatable.

Long before I met my husband, he used to do all his own automotive maintenance. At the time, he couldn't afford to have someone else change the oil or tune up the motor. On bitterly cold New England winter mornings, he would get up early and tinker with the car so he could get to work. He swore that when he became more successful he would never work on a car again. Since I've known him, he's been pretty much true to his word. It's perfectly okay to choose not to do something you hate and hire someone else to do it for you.

When You Want to Reward Yourself

Earlier I told you to make up a Rewards List. Several things on my list involve hiring someone to do something for me. Maybe it's a manicure or a facial. I sometimes treat myself by taking the car to a car wash rather than washing it in my driveway. For more money, on a really special occasion you can have your car detailed with all the little extras—even that "new car" smell!

Make a list of tasks you'd truly enjoy getting done for yourself, tasks you'd consider a reward. Add them to the Rewards List you keep in your planner/organizer. Put some money in your regular budget for celebrations and rewards, and give yourself a gift whenever you need a boost or want to say "Well done!" This list can be helpful for thinking of gifts for others in your life as well.

Hire Happily, and Avoid Getting Ripped Off

One reason people are reluctant to hire out certain jobs is because they're afraid they might not pick the right professional to do it. Many unprofessional "professionals" out there simply don't do a good job. How do you know you're getting the best one?

I've found a few helpful hints for hiring anyone, from a key employee to the cleaning lady. Follow them, and 9 times out of 10 you'll hire the right person.

First, it's important to know the job you're hiring them for. It helps if you actually know how to do the job you're hiring someone for or at least the basics of how it's done. If you don't, the person you're hiring should be able to explain exactly what the job entails and how they're going to accomplish it. If they can't or won't explain it, go on to the next person.

Next, do your research. Check the Yellow Pages or online and get a list of the people in your area specializing in a particular service. Then call your Better Business Bureau to see whether any complaints have been filed against them. Ask people you know and trust for recommendations. Ask for references and check them out. You might also try an online consumer rating service such as Angie's List (www.angieslist.com). This is such an obvious step, and yet people often ignore it and choose a professional without getting any background information.

Simplewise

Besides emergency repairs, some of the most common services people hire others to do are house cleaning, gardening, carpet cleaning, window washing, pet grooming, laundry, cooking, home maintenance, personal shopping, gift buying, reminder services, financial planning, and record keeping. Which ones make the most sense for you?

Be sure to interview the prospective "employee" before you offer someone the job. Write out a list of questions before you call to make the appointment. Ask whether they're bonded, if that's appropriate. Do they have the necessary licenses or insurance? How long have they been in business? What methods, equipment, or cleaning products do they use? What preparation will you have to do? Is there anything they won't do? Many smaller cleaning services do not do windows or carpet cleaning, for example. Do you get the feeling they want your business, or are they put off by your questions? If they don't act like they want your business, find someone who does.

You must also communicate clearly the results you want. Be sure you're on the same wavelength and that the job you need done is the job you hire to be done. Get a contract or letter of agreement if at all possible. Most cleaning services will want you to sign a contract at the outset. If yours doesn't, write a list of what you want done each week and give them a copy. Be sure to cover jobs you want done each time and those you want done periodically, with a schedule for getting them done.

Finally, don't accept shoddy work. Hold the professional accountable, and work with him or her until the job is done to your satisfaction. You have a right to get what you're paying for, so be sure you do. If necessary, withhold payment until the job is done properly. If, on the other hand, you're pleasantly surprised with more than you expected, let the person know, and perhaps even give a bonus. Let workers like this know you'll use them again and recommend them to your friends and neighbors. We all like to know when we've done well.

Black Hole

Don't hover over the cleaning staff. Be available to answer questions, of course, but don't stick your nose in where it's not needed, unless you have an arrangement where you're working on a job together. The next time the worker should see you is when the job is done and you're ready to evaluate it and hand over a check. If you don't trust someone to do the job right, why did you hire him or her in the first place?

Don't Clean for the Cleaning Lady

When you hire outside workers, it's their job to perform the work. Let go of the anxiety to clean before they arrive so they won't think you're a slob. This can be especially hard if you hire out a job you've done yourself for a long time. Remember, you're the customer, and you're not entering a popularity contest. If you called in a cleaning service because the house is dirty and you don't have time (or the desire) to clean it, they expect the house to be dirty. Let them do their job.

Do be sure you know what the cleaning service is specifically going to do and how much you're paying for individual tasks. Ask what their routine tasks (basic fee) include. Usually, these things are included in a basic cleaning:

- Dusting and polishing furniture
- Dusting open shelves, ceiling fans, air vents, baseboards, windowsills, and miniblinds
- Cleaning mirrors and picture glass
- Cleaning and towel drying bathroom tile, shower doors, toilets, sinks, countertops, and open shelves
- Cleaning the kitchen tile; sinks; counters; and the top, burners, and front of the stove
- Cleaning the top, front, and sides of the refrigerator
- Damp mopping floors
- Vacuuming all carpeted areas

Don't assume, however! Most dissatisfaction comes from the customer not communicating properly what is expected and the service not explaining clearly what their basic fee includes. Make a list and be sure it's all checked off before handing over a check.

Many tasks are usually *not* included in the basic deal:

- Cleaning inside the refrigerator
- Cleaning the oven and under the stove top
- Damp wiping baseboards, windowsills, door facings, and frames
- Cleaning up the fireplace
- Oiling and polishing kitchen cabinets
- Vacuuming or cleaning upholstered furniture

Of course, you can still get them done—for a price. If you want carpets cleaned; windows washed; floors stripped and waxed; and outside decks, porches, or furniture cleaned, you need to make this clear and find out what each task will cost.

If you decide you don't want to pay to have these specialized jobs done, doing some of them yourself either before or right after a commercial cleaning job will add value to what you've just had done. For instance, you may want to vacuum, shampoo, and rotate the cushions on upholstered furniture just before the cleaning service comes in and steam clean the carpets after they leave. Schedule outside services at a time when you can make the most of them.

Maybe You Just Need to Move!

Shocking idea, isn't it? But don't dismiss it too quickly. Are you still living in a four-bedroom house even though the kids are grown? Do you have a lawn you hate to keep and a big garden even though you don't like gardening? Maybe you just need to wise up, dump the old homestead, and move to a place that's easier to take care of.

What kind of maintenance does your home require? Do you live in a climate that requires a lot of extra work to keep up a house? Do you *have* to live there? Could you move to a planned community or condominium where much of the outside work is done as part of the regular monthly fee? Give it some thought. It's not for everyone, but it could be for you.

If not actually making a move, how about making some changes to cut down the work? Siding and simpler landscaping might be just the ticket. Just getting rid of certain plants might cut your garden maintenance in half. When a neighbor of mine moved in, she had all the rosebushes torn out and replaced with low-maintenance shrubbery. Although she enjoyed roses, she wasn't willing to fertilize, prune, feed, spray, and clip them each year.

Simplewise

If you're considering simplifying your yard work, hiring a landscaper might make sense, if only for a consultation on how you can change your yard from high maintenance to easy care. For suggestions on how to reduce yard work, consult *The Free-Spirited Garden: Gorgeous Gardens That Flourish Naturally* by Susan McClure. You'll know what you're talking about when you speak with a landscaper!

How about replacing plants that take a lot of care with native plants adapted to the environment you live in? These usually require less watering, fertilizing, and general care than plants that aren't naturally suited to a particular climate or soil. I've seen people replace a lawn with a field of wildflowers that doesn't need to be mowed, or simply let part of their property overgrow to merge back into the surrounding woodland. Simplify, and you'll save time (and money, too).

You're Hired, Kid

Should you hire your kids? This is a sticky question. Only you can tell whether this is a worthwhile arrangement. I don't believe in paying kids for things they should do anyway. After all, they live there, too! However, if there are bigger jobs that older kids could handle and you want to offer to pay them, that's up to you. *Offer* is the operative word here. If they don't want to do it, then that's the end of it.

By the way, I don't consider mowing the lawn a job worthy of extra pay. If you give your children a regular allowance, fine, but I've never liked the idea of tying that allowance to specific jobs. The subject of an allowance is separate from the chores a child or teenager is expected to do to maintain the house. Now if we're talking major work like rototilling, washing windows, or digging a ditch, then compensation makes sense. And all the principles of good hiring apply!

The Benefits of Bartering

The barter system is ancient. Before we used currency, humans bartered or traded for everything. The concept has made a comeback in recent years, and it can be a creative, inexpensive way to get things done. For example, my husband is a leather craftsman. Once he paid for his eye exam and pair of glasses with a beautifully hand-carved leather item, custom-made for our eye doctor. Not a single cent changed hands. For him, it was a matter of time and some inexpensive materials, but it reflected a skill the eye doctor doesn't have. In exchange, my husband received a service that requires a special skill. It was an even trade.

Black Hole

Don't try to hide the dollar value of what you receive as part of a barter arrangement. You must report it as income on your federal income tax. Be sure you know what your state income tax requirements are as well. Check out IRS Publication 525, "Taxable and Non-Taxable Income," for details on federal tax requirements at www.irs.gov.

This may be an excellent solution in many areas where you need something done but don't have the cash to hire someone to do it. You can exchange child care for cleaning services, sewing for home repairs—whatever you can think of. Just be sure you exchange products or services of equal value. It's also advisable that you get an agreement in writing and work out the tax consequences.

It's common when bartering to trade for full value. So even if you would normally give your friend Sue a discount on your hourly accounting fee, if you barter with her, swap your full amount for her full amount.

When Do You Need a Professional to Organize You?

Anyone can benefit from at least a few hours with a professional organizer, even if they've got things pretty well in hand. Why? Because professional organizers do this day in and day out. Believe me, they've seen just about everything, and they've solved problems in ways you and I haven't even dreamed of.

Good Reasons for Hiring a Professional Organizer

If you can't solve a particular problem no matter what you do, hire a professional organizer. I already told you about my problem with missing papers and messages. I thought I'd tried everything, yet I overlooked two simple solutions that were inexpensive and easy to implement. The professional organizer I hired solved the problem in a minute. Get the lion's share of the work done yourself if you can, and bring in a professional for the few things you just can't seem to get a handle on; that's the ideal situation.

If you're almost a hopeless case, hire a professional organizer. Okay, you've read this book (and many others, I'd wager) and you're just not making the progress you'd hoped. You can always hire a professional to work with you until you get your problem licked. This won't be cheap, mind you, but it may be the only way to go—you're desperate! A good professional will work with you on one area at a time—just as I did in this book. In fact, I've had professional organizers tell me they've used my book with their clients and assigned them homework from it to do before their next visit! You'll get a list of things to do before the next session and then pick up where you left off. You can concentrate on one area or keep going until you've done it all. That depends on you and your pocketbook. Consider this "organization therapy."

If you need to nudge others and haven't been able to do it yourself, hire a professional organizer. As I mentioned earlier, sometimes people take direction from an outsider better than from someone they know. You may see the problem clearly, but a profes-sional will know all the tricks for getting cooperation and getting the job done. Besides, when someone's paying for the advice, sometimes they're more likely to use it!

If you need a jump-start, hire a professional organizer. If getting organized seems overwhelming and you aren't able to get going, a professional can be just the push you need. A professional organizer can sit down with you and help you break up the whole into manageable chunks, setting priorities and following up with you over time.

 Simplewise _____

One effective way to use this book along with a professional organizer is to take one unstuffing or organization project I've outlined and tackle it yourself. If you feel you need additional help, bring in a professional to augment that particular project. You'll save money and get the best from your organizer!

If you need help to stay on track, hire a professional organizer. It could be you've done a mammoth job of unstuffing and organizing the heck out of your life, but things seem to be going back to the "old way." Maybe what you need is a periodic checkup! Share your goals with your professional organizer, and ask to be called for a quarterly checkup session (or more often if needed). You and your organizer can refine your systems, pull you back to your goals and priorities when you get side-tracked, and set up better maintenance schedules. Sometimes it helps to have a partner in crime.

If you've experienced a major lifestyle change, hire a professional organizer. Perhaps you've gone out on your own and have moved your office into your home. Or maybe you've been a stay-at-home mother and have just reentered the workforce. Any time you experience a major lifestyle shift, organization systems that worked before may suddenly not fit anymore. A professional organizer can help you adapt and revamp for the way you live now.

Finding a Professional Organizer

To find a professional organizer, follow the same procedures for hiring someone I outlined earlier in this chapter. As a jumping-off point, I recommend contacting the National Association of Professional Organizers (NAPO) by calling 847-375-4746 or visiting www.napo.net. This nonprofit organization has annual meetings for organization professionals where they exchange innovative ideas and solutions for problems. They also have many local chapters located around the country, an annual membership directory, and an online organizer finder.

You can hire a professional organizer to help you with your home, your business, or both. Some specialize in one or the other, so be sure to ask. If you are computer-based, you'll probably want a professional with computer expertise. Don't be afraid to ask about qualifications or experience. If you're doing some heavy-duty revamping of complicated business systems in your organization, you want someone with the ability to handle such an in-depth project.

Ask upfront about pay schedules. Many organizers charge by the hour, but some charge by the project and will give you an estimate. They may even have a "frequent visitor's plan," whereby you get a discount for a longer-term arrangement. Be sure to ask about travel pay as well. This may be a considerable expense if your organizer is traveling some distance to reach you.

A good professional organizer will call after a session to see how you're coming along, and you'll probably want to schedule a checkup after you have a chance to work with the new system.

Also ask whether you or your organizer will provide supplies. You have to pay for them either way, but your organizer might mark them up—or may get them for you at a discount. Ask about his or her policy and compare prices.

Some professional organizers do a lot more than just organize you. Some have personal shopping services, where they get your sizes and shop for clothes and bring them to your home, where you try them on. You pay for what you keep, and your organizer returns the rest.

Others have gift-reminder and -buying services. You give your organizer information about birthdays, anniversaries, and anything else you want to be reminded of, and they'll send a gift and a card for you at the appropriate time. This is too impersonal for my taste, but may be just what you've been looking for.

Visualize It

Close your eyes and imagine you had unlimited time and money to work with a professional to help you organize your life. What areas would you tackle that you haven't dared to so far? If you didn't have to do the work, what would give you the most pleasure to just snap your fingers and have it all handled? Can you take a piece of that fantasy, perhaps just one phase or step, and give it to a professional to help you with it?

There's no shame in admitting something is over your head or you just could use some help. Whether it's a specific task that a professional could remove from your to-do list or an organization overhaul, weigh the pros and cons. Then farm out whatever your budget (and psyche) can handle.

The Least You Need to Know

- There are many good reasons to bring in an outside service or expert to help you clean or otherwise get organized.

- If you follow some specific steps before making the final decision to hire someone, you can maximize your chances of having a mutually beneficial experience.

- It's common for people to have trouble letting someone else do tasks they've normally done. Let the person do his or her job, and sit back and enjoy the results.

- You may not need to hire professionals to help with the work; you may simply need to cut back on the work. Moving into less-demanding quarters or making some time- and work-saving home improvements could be a solution.

- Alternatives to hiring an outside contractor may be to hire your kids or to barter services.

- There are many benefits to hiring a professional organizer, and one of the best ways to use one is to do as much as you can on your own and then consult a professional for specific areas where you need help.

Part 7

Now That You're Organized, Keep It That Way!

Congratulations! You've come a long way. You've got the essentials in your life unstuffed and organized. Now you need to know how to maintain your new systems, figure out how to fix them if they start breaking down, and be able to adjust what you've learned for your particular lifestyle and the different stages of your life. What works today may need some tweaking or even total revamping tomorrow.

And finally, hectic though the holidays may have been in the past, they're not going to throw you off track this year! In fact, you're going to enjoy them from the cool vantage point of someone who's got it all together and celebrate their true meaning—and you're not going to break the bank either!

Chapter 18

Minimum Maintenance: Strategies for Staying Organized

In This Chapter

◆ Strategies for keeping your life organized and in working order

◆ Moving to the next level and switching to high gear

◆ Avoiding pitfalls and backsliding

◆ Dealing with system breakdowns

After you do the major reorganizing projects outlined in this book, all that's left is to maintain the systems you adapted for yourself and enjoy your newfound free time. The key to maintenance is simple—do a little each day, *every* day. This chapter helps you solidify the progress you've made and look for ways to move to an even higher level.

Don't panic if your efforts seem to erode or even come unraveled sometimes. You'll learn some practical ways to get back on track and keep it from happening again. Don't worry if you're not there yet. You're not behind, and you don't need to catch up! Just keep on working from where you are, and if you've stalled, you can always start again.

The Bottom Line

We've covered a lot of ground together. Do you feel a little overwhelmed? That's okay. It happens. Ask yourself, "Have I tried to do everything at once?" If the answer is yes, this is a good point to step back and take stock.

Pat yourself on the back for what you've accomplished, and don't be stingy with self-praise. You've earned it! To get over the hump, focus your time and resources on the areas that cause you the most grief, confusion, money, time, or stress. That's where the dividends will be the greatest.

What's *your* bottom line? Do you desperately need to get your finances on an even keel or everything else will soon fall apart? If so, do that first. Are your disorganization and inefficiency in certain areas causing real problems with your significant other, housemates, or co-workers? Then working on those areas are your first priority.

Decide on the basics that make your life work (or not), and do them no matter what. The basics for most people would be ...

♦ Getting bills paid on time, and getting out of debt.

♦ Having the dishes done every day and being able to prepare nutritious meals with a minimum of fuss.

♦ Doing the weekly grocery shopping and having storage for food that allows you to find what you've bought.

♦ Getting adequate rest, nutrition, and exercise.

♦ Having your house tolerably clean so you feel comfortable coming home to it. I'm not saying *perfect*, mind you, just a level of clean that works for the stage where you are now.

> **Black Hole**
>
> Taking care of yourself isn't for later. It's definitely a part of minimum maintenance to do now and always. Without the captain, the ship loses direction. Be sure *you* are part of the bottom line.

- Doing the weekly wash and having a closet full of clothes that fit and are in good repair.

- Getting to work on time and keeping up with your assignments.

- Keeping track of appointments.

- Maintaining your automobile (if that's your main mode of transportation).

The systems I've outlined for you in this book for these areas should handle them for you in a hurry. Have in mind an absolute minimum level of order that you won't go below, and stick to it. That's your *bottom line*. You can always do better later, but maintaining this bottom-line organization gives you a good foundation on which to build. Remember, perfectionism is your enemy. It will debilitate you and distract you. Strive for *good*, not *perfect*.

Get Regular Tune-Ups for a Smoother Ride

Just like maintaining your automobile, maintaining your organization systems takes regular checkups and even periodic part replacements. Some regular maintenance tasks will keep everything humming.

For example, add to your Master List the projects you didn't get to while you were working with this book. You've been concentrating on high-priority tasks and major life systems, but you probably came across tasks and projects you know need to get done at some time. Capture them so you can schedule them for the future.

Schedule regular maintenance days. Have a closet-maintenance day, a file-maintenance day, a car-maintenance day, a food-and-kitchen-maintenance day, and a financial-maintenance day. If it only takes half a day, treat yourself to an afternoon off.

Create checklists for maintaining various areas of your life, and make copies. For example, you could make a food and household supplies inventory list. Or how about a spring cleanup list for the outdoors? Why reinvent the wheel each time when you can save the time and energy for other things?

When you set out on your maintenance mission, look carefully at the new systems you've created and ask these questions:

- How's my system working?

- If it's not working well, where and how is it breaking down?

- If it's working pretty well, is there anything I can do to improve it?

◆ Have I learned any new tips, methods, or ideas to try? Have I found any new storage solutions or organization products that might work better than what I have in place now?

◆ Are there any ways I can streamline this system, make it more efficient, or save additional time?

◆ Is there any way I can make my system more aesthetically pleasing? For example, I have some cardboard organizers that I know will do the trick. My next step is to find or make something more durable and nicer looking. The idea is working, but I can still improve on the way it looks.

Simplewise

New products are constantly being developed as more people take organizing their lives seriously. Browse hardware, business-supply, craft, and department stores for new space-saving ideas. Check out the many new organizing products stores, catalogs, and websites for new solutions. Write down the measurements of problem areas in your planner/organizer in case you see something that might work.

Making and keeping appointments with yourself for evaluating and planning is essential to maintaining your organization systems. If you pick a regular time slot, it will become a habit—something you actually look forward to. For me, planning time is Sunday evenings. I curl up with the three C's—a cat, a comforter, and a cup of tea—get out my planner/organizer, and do everything from reminding myself of my mission statement, goals, and plans, to deciding on the week's menus and making out a shopping list. Find a time that works for you, and make an enjoyable event of it. Consistency is the mother of habit, and pleasant rituals help make it easier to be consistent.

Continue to reward yourself for the strides you're making. Praise yourself. You'll discover that the rewards of the changes themselves are self-reinforcing. Cooking in a kitchen that's efficient, orderly, and clean makes it more fun to cook. Opening the garage door and seeing everything in its place, in working order, and well maintained is a reward in itself. Every time it takes me one step and 5 seconds to retrieve an account number or balance, I get this smug, self-satisfied grin on my face. It works that way—honest!

Taking It a Step Further

But don't stop there! There are more tune-up ideas you can put into practice. For example, make a list of self-improvement or inspirational books to read, seminars you'd like to attend, or audiotapes or videotapes you'd like to purchase or borrow, and use these items regularly. Reinforce your new habits, and build on them by feeding your conscious and unconscious mind with positive messages.

Set up a "brain trust" or resource network of positive, organized, motivated achievers. When you unstuffed your relationships, you eliminated those that dragged you down. Build new ones with people whose goals are to constantly improve themselves and make their lives and the lives of those around them better. Tap this network when you're looking for new ideas, and share ones you've found that work. Meet regularly with the people in your life—and be sure you listen!

Keep writing down your goals. In fact, try keeping a journal so you can express your thoughts on your self-improvement journey and later, look back and see how far you've come. Always ask "Why not?" instead of "Why?" when you're contemplating something.

Continue to develop yourself and look for ways to contribute to the lives of other people. If you need something, give it away. In other words, if you need understanding, give understanding. If you need love, give love. There's more power in this than you may realize.

If you're having a problem with something, study people who have solved the problem effectively. Find models for success. And when you find a system that works, see if you can apply it to some other area of your life. You may need to adapt it somewhat, but see if you can standardize it in some way.

Simplewise

Make a list of resources you know you can count on, and keep it in your planner/organizer. Include companies that sell supplies you use most often and their toll-free numbers or websites, dependable people you can call to hire for various tasks, organized friends with whom you can brainstorm, and books you refer to regularly. Whenever you're stumped or things don't seem to be working quite right, turn to your resource list for help.

If you pay attention every day to honing your life-management skills, the results will be enormous. Organization and simplification give you a feeling of control and self-confidence. From there, you can accomplish anything.

Lists, Schedules, and Files Revisited

You're probably tired of hearing it, but I'm going to say three things one more time. If you missed them before or they didn't sink in, now you have no excuse!

First, lists are your friends. Your Master List is one of your most powerful tools. It keeps you from forgetting things you must do and helps you get in touch with your real desires. Lists hold you accountable, and they let you see all you accomplish as you check off the items. Eventually, some things will become automatic and you may not need a list (such as your daily cleaning list). But keep it handy in your planner/organizer anyway, so you can check up on yourself periodically and see whether you're beginning to slide. If you are, you can use the checklist again for accountability.

> **Word Power**
>
> Our remedies oft in ourselves do lie, / which we ascribe to heaven.
> —William Shakespeare

Next, schedule, schedule, schedule! Make appointments to do things on your list. Make appointments with the key people in your life. Make appointments with yourself. Don't just put it on the list, set a time to *do it*.

Finally, set up efficient files and purge them regularly. A good filing system keeps the mounds of paper in your life moving. When it's filed, it's out of the way and you can retrieve it when you need it. By purging regularly, you keep those files fresh and useful.

If you haven't finished setting up or revamping your files, this should probably be a high priority. If they need purging, do it promptly. You'll create space, and you'll be on top of what's there.

If Things Start Breaking Down

It's not unusual to experience some amount of breakdown even if you worked hard to get things in order and you thought you had it licked. Don't despair, and don't pack it in. Just step back, and ask yourself, "What's happening here?"

What's Going Wrong?

You may be trying to do too much at once. Do one thing well and completely. After you master that, move on to the next. Choose the problem area that came up during some of your visualization exercises and work on that first. You'll see an immediate impact.

The area that kept coming up for me when I first committed to getting myself organized was our household finances and records. It loomed over me, aggravated me daily, and caused resentment. When I finally said, "Look, I'm going to make this work, and I'm going to make it as easy on myself as possible," things immediately got better.

I organized our financial files, got on a regular bill-paying schedule, computerized with financial-management software and electronic bill paying, and rounded up all our back-tax information and transferred it to uniform boxes. Then I hired a financial planner to help me develop an investment plan and set up a flow system for incoming bills, checks, and financial statements.

Concentrating on this one area had an enormous effect on my disposition, sense of control, and ability to lay my hands on anything financial in seconds; it actually made tasks I dreaded—such as bill paying—almost enjoyable. After my success in that one huge problem area for me, I was so charged with energy I was almost self-propelled. Choose what most annoys you or gets in your way. The rewards you'll experience will get you moving again.

Visualize It

Review your day yesterday. Close your eyes and see it in as much detail as you can, exactly as it happened, from morning until you laid your head down at night. Where did problems come up? Is there a pattern? How could you have solved or prevented those problems with what you now know about organization? Write down what you discover, and set aside time this week to concentrate on these areas.

Don't forget to delegate, either by getting people to take more responsibility at home or at work, or by hiring out some work. The latter solution may only be temporary until you get organized in that area. If things are breaking down, it may mean other people aren't pulling their weight.

Experts say it takes 21 days to form a habit. Are you giving yourself enough time? You may be expecting too much, too soon. You didn't get disorganized overnight, and it will take longer than a day to fix it.

Getting Back on Track

Now let's look at some tricks I use to get back on track when things seem to be slipping.

> **Black Hole** _____
>
> When obstacles appear, you may be tempted to give up and go back to the old way. Resist the urge to abandon what you're doing altogether just because some of it isn't working right now. Rewrite the plan; don't scrap it!

Make appointments that will force you to focus. If you're losing control of your finances, call your financial planner to do a portfolio or budget review. If the house has gotten away from you while you were working your organization plan in other areas, make an appointment for a cleaning service to come in. You'll have to straighten up at least a little bit before the service can do their work, but don't clean, just get things out of the way. In fact, purge while you're at it!

Entertain—really, this works! Invite your mother-in-law or your boss (or maybe just imagine they're on their way over). Imagine them going through every room in your house. Imagine them going through your closets, your files, your kitchen, and your garage. If you're single, invite a date over. Before that special someone gets there, the floor and countertops will be clean enough to eat off of!

Get an estimate for a cross-country move. When you get the estimated cost of moving all that junk, you'll start unstuffing your house like you wouldn't believe. Just imagine packing it all, too!

Terminating Time Wasters, Overcoming Organization Ogres

If you're not getting where you want to be as fast as you expected, you may be the victim of a time waster or organization ogre. Let's go over what to look for and ways to fix it.

Don't fall into the television trap. Analyze your TV-watching habits. Although it's easy to mindlessly sit in front of the tube to "relax," it can rob you of precious time with very little return. I have more than a few friends who have ditched their TV altogether, but I'm not telling you to do that. I do suggest you choose your TV programs carefully and put them on your schedule. Don't just sit down in your easy chair and zap the remote to while away the hours. Use your VCR or DVR to selectively record programs to watch when you want. And you'll save time by fast-forwarding through all the commercials.

Don't succumb to interruptions. You may undermine yourself by allowing too many to stop you. Of course, not all interruptions can be avoided, but many can. Don't just accept them—control them. Set aside a period of time that you don't take any phone calls. Let voicemail do its job. If people drop in, tell them you have an appointment (you do—with yourself) or that you're on a deadline and will see them when you're done.

Don't procrastinate. Do a procrastination checkup by going back to Chapter 3 and reviewing the section on procrastination. Keep giving yourself the message, "Do it now!" Make that your new mantra.

Don't go without a plan. You may have done a great job of identifying your goals but failed to work out a manageable plan, breaking things into smaller chunks and adding them to your schedule. Goal-setting is an important step, but it doesn't go far enough. Set aside time to plan if that's what's hanging you up.

Don't allow stuff to reaccumulate. Keeping your life from becoming overrun by "stuff" is an ongoing process. If your system worked great for a while and then started to bog down, you may have fallen into the Acquisition Trap again. Do a clutter inventory, and pare down right away. Stop allowing junk to come into your life (including junk relationships), and get rid of what junk already has. Remember, too, if you buy something that's better than what you have, don't keep the old one.

Simplewise _____

Ask your friends and family to stop giving you stuff. Tell them you'd rather they spend time with you, contribute to a worthy cause in your name, help you with your organizing chores, or create an experience for you. Share with them how hard you've worked to unstuff your life and how much you're enjoying your newfound space.

Don't make things too complicated. Simple is better. You may have packed away umpteen widgets in neat little boxes with color-coded cards to tell you where everything is, and cross-referenced and dated every piece. The chances you'll keep up such a complicated system are slim, though. If you stick with the KISS principle—Keep It Simple, Sweetie—your systems will be less likely to break down.

Don't give up too soon! If your system doesn't work the first time you try it, you may be tempted to scrap it entirely and give it up. Not so fast! It may just need some fine-tuning or some simple repetition to get it up and running.

Don't rest on your laurels. I said to reward yourself, but I didn't say you could stop there! Enjoy your successes, do something nice for yourself, and move on. Continually ask, "What's next?" This is your other new mantra.

Don't be too much of a perfectionist. Have you become an organization zealot? Are you spending too much time doing everything perfectly instead of just getting it done? Somewhere between a neatnik and a slob is a functional, comfortable level of order we can all strive for. You can always go back and do it better, if and when you have the time, but I'd rather be out walking in the sunshine or spending time with my husband! Organization is a tool to master, not your master.

Finally, don't forget to include *you* in your maintenance plan. If you leave yourself out, everything will break down. Be sure you renew yourself in the four basic areas: physical (exercise, rest, and nutrition), mental (reading, learning, organizing, and planning), social/emotional (relationships), and spiritual (prayer, meditation, nature, and creative expression). Include activities each week to fine-tune, maintain, and improve all four areas. Seek a balance.

Can Your Computer Keep You Organized?

If you have a home computer, you may be underestimating it as a tool to help you maintain your organization systems. One of the best ways a computer can help is as a reminder tool. Plenty of software packages are available for scheduling appointments. Even if you don't use a program for your day-to-day meetings or tasks, program it for major maintenance reminders.

Black Hole

Computer-based solutions are not always the most time- or cost-efficient. They're also not always the most mobile or adaptable. Before you make a major changeover to a computer program, consider the low-tech solutions as well as the high-tech.

Some organization software has the ability to create audio reminders, little alarms that sound when it's time to do something important. You can use this feature to reinforce maintenance chores that may be easy to forget, such as quarterly file purging, early tax preparation, or regular oil changes. Or use it as a reminder for birthdays and anniversaries. How can you make this work for you?

If a paper-based system you're currently using for some task doesn't seem to be working well or takes longer than you think it should, maybe there's a computer program or online tool that does it better. Stay on the lookout for any technology solutions that might help keep you on track. You can vote on stock proxies, buy and send gifts, track packages, look up phone numbers and addresses, send greeting cards, and file your tax returns online. More and more vendors are going paperless for their billing and statements. Most of these services are free. Why not take advantage of them?

Some programs, including recipe, personal record keeping, and financial software, require some heavy setup, but after the initial data is entered, they're quick and easy to maintain. Weigh the investment in time and money needed for setting up a program against the time, money, and clutter savings in the long term.

Aesthetics Essentials

My first aim in writing this book was to help you get things functioning more smoothly in your life. When that happens, you can move to the next step, which is making what already works more beautiful. Order in itself is beautiful, in my opinion, and after you have a basic level of order and simplicity in your life, you can then turn your attention to making it even more aesthetically pleasing.

You can use the free time that results from being organized to pay more attention to details, including aesthetics. I have two rules, however. First, if something looks nice but fails to do the job I created it for I opt for the less attractive tool that works. And second, if it isn't functional, it needs to go—unless it truly adds pleasure and beauty to my life.

I've tried lots of household paper-sorting systems, including ones made of wicker and other decorative materials, but the one that works best for me is a horizontal cardboard cubby system that fits on a shelf. Someday I may have a more attractive wooden one made, but until then, I'll take my ugly organizer over the decorator ones anytime!

There are lots of little ways, however, to add some beauty to otherwise mundane aspects of daily existence. Here are a few:

- After you get your closet organized, decorate the inside with colored hangers, attractive boxes, and picture postcards or posters on the unobstructed wall space. Change them periodically when the spirit moves you.

- Put fresh flowers on the breakfast table regularly, and maybe a single bloom on your nightstand next to your bed.

- Cover recipe binders with wallpaper scraps or coated gift paper.

- Add scented sachets to your closet and drawers.

◆ Have a pretty, well-stocked basket of stationery within easy reach, filled with postcards, note cards, stamps, and an elegant letter opener you can grab when you have a few minutes to do your personal correspondence.

What other ways can you think of to make your personal world a more beautiful place?

Simplewise _____

Alexandra Stoddard has made a study of adding beauty to everyday rituals and spaces in simple ways. For some inspiring ideas, read one of her many books. *Living a Beautiful Life: 500 Ways to Add Elegance, Order, Beauty, and Joy to Every Day of Your Life* and *Living Beautiful Together* are two of my favorites.

You Have a Dream!

Being organized doesn't mean becoming a drudge. On the contrary, it should mean you're pounds lighter, experiencing a freedom you've probably never known.

If you find yourself burdened, a slave to your schedule, then you've lost sight of the purpose of getting organized—to fulfill the mission you said you wanted in life! Go back to the beginning and take another look. Review Chapter 2. Redo some of the exercises. If you need to, get some additional help with developing a mission statement and formulating your goals.

Reviewing and perhaps redoing this groundwork may make the difference between being a drudge and a dynamo! Tapping back into your real desires and passions can't help but infuse your efforts with new zest and energy.

Allow yourself time and space to wish and dream. Exercise your visualization muscles. There are good books and tapes on developing and using visualization techniques to help you as well. These techniques are enjoyable because they activate the unconscious, invigorate the imagination, and teach you how to employ your fantasies to help you identify what you really care about in life. (I've listed several tools and how to obtain them in Appendix A.)

Getting organized around your true desires for a fulfilled and joyous life is fun. If it's not, you're doing something wrong! Give yourself the time and space to embark on this important exploration—it will fuel everything you do.

Let the Seasons Tell the Time

Since first developing my own organization plans and implementing them, I've learned a trick that has added a new dimension to tasks that need doing every year: key them to the seasons. This is how our ancestors made sure things got done on time! I find it adds a wonderful rhythm to life, when what I do works along with the changes in nature.

Winter is a time for turning inward. There's not much that can be done outside, so I can focus more on the house's inner workings. This is when my life centers around the hearth and my own goals and dreams. It's a time for taking stock and planning. Chores such as cleaning out drawers and closets seem perfect for this time of year. Detail work, such as mending and sewing, takes precedence.

Spring means clearing out. There's a reason why it's called "spring cleaning." That's the season when the earth is waking up and activity begins to heighten and move out-doors. What better time to unstuff, have a yard sale, and get the family car in shape?

In summer, we can shed our heavy clothes, live more in the fresh air, and schedule tasks such as painting and refurbishing for a time when windows can remain open and cleanup is easier.

The fall, harvest time, is a time for reaping the rewards of our industry, making prep-arations for the coming cold weather. This is a good time to survey your disaster preparedness, food storage, and batteries.

What are your seasonal rituals?

Make Maintenance a Celebration

I can't encourage you enough to make organizing your life and maintaining your organization systems joyous and celebratory. Growing a happy life is something to celebrate! Add silly (or serious, if you like) rituals, songs, rhymes, readings, music, and dance to your celebrations. Add whatever trappings make them fun. Make up your own holidays to both celebrate and serve as a reminder, or key them to our mysterious past if you like.

Each February 2, for example, I celebrate Candlemas (or Imbolc, if you prefer its Celtic name), an ancient holiday that has since been transmuted into Groundhog Day, which reminds us of the longer days to come with the spring. I air out the house (whatever the temperature), imagine any stale influences taking flight out the windows, take an inventory of my spices and pantry staples, light candles throughout the house, and welcome the coming of the light and the green of spring. All winter holiday decorations and seasonal cooking utensils are carefully put away in long-term storage for next year. I begin collecting all the statements, documents, and receipts for taxes. I drool over seed catalogs. The actual celebration of this event when the date appears on the calendar adds a depth and a richness to it that grows in meaning each year.

Simplewise _____

To learn more about seasonal celebrations, find a copy of *Mrs. Sharp's Traditions: Nostalgic Suggestions for Re-Creating the Family Celebrations and Seasonal Pastimes of the Victorian Home* by Sarah Ban Breathnach. It offers a perspective on the old-fashioned way of observing seasonal changes.

Whatever your nationality or religious faith, look for ways to integrate daily tasks into larger events and celebrations already meaningful to you. Find out what seasonal tasks were associated with these dates and adapt them to your own. At least try it. You may like it!

The Least You Need to Know

♦ Finding and maintaining your bottom line is the best foundation for keeping your life organized.

♦ Lists, schedules, and an efficient filing system are the fundamental tools for maintaining an organized life.

♦ If your organization plan starts to break down, you can take specific steps to identify problem areas and get yourself back on track.

♦ If your system is functioning well, you can add beauty to everyday spaces and rituals.

♦ Providing time and space for you to fantasize, visualize, wish, and dream is crucial to successfully building and perpetuating order and high performance.

Chapter 19

Organization Styles for Different Lifestyles

In This Chapter

- ◆ Adapting your organization plan to your current lifestyle
- ◆ The importance of changing your plan for changes in lifestyle
- ◆ Tips for single parents, caregivers, singles, widows, and widowers
- ◆ Resources for the special needs of frequent travelers

The basic organization principles I've given you so far in this book apply regardless of your age, living situation, or financial status. Whether you're a student or a retiree, live alone or with a large family, getting organized will make your life better.

In this chapter, we look at how you can adapt these basic principles to your specific lifestyle and status, concentrating on the areas of food, clothing, shelter, people, money, and work.

All by Yourself

According to the latest U.S. census information, men and women are marrying later than ever before, and 1 in every 9 adults lives alone. If you have the house or apartment all to yourself, it's easier to implement an organization plan that works for you. You don't have other people to mess it up!

You may live alone by choice; you may be a student living on your own for the first time or a professional seriously pursuing a career; or you may be divorced or widowed. Whatever your situation, being single presents its own organization challenges, whether you're beginning your adult life or are well into adulthood.

Young and Single

If you're young and single, chances are you have a fairly social lifestyle at this stage of your life. You may not eat at home very often. You're more likely to rent a house or apartment than own your own home, and you may move several times before settling in one place.

Although you may not yet be building equity in a home, it's important that you begin budgeting now, so you can keep a close watch on where your money goes and plan for emergencies. Now is also a good time to think about the future with a small investment fund. If you're not sure of the best way to begin investing, speak to a financial planner or educate yourself through an investment club or seminar. Organize your financial life now by setting up filing and bill-paying systems. You will be way ahead of the game when things get more complicated later on.

Start organizing your work records now, too. Keep employment information and reviews in your files. Think ahead about references for future employment. If you're a student, your professors will be among your first references, so keep them in mind. Organizing to find a job might be a top issue soon, if it's not already. Now is the time to think about that resumé and begin collecting the information you need to write a good one.

Although you may be inclined to eat out a lot, with some simple kitchen tools and basic ingredients, you can create meals that are more nourishing and easier on the budget than eating out or ordering in. It's easy to get into the junk food habit when you live alone, but it's expensive and doesn't promote good health. Even if you only cook for one, treat yourself like a guest. Sit at the table, not in front of the TV. Put on some dinner music, and set the table. Enjoy a good, wholesome meal you prepared just for you.

Go back to Chapter 11 and review the information on bulk cooking, quick cooking, and slow cooker cooking. Experiment to see which methods could work best for you. If you're simply not in the mood to cook after a hard day at work or school, try cooking only a couple of times a week and freezing single portions for other days. Soups and stews work well for this, as do many pasta sauces and casseroles.

If you're on a tight budget, you can often find good used cookware at garage sales and thrift stores. Whatever you can't find there, purchase from reputable companies and try to buy the best quality you can afford. Here's a list of the basics:

- 10- or 12-inch nonstick skillet
- 1- and 2-quart saucepans with lids
- 5-quart Dutch oven with lid
- 8- or 10-inch high-carbon, stainless-steel chef's knife
- 3-inch paring knife
- Sharpening steel and whetstone for sharpening knives
- Large cutting board (plastic or wood)
- Wooden spoons of various sizes
- Slotted spoon
- Ladle
- Plastic spatula for nonstick cookware
- Rubber spatulas, large and small, for scraping out bowls
- Tongs
- Set of measuring spoons and measuring cups
- 2-cup glass measuring cup
- Mixing bowls in various sizes
- Grater
- Baking/roaster pan
- Large strainer or colander

Simplewise

For helpful tips on cooking for one, check out *Going Solo in the Kitchen* by Jane Doerfer and *Serves One: Meals to Savor When You're on Your Own* by Toni Lydecker. You can join the Cooking for One or Two Recipe Swap online at www.kitchenlink. com and search www. foodnetwork.com for episodes on "cooking for one."

- Can opener

- Corkscrew and bottle opener

- Oven mitts and trivets

- Kitchen towels

- Kitchen shears

- Vegetable peeler

- Microwave-safe storage containers

- Jar and bottle opener

Of course, you'll add to your collection as you cook more or if you decide to bake, but these are the basics. Add one good, basic cookbook such as *Joy of Cooking*, the *Fanny Farmer Cookbook*, or the *Better Homes and Gardens New Cookbook*, and you're all set.

You're probably doing your laundry out, but because you're only one person, the weekly trip to the Laundromat shouldn't be too taxing. Take advantage of off-peak hours, but don't compromise your safety. The typical dinnertime, between 6 and 8 P.M., is usually a good time for doing laundry and grocery shopping.

Because you're just starting out, you can unstuff and avoid the Acquisition Trap right from the beginning. Make careful selections, and buy quality things. It's better to buy quality used things than new, cheaper ones of inferior quality. When selecting furniture, remember that you'll likely be moving it several times. Stay away from massive pieces that need special handling or may not fit through the door or up the stairs of your next apartment.

Simplewise _____

There's a great book called *Where's Mom Now That I Need Her? Surviving Away from Home* by Betty Rae Frandsen, Kathryn J. Frandsen, and Kent P. Frandsen. It explains basic food preparation, simple first aid, laundry and clothing repair, stain removal, and lots more basic survival information for starting out on your own. A second volume, *Where's Dad Now That I Need Him? Surviving Away from Home*, handles the "guy" stuff Dad would teach you.

Older and Single

If you're older and single, you also have total control of your environment and destiny, but you're at a different stage in life than the young single. You may be living alone as an intentional lifestyle, or you may be divorced or widowed and have no children at home.

One great challenge for you could be balancing alone time with social activities. It may mean forcing yourself to get out and be with other people. If you have a career, you'll have more opportunities to socialize, but if you're no longer in the work force, you may have to make a conscious effort to involve yourself outside the home.

Add some activities to explore to your Master List. Using your planner/organizer to schedule specific activities will remind you of your social needs. Join a book or political discussion group, take up a hobby, volunteer, or get involved in your community. There are lots of opportunities to meet new people and contribute your skills and experience.

Statistics show that women make up the largest number of those surviving a spouse. Many women haven't had responsibility for the finances during their married years, so developing money-management skills becomes crucial when they're on their own. If you're in this situation and haven't done so yet, taking stock of your finances should be your number one priority. If you and your husband had a financial plan, it needs to be revised for your new circumstances.

Black Hole

If you're alone due to the death of a spouse, one delicate issue is what to do with the departed loved one's things. It's hard to say when is the best time to pack up your spouse's belongings and pass them on, but at some point it will make sense. Don't let others push you or think you should do it right away. If you need support, have someone go through the process with you.

Now that you're cooking for only one person, you can cut down the ingredients for your favorite recipes or make the same amount you did for two and freeze the rest for a later meal. Be sure you don't give in to the "why bother?" syndrome when contemplating a meal just for yourself.

My recently widowed friend Edith, who loves to cook, decided she missed cooking for other people more than she realized, so she now regularly invites friends over for dinner. Everyone pitches in with ingredients, but she does the cooking. Guests help with the cleanup, too. This gives Edith great pleasure and stimulating evening conversation. She eats more nutritious meals than she would if she were only preparing food for herself. And her guests don't have to cook that night! It's a good deal all around. Don't be afraid to try offbeat ideas. They're often the ones that work the best.

Single-Income, Dual-Parent Families

Some couples feel the sacrifices they must make to have one parent home at all times are worth it. One partner may give up his or her income altogether, or each may have a part-time arrangement so they can share child-care responsibilities.

For couples embracing this lifestyle, organization issues usually focus around thrift and scheduling child care. Time-management issues will likely be different as well. With reduced income, the family is choosing a quality of emotional life over material things. Extra-careful budgeting, cooking from scratch, and even having a vegetable garden and sewing some of the family's clothes might be part of the plan. Children can be brought into these activities and, in fact, taught valuable self-reliance, organization, and time-management skills. If children understand the reasons for the tradeoffs and are made a part of the process, they'll be more willing to cooperate.

Simplewise

Subscribe to "The Dollar Stretcher," a free e-mail newsletter filled with useful suggestions for those trying to get by with less, at www.stretcher.com.

Steve, a writer friend of mine, and his wife, Leslie, decided they both wanted to be highly involved in the daily life of their new baby. Leslie is a schoolteacher, and Steve was a technical writer. Steve left his job to become a home-based freelance writer, while Leslie kept her teaching job. Together their two present incomes equal roughly half of what they were making when both worked full-time. During the summer, Leslie takes over the child-care duties so Steve can develop his writing business. During the school year, Steve has to juggle caring for the baby with getting his work done. He can handle some of it at night and on weekends, but when deadlines loom, he sometimes needs help.

One solution is in-home child care, where the parent is still available, and the babysitter tends to the child's needs while the at-home parent works. Another is a trade situation, where several at-home parents trade off caring for each other's children one day a week. Steve opted for the latter.

If one parent takes on the role of at-home child-care provider, it's important that the other spends time with the children and gives the at-home parent some private time. Negotiating these times, as well as the cleaning duties, are key issues. It's all too easy to assume that the at-home parent is responsible for cooking, child care, and keeping the house clean. No fair! Those duties should be shared. How they're divided up needs to be negotiated and jobs scheduled.

Dual-Income Couples

For working couples without children, meshing schedules and sharing housework are the key organization issues. Because they tend to be very career oriented, DINKS—dual-income, no kids—can sometimes forget how important it is to pay attention to their primary relationship. Over time, they may grow apart. If you fall into this lifestyle category, be sure you see to it there's adequate focus on your significant other, not just your own personal ambitions.

The only time available for maintaining both the house and the relationship is evenings, weekends, and vacation time, so it's important that both partners share their schedules and commit to certain chores around the house. This group can often benefit from hiring outside help, and they're more likely to have the income to do it. Doing housework chores together is another solution, building some fun and communication into what needs to be done anyway.

Another time for sharing and reconnecting is during the preparation and enjoyment of the evening meal. Make these times special by planning menus and perhaps doing some food preparation ahead of time (see Chapter 11 for meal preparation strategies), so you can concentrate on making mealtime hassle-free and relaxing. Light some candles, use fancy cloth napkins, hold hands, and talk!

Dual-Income Families

Organization issues for families where both parents work are likely to revolve around child care and work-related topics, in addition to household chores and meal preparation. The working couple knows that spending time with the children needs to be one of the highest priorities, but it can be tricky. Balancing the personal need for downtime and renewal against the needs of the children isn't easy. And again, who does the housework? All too often it's the working woman who ends up trying to do it all. No fair, guys!

Planning and scheduling come to the rescue here. So does finding ways to get things done and spend time with the kids at the same time. Who says washing the car has to mean time away from the family? It can mean a fantastic water fight and a cleaning session at the same time. Even the dog may get a bath.

If you're clear about your mission in life and you write down your goals, develop a plan, and work on it each day, you'll raise great kids (a worthy life mission) and get ahead in your career. It doesn't just happen by accident.

Black Hole

Like other families, dual-income families need to look at accumulating money for college tuition, so financial planning and careful budgeting are high priorities. But because time for managing investments is most likely hard to come by, finding a good financial planner is crucial. Review Chapters 14 and 15 to get your finances in shape for now and the future.

Single Parents

The adult of a single-parent family has to do it all. There simply is no one else, or so it often seems. It's a tough place to be. I know—I've been there. If you become a single parent through divorce, besides all the challenges you face, you may hear from out-siders and the media that your home is "broken." Well, I never accepted that, and neither should you!

Sure, it's best for kids to grow up in a healthy two-parent household, but when you're going it alone, there's no reason not to have a great family! Just recently I read a list of ways single-parent families have unique strengths. I thought I'd paraphrase some of them for you.

First, just because a family has two parents doesn't mean it's healthy or happy. If there was an unhealthy situation before, a single-parent situation is vastly superior. Now the children may have an opportunity to bond with both parents separately, without the discord that existed before.

Single parents have more flexibility in planning time with their children. They don't have the regular demands and distractions of another adult. When the children are with each parent, they can have exclusive attention and the individual parent may be more attuned to their emotional needs.

Single-parent households can be more interdependent. Single parents depend more heavily on cooperation from each family member, and children are more likely to pitch in voluntarily. I'm convinced my children are the responsible adults they are today largely because they learned responsibility early. They felt needed and rose to the occasion.

Children in single-parent households are often exposed to a wider range of experiences. Rather than getting a baby-sitter (which I couldn't afford), I took my children to college classes with me, to work on my college newspaper, to the library, and on field trips. When I organized the company Christmas party, they were the elves.

In divorced families, children can experience two totally different spheres. They get a wider view of life, and besides, they get two birthday parties and two Christmases!

Of course, single parents have their work cut out for them as well. Certain standards may have to be lowered, especially those surrounding housework. But order and organization are even more important in a single-parent household. Because there's so little time, things need to be streamlined to operate as efficiently as possible.

The once-a-week food preparation method worked well for me when I was a single parent with young children. I shopped and cleaned on Saturday while the children were with their father and cooked the week's meals on Sunday afternoon. The children knew what was scheduled for when, so even if I got home late they could get things started. If the meal was frozen, I took it out to thaw in the morning before I went to work. We had good, wholesome, home-cooked meals that were within my budget, and I didn't have to cook after a long day at the office. The slow cooker was the other workhorse in our household.

Simplewise

The National Organization of Single Mothers (www.singlemothers.org) is an award-winning organization that helps new members form or join local support groups. There's a great site just for single dads, too: www.singledadnetwork.com.

Two of the biggest issues for the single parent are making sure the children aren't alone when they come home from school and someone is always available in an emergency. Some school systems have after-school programs for "latch-key kids." If you don't live in an area with support programs for single parents, you may want to consider relocating. You can't do this alone, and it helps to live in a community where you can get some help. Look to church groups and single-parent organizations as well.

For emergencies, the best system is to have several people who can cover for you in case you can't be reached. Line up in advance the relatives, friends, or neighbors you can trust. You also need to cover the times the children are sick and you have to go to work. A redundant system with several backups is the way to keep things covered no matter what.

It helps to work for a company that's pro-family. You should never have to choose between your job and the well-being of your child. There are organizations that rate companies in these areas. Do some research (start with your local research librarian). When you go job hunting, have this objective clear in your mind. You're more likely to find what you want if you firmly plant the idea in your mind before you start looking.

On the financial front, you need to provide for your children in case something happens to you. Get all the benefits you're entitled to at your workplace and through the local, state, and federal governments, whether you're divorced or widowed. Think through what you want done with and for your children if you die or become seriously ill. Name a guardian who will have immediate access to all your financial information. Organize it the way I outlined in Chapters 14 and 15, and show the person you choose how you have it set up. Be sure to include any special information about the children this person may need to know, such as medical history or special needs.

Simplewise

Although it's not something we naturally want to discuss, it would be a good idea to get a feel for what your children would want if you couldn't be there to take care of them. Choose a time to carefully broach the subject, reassure them that nothing's wrong, but tell them you want to be certain no matter what the future brings, they're always taken care of. Take their wishes into consideration when choosing a guardian.

The Empty Nest

I can address the empty-nest change in lifestyle, because I'm smack dab in the middle of it! When the fledglings fly from the nest, Mom and Dad can be anywhere from their 40s (if they started a family early) to well into their 70s and older. The issues for empty nesters are somewhat different depending on age and financial status, but certain things crop up regardless of when your little birdies fly the coop.

One such issue is deciding when to take over the kids' rooms. This can be more trouble than you might think. When my oldest daughter left for college, I immediately moved my office into her bedroom. I had been using the dining room, but there was too much activity there for me to work effectively and I couldn't keep my papers in order. She was crushed. I was looking at it from a totally practical standpoint; her reaction was purely emotional. I never intended to make her feel she wasn't welcome (I had a bed fixed up in the family room downstairs), but that's how she felt. What can I say? I goofed! It's a good idea to find out from your kids how they feel about using their old space *before* you make changes.

On the other hand, don't become a storage facility for your grown kids. As soon as they're on their own and settled semipermanently, they need to decide what to take, what to toss, and what they'd like you to hang on to (for a while). Keep the last category to a minimum. Strike a balance between keeping a place for your grown children and moving on to the next stage in your lives.

Now is a good time to reevaluate your finances. Your children may have their own benefits at work, so you'll be able to make some changes there. As a gift to each child, one year we arranged for them to have a professional financial planner where they live draw up a complete financial plan for them, while we did the same for ourselves. Rather than contributing more clutter to your children's lives, why not give them something they can really use?

Black Hole

Be sure you transmit the right message to your kids! You want to make them feel that they're loved and can always come home if they need to. But you also want them to be independent and self-sufficient, solving their own problems and forging their own future. Strive to create this balance—both offering support and letting go—in your organizing plan.

The Open Nest

These days, more adult children are living at home than ever before. When older children come back home to live, it shouldn't be on the same basis as it was when they were children. They are now housemates, and they need to understand that right from the get-go. Negotiate their household share of the cooking, shopping, cleaning, and financial requirements. Expect them to behave like adults, and resist the temptation to treat them like they're young children again.

It's also a good idea to have a defined period of time for this arrangement. Is it for 6 months? A year? Don't wait until they've moved in to discuss these things. Get things out in the open from the start.

You need to work out storage arrangements, too. If they have furniture, where will you put it? You have to make room, they'll have to find a solution, or someone will have to pay for a storage facility rental. Will you be eating together, or will your adult child be responsible for his or her own meals? If the latter, will they be shopping for their own groceries? Do they understand they'll be cleaning up after themselves? What about laundry? Discuss these issues up front to avoid misunderstandings and hurt feelings later.

Caregivers and Extended Families

Having an ill, disabled, or aged family member in a household creates several crucial organization issues. Laying out the home in an efficient manner is essential to saving steps for caregivers and making it easier for a loved one to care for him- or herself as much as possible. Much has been written on this topic, and contacting one of the various organizations that addresses your particular situation would be an excellent idea.

You may need to rethink how you store things and how you shop. Perhaps smaller sizes would make it easier for a disabled or aged family member to prepare meals. Many ingredients now come prechopped or semiprepared, making it less labor-intensive to put together a dish. Lower shelving might help, or perhaps simply relocating essentials to an area within easy reach will do the trick. Some simple aids might contribute to independence as well.

In some cases, you may need a home health-care aide to assist you, even if only temporarily. Contact your local social-services agency and ask for referrals. A professional might know simple techniques to make things easier or be able to point you toward helpful equipment and tools.

Simplewise _____

To find a caregiver support group, contact the American Self-Help Clearinghouse at www.mentalhelp.net/selfhelp. You'll find information on self-help organization chapters in your area and how to contact the headquarters of a national organization that addresses your needs.

The role of caregiver needn't fall to one member of the family alone. Everyone can be involved, sharing scheduled time and responsibilities. Even small children can give the primary caregiver a hand, and older children can provide much-needed relief.

Blended Families and Dual-Custody Arrangements

With more than half of all marriages ending in divorce and many divorced partners remarrying, new solutions have evolved to handle parenting by more than one set of adults. These arrangements can work if everyone involved keeps their main priority in mind: the welfare of the children. Beyond this, organizing for smooth transitions from one residence to the other is imperative.

In some cases, as many as five sets of children are involved in the blending of families: the divorced couple's, each of their new spouse's kids, and children from the two new unions. The challenges are enormous but are being met by real people every day.

My friend Katie and her husband have a dual-custody arrangement with Katie's children. Both she and her ex-husband live in the same neighborhood, so the kids attend the same activities, they just go home to a different house every other week. Certain basics are duplicated in each household, and personal areas are designated for each child to call his or her own. Certainly, this arrangement would not work for everyone, but when adults put their efforts into cooperating and promoting their children's welfare, it's amazing how well children adapt and thrive.

Ideally, in a dual-custody situation, chores assigned to a child in one household should also be assigned in the other. This reduces the feeling of disruption in a child's life and also helps both households keep working efficiently. Both parents need to work together to create consistency and see that one doesn't undermine the discipline efforts of the other.

Scheduling regular family conferences is crucial to keeping communication flowing and resolving logistical issues before they get out of hand. If a child is being disciplined in one household for unacceptable behavior, the adults in the second household need to know what's going on and, hopefully, support those efforts.

The Road Warrior

I covered the needs of the home-based worker at length in Chapter 9, but one lifestyle I only touched on was that of the road warrior or frequent traveler. Whether you're self-employed or working for someone else, your job may involve a great deal of travel. This lifestyle brings up a whole host of special organization issues. To name a few …

Who handles things while you're away? If someone is holding down the fort at home or at work, you may naturally be tempted to dump everything on him or her. How fair is that? You need to be organized to handle your daily tasks on the road. If you normally pay the bills, consider an electronic bill-paying service and computer cash-management program on your laptop (with built-in modem, of course) or your

Internet-equipped cell phone, which makes handling this stuff on the road pretty easy. If this won't work, see whether your bank has an automatic bill-paying service. If it doesn't, you may want to look for a new bank. Look for other ways you can take care of the same responsibilities while you're traveling that you do when you're at home.

What happens in an emergency? Have people and services lined up for everything that might go wrong, from a flooded basement to a sick pet.

Black Hole

If you live alone, don't forget to designate someone to keep extra keys so he or she can get into your home or apartment in an emergency—and so you can get in your home if you lose your keys. Trusted neighbors are ideal, especially if they're home during the day.

What if people need to get in touch? A detailed itinerary with accurate information about where you'll be at all times is crucial. Be sure to include phone numbers. If things change en route, amend the itinerary as soon as you know. Leave this information with all the key people back on the home front.

I've been a "road warrior" myself at various times, and I know many other writers and business people who spend a lot of time in planes, trains, and automobiles. Here are a few tips I've put together from my own "road show":

Have portable everything! Consider bulk, weight, and durability in things such as luggage, clothing, computer equipment, and personal appliances. Look for small-size toiletries and small containers you can transfer things into. Make frequent use of resealable plastic bags for individual items that can leak.

Be sure to get some exercise. Select accommodations where you can walk safely, or ones that have exercise facilities indoors. Schedule time in your planner/organizer for exercise just as you would if you were at home. You'll feel better, and it's a great stress reliever!

Eat a balanced diet. Stay away from fast-food places, and try to eat balanced meals that aren't too rich. Ask the locals to recommend places that fit the bill. And take your vitamins! If I'm going to be in one place for a few days, I often get meals from my favorite take-out: the grocery store! Fruits and vegetables can be kept on ice from the hotel or motel ice-maker. Some cooked chilled shrimp with cocktail sauce and a salad add up to a delicious, light meal that's easy to put together in a hotel room. My husband and I, tiring of rich restaurant food, have often made a repast of fruit, cheese, and hearty bread.

Pack light. Most experienced, heavy-duty travelers recommend packing everything into your carry-on luggage. If you can't get it into your carry-on (check your airline's requirements), don't take it. That way you don't have to wait in line for your baggage or run the risk of losing it between stops. Not to mention that some airlines are charging fees for checking luggage these days. If you're away for a long time, you can use hotel laundry services or a Laundromat. If you know you'll need to accumulate stuff on the road, such as brochures or conference materials, pack it up and ship it home.

Stay in touch. Make regular calls home if someone there is taking care of things for you. Tell them how much you appreciate their help and support. If you're in a relationship, communication is essential. Most people I know with heavy travel schedules who are in a relationship call home at least once a day. This gives the one at home base the opportunity to involve you in important decisions and gives you a feeling of connectedness, even if you can't remember which city you woke up in this morning. Cell phones with e-mail make this all the more simple, but there will be times when you simply can't be reached, so be sure you check in.

Dress for travel success. Invest in lightweight, easy-to-care-for, mix-and-match separates. Women actually have it easier in this area because male business travelers generally have to cope with bulky suits. Many clothes travel best rolled rather than laid flat. And wear only comfortable shoes.

Don't bring it home. Restrain yourself from bringing home clutter from your travels, either for yourself or as souvenirs for those who stayed behind. E-mail often. Write long, love-filled letters. Use the video cam on your laptop to say goodnight. Share your feelings. Tell them you miss them and what you love about them. Those things are better than souvenirs any day!

Visualize It

Take some time to think about your present lifestyle. Has it changed recently? What are the positive things about your particular situation? What are the unique challenges that might be helped with planning and organizing? Are finances the greatest area of concern? Or does finding time for intimacy need more of your attention? If you could change one thing about your current lifestyle, what would that be?

Two good books to help you learn the ropes of serious business travel are *Road Warrior Survival Guide* by Greg Rosner and *Keeping Your Family Close: When Frequent Travel Pulls You Apart* by Elizabeth M. Hoekstra. These can provide plenty of tips to help make both travel and returning home easier for everyone involved. And speaking of coming home, be sure to detox from your trip as soon as you can. Listen first to what's gone on at home and then tell your tales from the hinterlands.

Whatever your particular circumstances, you can adapt an organization plan to suit them. It's not a one-size-fits-all world. Know the specific challenges and advantages of your lifestyle, and create a plan that works best for you.

The Least You Need to Know

◆ You can adapt the basic principles of organization to every lifestyle.

◆ You can organize for the way you live now and for future changes by changing emphasis and priorities.

◆ Key activities for adapting your organization plan are negotiating, scheduling, and planning.

◆ Whatever your situation, strive for balance between the physical, mental, emotional, and spiritual.

Chapter 20

Seasonal Stuff: Ensuring a Year of Happy Holidays

In This Chapter

- ◆ Making your holiday schedule less hectic
- ◆ Creating a holiday season less about stuff and more about fun
- ◆ Time- and money-savvy holiday gift-giving tips
- ◆ Conquering holiday storage problems

We all know the recipe for ruining the holiday season: start with unreasonably high expectations, heap on a good dose of guilt and a dash of procrastination, let simmer with family differences and distances, try to do too much, and garnish with a little flu bug. No wonder you'd rather spend the holidays alone in Timbuktu!

If you've become a Grinch, why not turn things around? Make this the year you truly look forward to the holidays with wide-eyed enthusiasm and delight.

Goal-Setting, Holiday Style

There are those words again: *goal-setting* and *planning*. Do the holidays have a way of just happening to you? When you don't focus early on how you want things to be, they can take on an unintended and unruly life of their own. But if you start out with clear intentions, you're more likely to create what you intend.

Granted, getting in touch with your inner desires when it comes to the holidays may not be as simple as it sounds. Holidays are fraught with emotional triggers and baggage that are often very complicated and not wholly clear. I think you'll agree, however, that it's easier to navigate a minefield when you know where the bombs are buried.

Visualize It

Close your eyes and imagine your ideal holiday. Imagine it the absolute best it could be. Start with Thanksgiving and make your "movie" go all the way through New Year's Day. Who would be there? What kind of food would be served? How are things decorated? What is your mood? Be free in your imaginings. This doesn't have to be like any holiday season you've ever known. Write down the major elements of your movie. If you imagined going out into the woods and cutting down your own Christmas tree, write that down. Keep your list close by. You're going to use it later.

Creating a great holiday is a lot like orchestrating a great party. Imagine you're putting on a play or making a movie. You have a script, props, scenery, various players, and a director. Everyone's the director in their own holiday pageant, whether they know it or not. Why not accept the role and make the production your own?

Your Personal Holiday Planning Book

Some years ago I made a holiday binder I now rely on every year to make our holidays bright. It's a standard-size loose-leaf notebook, with colored dividers and lined three-hole-punched paper. My categories are Cards, Crafts, Décor, Food, and Gifts. I use it for Thanksgiving, Christmas, and New Year's planning each year, plus it comes in handy for other special occasions. Other possible categories you might want to add could be Parties, Menus, Lists, Songs, Traditions, Budget, or anything else you want to keep track of.

I have our Christmas card mailing list on a label program. Each year I revise it, making any necessary changes, additions, and deletions; print it on regular paper; and add to my planner behind the Cards divider. Each year, I use that printout to make notations and to revise my label program when card-sending time arrives.

Under Crafts, I keep directions for making decorations or ornaments we especially liked that year or ones I want to try next year, along with any notes that might be helpful. If I make ornaments to give away, I sometimes take photos and add them. Crafts are a big part of our holiday celebrations, but they may not be your thing. Edit your Holiday Planning Book accordingly.

The Décor section contains ideas for decorations, inside and out. If I see something in a book or magazine, I photocopy it or tear it out and add it to my binder. I do the same for printouts from my Internet wanderings. If you create a decorating scheme you're especially pleased with, take a picture and put it in your binder so you can duplicate it the following year.

The Food category contains copies of our traditional family recipes. I also have these recipes elsewhere, but I find that during the holiday rush, it's nice to have them all in one place—a sort of personalized family holiday cookbook. I also keep menus and shopping lists. (You can store these in plastic sheet protectors.)

Under Gifts, I keep gift lists and any notes on what people might mention during the year that they'd like for Christmas or "someday." If you see an item in a catalog, you may want to make a note of it here. Having gift lists from the past reminds me of what I've already given so I don't duplicate.

You could also have a shopping list page and a to-do list for next year. When the season begins to draw near, that can become your head start. You can make a copy of the shopping list and keep it in your planner/organizer so you can buy stocking stuffers or even major gift items when you see exactly what you want, no matter what the time of year or when items are on sale.

The Holiday Planning Book is just for you and can be as elaborate or as simple as you want or need. You can have several volumes for various family celebrations. I believe that once you begin to assemble it, your Holiday Planning Book will fast become as indispensable at your house as it is at ours.

Making a List and Checking It (at Least) Twice!

Referring to the Visualize It exercise earlier in this chapter, use your list to decide which holiday activities mean the most to you. It might be baking cookies, making donuts or latkes for Hanukkah, having a tree-trimming party, going out caroling, or extravagantly decorating the house. What activities would give you the most pleasure? The greatest kick? Which would cause you the most pain or disappointment if you didn't do them?

Now decide on the top three or four and break them down into the main tasks needed to make them happen. Caroling might be as simple as finding a group that organizes such an event, getting the music together, practicing a few times, and putting the date on your calendar. The best time for advance planning is a couple of months before Thanksgiving so you have time to really play with your ideas, reserve time on your schedule, and prepare ahead.

Black Hole

One cause of holiday disappointment is family members having different priorities or emotional attachments to different traditions. Try the "ideal holiday" visualization (presented earlier in this chapter) with your family. Look for ways to fulfill some of each person's fantasy, and compromise on the rest. You may be surprised what comes out of this session!

Be realistic about your schedule, your budget, and your skills. Look for ways to get others involved and committed to helping with cooking, cleaning, decorating, and shopping. Whatever events or activities you choose as your holiday centerpieces, make plans and throw your whole heart into them. The more energy and focus you give the things you care about, the more fulfilling the holidays will be.

Make menus and gather the recipes early. If your family is like mine, certain traditional favorites must be on the table or there's a revolt! But it's fun to experiment with new side dishes, appetizers, or desserts from year to year, as long as the absolute "musts" are still on the table. By planning ahead, you may be able to stock up on some ingredients at bargain prices.

The same goes for your gift list. By having in mind what you're giving each person well in advance, you can shop here and there instead of putting in a few grueling days close to the holidays. I know you've heard this advice many times before, but it really does make the season much more enjoyable if you shop ahead. And it's easier on the budget to spread out holiday buying over as wide a period as possible.

With online shopping, there's a whole gift universe out there at the touch of your fingers. You can also do your research online but pick up the actual item locally to save shipping charges.

Some years I've had a "signature" gift that I bought or made for everyone on my list. Some things I've done in years past were bath and body products I made myself, gourmet coffee and spice blends in a pretty basket, a crocheted scarf handmade by me from some really beautiful imported yarns, and an elaborate beaded ornament for each person's tree that was pretty enough to leave out all year round. This method of gift giving makes it easy to plan, and you can get started early because you know what you're giving. A word of caution, though: with handmade gifts you really *must* start early or risk working your fingers to the bone until midnight on Christmas Eve! Another plus to one-size-fits-all gift giving—you can use the same wrapping method for everything!

Finding Time to Get It All Done

First and foremost, realize that you *can't* get it all done! Just accept there will be things on your list that won't make it into reality. If you put your list in priority order, so what if the items on the bottom bite the dust? You did the things you wanted to do most, and that's the key.

Remind yourself who the most important people in your life are (remember your Quality Circle from Chapter 8!), and commit to pleasing them first. And remember, the most important person on that list is *you.*

Simplewise _____

Watch *National Lampoon's Christmas Vacation* at least once this holiday season. Sure, you can get teary-eyed over *It's a Wonderful Life* or *Miracle on 34th Street,* but when you need to come back to Earth, let Chevy Chase's disastrous attempt to create the "ideal" holiday add some humor to your holiday cheer and remind you of what's really important.

Sit down with your family and negotiate their share of the work. Make a list of holiday chores, and let them choose those they'd most like to do. You won't get help if you don't ask.

Hire some help. Sure, you want to do the good stuff yourself, but who says you can't hire someone to do the stuff nobody wants to do? My friend June has a cleaning service come in before the holidays and has her carpets done as well. It's the only time she gets this outside help. She throws a big bash on Christmas Eve and has the wine and champagne delivered. She always makes a few traditional dishes herself, but she supplements her favorites with others from a caterer. This allows her to concentrate on the things she enjoys most.

Simplewise _____

Remember, when you dele-
gate, things may not be done
exactly the way you would do
them. Especially at holiday time,
standards and expectations can
be impossibly high. Decide on
the desired results and let the one
who does the job do it his or her
way. This will probably yield the
best results, too.

Consider hiring a baby-sitter while you do your
shopping or, better yet, trade a couple of days with
other parents.

Hit the mall as a family, with one parent taking the
kids for the morning while the other shops solo. The
whole family meets for lunch at the food court, and
the kids switch and shop with the other parent.

Learn to combat "the perfects." Instead of aiming
for the perfect meal, the perfect tree, or the perfect
gift, be present in the moment and make it wonderful as only you can.

Finally, don't beat yourself up. Don't tell yourself you've somehow failed because you
didn't make the cranberry relish. Don't berate yourself because you couldn't afford
all the gifts the kids asked for. Don't whip yourself because Aunt Jane asks why you're
still single this holiday season and tries to fix you up with the deliveryman. Decide not
to accept the guilt! Remember, a holiday isn't any one moment. It's larger than that.

Christmas in July (and Other Time-Savers)

For most of us, the holidays seem to creep up on us and suddenly there's only a few
weeks left to do everything. Well, get a real head start—in July! When the kids are
home from school and that familiar "I'm bored!" chorus starts ringing through the
house, tell them to get ready to celebrate the winter holidays. Put on Christmas
music, don your Santa hat, and get out your Holiday Planning Book. (This works for
any holiday, by the way!) Assemble craft materials, go through old magazines and holiday craft books, try out new cookie recipes, or make up the family's gift lists. Are
there any decorations that need repairs, spiffing up, or even replacement?

Dust off the holiday sheet music and make copies. Make a nice cover, bind them, and
you're all ready for a musical gathering or caroling. Start practicing the harmony
parts now! Talk over party possibilities, and begin planning decorations and menus.
If you don't use them this year, they'll probably come in handy some other holiday
season.

When you have Christmas in July, there's time to experiment and an opportunity to
hone new skills so gift making can be relaxed and creative. It's like having a buried
treasure put away for just the right moment!

You Shouldn't Have! Giving Great Gifts

For some people, the holiday season is one enormous Acquisition Trap. They spend too much, enjoy too little, and pay for it for the next 6 months. The holidays aren't about getting or having, they're about doing and being. This year, give things that won't add clutter to the lives of the people you love and won't bury you in debt.

For instance, give something really useful you know an individual wants or needs (even if it isn't what *you* want to get for them). You can even ask directly. If your favorite crafter really wants a glue gun or a band saw, make that her gift.

Or give something consumable—a special liqueur, a monthly fruit or flower club, bath salts, or a homemade cheesecake. Make it yourself if you have the time.

You could also make a donation to someone's favorite charity. If you don't know which one it is but you know he likes animals, adopt a wolf, a dolphin, or a manatee in his name.

Give gifts that emphasize the tradition of the holiday, not the commercialism, such as homemade holiday treats and decorations. Don't put the focus only on the children, but also on the elders in your family and community.

 Simplewise

You can adopt a wolf through Wolf Haven International in Tenino, Washington (1-800-448-9653 or www.wolfhaven. org). Your gift will include a photo of your chosen wolf and a subscription to Wolf Haven's newsletter for the year.

If you don't subscribe to the religious part of the holiday but love the seasonal associations, make your gifts reflect the season and its symbols, with decorated evergreen arrangements or ivy topiaries for the winter holidays.

For something really personal, give something only you can give. Make a collection of meaningful photographs. Record an audiotape of you reading your favorite poems or a videotape of your locale if you're far away. Write a song. Draw a picture. How about compiling a family cookbook? Solicit contributions from everyone, type the recipes on your computer, lay out the book, and have it photocopied and bound. From now on, no one will be calling at the last minute for your famous crab dip recipe. *It'll be in the book!*

Give something that grows. Start bulbs that will come up during the dark winter months—an amaryllis, paperwhites, maybe a crocus. Include watering and planting instructions. Or start some houseplants from cuttings of your own. Include care instructions.

Black Hole _____

Some people hate practical gifts such as appliances or tools. For the practical-present-hater, give something that's pure indulgence, such as some sinfully rich chocolate or sumptuous bath oil. Note, too, the people on your list who thrive on practicality!

Give experiences instead of things: a balloon ride, a Jeep tour, a picnic, a massage, a day at the movies, a trip to a museum, tickets to the ballet, a concert, or sporting event—whatever will tickle the recipient's fancy.

Give gift certificates to favorite stores, restaurants, or service providers. Or make your own gift certificates, customized for the people you're giving them to. You can offer baby-sitting, cleaning, hugs, afternoons together, foot massages, or a weekend getaway.

Divide the giving. In some families, each buys for one person by drawing his or her name from a grab bag. That way, the recipient can get something more substantial, and the giver only has one person to worry about.

Set a limit on spending. One way is to use cash only—no credit cards. When you lavish gifts on your children and put yourself in debt, think, "Are these the lessons I really want to instill in my kids?"

Use mail-order catalogs or Internet shopping sites. They allow you to avoid the crowds and make it easier to map out your spending. You can also use your computer to help map out local shopping trips to maximize your time and gas mileage. For specific items, go to www.switchboard.com to find phone numbers of stores in your area. Call ahead and see whether they have the item in stock or have extended holiday hours. The site even gives you a map and directions!

Put aside a few small gifts for serendipitous giving. Include a couple of items for adults and some for children. A book of holiday verses, a pretty box, some stationery, some crayons with a holiday coloring book, or some homemade gourmet coffee or hot chocolate mixes (I make these up in big batches) are all good things to stash away "just in case."

Let the store (or mail-order company) do the gift wrapping and shipping. It's worth the extra couple of dollars so you won't be running to the post office at the last minute trying to make the deadline if you have gifts to mail.

Give yourself a present! That's right. You deserve it. Wrap it up and put it under the tree.

Most of all, give of yourself. Give your attention, your listening ear, and your love.

Stellar Strategies for Holiday Entertaining

Because the holidays are more hectic than most times of the year, if you throw a party, you need to give it extra thought and planning.

You'll probably have to be creative with the calendar, because so many events are competing with each other at this time of year. Consider throwing a party just before or right after Thanksgiving—a sort of "launch-the-holidays" party. Combine Hanukkah and Christmas in an interfaith family, or celebrate Twelfth Night, a medieval tradition that falls after Christmas. Or how about having your party the week after Christmas but before New Year's or perhaps the weekend after New Year's?

Open houses work well because people have more flexibility to fit them into their schedules. It's often easier to merge your professional and personal worlds in this less-formal setting. An open house works well for a tree-trimming party. Be sure to have the lights already strung before guests arrive. A potluck might work better for a menorah lighting, with guests arriving at a set time.

Simplewise

Don't forget to pay attention to presentation. It can turn the mundane into the spectacular. Sprinkle gold glitter or confetti over tablecloths before you lay down the silverware or serving dishes. Make use of greenery and seasonal fruits, berries, and nuts. Enhance candlelight with mirrors and inventive candleholders. Scan magazines, books, and websites for creative presentation ideas that don't cost a bundle.

If you're just starting out on your own, ask your guests to bring an ornament for the tree. It's a great way to start your own collection, and what your friends bring can be amazingly revealing. You can also provide a few simple materials for making ornaments for those who forget to bring one.

Don't be afraid to do something different with your holiday entertaining. How about a cookie-exchange party? Everyone brings a couple of dozen of his or her specialties, there's a quick sampling, and each guest ends up with an enticing array of goodies.

How about an ornament- and decoration-making workshop? I've done this for the past several years, and it's always a hit. I provide lots of craft materials, a big newspaper-covered table, some craft books and magazines, and plenty of finger foods and refreshments. Then we play!

Do a historically oriented Christmas party. You might try a medieval, colonial, or Victorian theme. Slant the decorations, foods, music, and customs toward whatever historic direction you choose. If you have a costume that reflects the era, wear it to set the mood.

Cocktail parties work well because they can be held early in the evening and guests can still fit in another engagement that night. Or consider a party for the other end of the meal. Dessert and champagne is elegant and relatively easy to do.

How about a day-after-Christmas brunch? I'll bet you have enough leftovers to pull off this one without even hitting the supermarket!

Decorations can be traditional or modern, fussy or uncomplicated, depending on your taste. Take pictures of your most effective ones so you can duplicate them.

Finessing the Family Tug-of-War

"Whose house do we go to for Christmas (or Hanukkah) this year?" Is that a familiar question at your house around Thanksgiving? Or how about this variation: "Who gets the kids this year?" Conflicts over who gets to host the family holiday celebration or, if you're divorced, who gets the kids on what days, can wreck even well-laid plans. If you're newly married or newly separated, I can understand this being an issue, but if it's a problem every November, I suggest you come up with an enduring solution this year.

Some couples spend Thanksgiving with one set of parents and Christmas with the other. Others alternate each year. Because Hanukkah is 8 days long, there's plenty of opportunity for equal time. The same arrangement can be worked out between divorced couples. My ex-husband and I used to alternate Thanksgiving and split Christmas Eve and Christmas Day. The kids and I made our celebration on Christmas Eve, and he usually took them for Christmas Day. As long as the children know what the plan is and all the kinks have been ironed out ahead of time, this can work quite smoothly. The important thing is not to let it ride each year. Come to an agreement on how it's going to be each year, and stick to it. Then there are no surprises, and the one who's going to be without the children can make alternative plans.

If you're going to be alone on Thanksgiving, Hanukkah, or Christmas, why not invite someone else who's going it solo to spend the holiday with you? Other singles are bound to be in the same boat, and if you're feeling a little self-pity, they're sure to understand. If you'd rather not be with other people, plan a special trip. Book a room at an inn or B&B, sign up for a cruise, or stay in a rustic cabin and get away from it all. Whatever you do, prepare yourself and do something. Don't let it sneak up on you.

Just because the family isn't together on a particular holiday doesn't mean you can't celebrate the spirit of the season together at a different time. Institute some creative family traditions that aren't just for a particular day. Make tree-trimming a regular event with specific rituals you repeat each year. Have an annual light-gazing tour or go window shopping. Volunteer each year to work at a soup kitchen or to go caroling at a local nursing home.

Now that our children are spread far apart across the country and don't usually visit until Christmas, we've begun a tradition for Thanksgiving. We call it Orphan's Thanksgiving. Anyone in our circle of friends or neighbors who doesn't have a place to go for Thanksgiving can come to ours. If it ends up being a crowd we do it as a potluck and move or add furniture as needed. One year we had 21 "orphans" for a sit-down Thanksgiving dinner! Everyone had a ball, hosts included.

 Black Hole

Trying to accommodate everyone's wishes will leave you angry and exhausted. You can't be everywhere and please everyone, so decide with your own family what's most important to each of you and honor those things first. Even extended family and friends are less important. Gently make changes and assert your wishes, and don't back down.

If You Must Travel

With extended families spread out from coast to coast, someone will probably have to travel at holiday times. Sometimes it's worth bringing the family to you (tickets become presents), but sometimes this just isn't possible. If you're going to travel for the holidays, here are some ways to make it easier:

- Book flights and accommodations well ahead of time.

- Travel at odd hours to beat the rush.

- Ship gifts ahead so you don't have to carry them with you. Do the same thing on the return trip with the gifts you've received.

- Travel light, and prepare for changes in climate. We live in the Southwest, and if we're traveling back East in the winter we need to arrange to borrow warmer clothing to wear while we're there. (I got rid of my down jacket years ago!)

- If you're driving, prepare for bad weather. Have emergency supplies such as a flashlight, blankets, and flares, and watch the weather reports.

Travel happily and be safe!

Holiday Storage Snags

What to do with all those bows, lights, ornaments, gift wrap, and boxes? Well, first of all, if you have some you haven't used for the past 3 years, you know where they go! After you unstuff using the box method you should know in your sleep by now, the next thing is to gather the proper storage materials so you don't end up having to replace things because they're crushed or broken.

I've used a divided ornament box for umpteen years now, and I've never unpacked a broken or damaged ornament. These boxes work great for ornaments that are a fairly uniform size, but some of the larger or unusually shaped ones need to be wrapped in tissue and put in a separate box.

Group all your holiday decorations and ornaments together, and label them clearly so they'll be easier to retrieve next year. They can be stored in less-valuable deep-freeze storage space because it will be a whole year before you'll need them again.

Simplewise _____

If you find you've acquired more ornaments and decorations than you can use each year, share the ones you no longer use with a young person just starting out on her own or someone who's lost his belongings in a divorce or disaster. You'll lighten your load and help put the "happy" back into someone's holiday.

Try to buy just enough wrapping paper so you won't store it a whole year. I use colored tissue for everything throughout the year and customize it with colored ribbon and stickers for the occasion. With the popularity of angels, you can use angel paper for a variety of special events. Glossy plain white, red, gold, or silver paper lends itself to any gift-giving purpose.

If you use all-occasion paper, don't store it with the holiday stuff, but somewhere more accessible because you'll be using it throughout the year. Gift-wrap organizers work quite well. You can also stand up rolls of paper in a wastebasket or deep bucket in the bottom of a closet. Ribbon, flat paper, gift cards, stickers, and rubber stamps (another way to customize gift wrap) can be stored in a flat box on a shelf, clearly marked. Another idea is to use one of those large, flat sweater storage boxes and store everything under a bed.

Other decorations such as artificial wreaths, garlands, menorahs, figurines, and banners should be put away carefully, protected with tissue or newspaper and a sturdy box, labeled, and put in a clean, dry place. Consider the effects that extreme temperatures, dampness, and dryness might have. I once stored a beautiful tree-top angel in the attic, not thinking about how hot it got up there in the summer. The next Christmas, our beautiful angel was a melted mess.

Special corrugated boxes for storing wreaths of various sizes work very well, or you can construct your own. Untangle lights before you put them away, and wrap them around stiff cardboard. Some boxes are specially designed for storing lights.

Don't get carried away keeping packing materials. Unless you ship regularly throughout the year, get rid of this stuff (recycle!) and buy (or start accumulating) new packing materials a couple of months before the holidays. Storing bubble wrap or Styrofoam peanuts for 12 months can mean it's unfit to use when you need it anyway. The same is true of boxes for shipping. Figure out how many you need and in what sizes for the gifts you have to ship, and be on the lookout closer to the holidays. This is just one more reason to get your gift buying done early!

Finally, It's All Up to You

What I like most about the holiday season is the time it allows for reflection. It's a time of renewal and excitement about the year ahead. When else do we get to sip a glass of brandy, sit in front of a crackling fire, and contemplate the meaning of family or revel in our good fortune? Whether it's a deeply religious holiday for you or more of a seasonal festival, why not make it a time to be thankful for the abundance and natural beauty around us? Force the hubbub into submission, and insist on a holiday filled with fellowship, appreciation, and joy. The holiday spirit is, after all, *your* spirit!

The Least You Need to Know

◆ Planning and scheduling are the keys to turning your holidays from madness to merriment.

◆ Sensible gift giving means less clutter for the recipient and more enjoyment for the giver. Keep a careful watch for signs of the Acquisition Trap hidden in your holiday celebrations.

◆ Holiday entertaining requires choosing a date early or picking one that has less competition. Creative party ideas can forge new holiday traditions.

◆ Preparing for family issues ahead of time and negotiating standing arrangements can reduce holiday anxiety and conflict.

◆ Basic organization principles make storing holiday paraphernalia a simple chore.

◆ By controlling your focus and state of mind, you can make any holiday a happy one.

Resources

Here, all in one place, is a list of resources to help you develop your own personal organization plan. To make it even easier to find what you're looking for, I've grouped them by chapter. In some cases, I've repeated sources that were part of your reading, just so you could have them where you need them as you work through various areas in your life.

Chapter 1: Where Do I Begin?

Books

I Could Do Anything If I Only Knew What It Was: How to Discover What You Really Want and How to Get It by Barbara Sher (Dell, 1995).

The Magic Lamp: Goal Setting for People Who Hate Setting Goals by Keith Ellis (Three Rivers Press, 1998).

The 7 Habits of Highly Effective People: Powerful Lessons in Personal Change by Stephen Covey (Simon & Schuster, 2004).

Wishcraft: How to Get What You Really Want by Barbara Sher and Annie Gottlieb (Ballantine Books, 2003).

Software

GoalPro 6.0
This Success Studios Corporation software helps reinforce your goal-setting skills and manage your goals. Download a free trial at www.goalpro.com/trial.

Chapter 2: It's All About *Stuff* and *Time*

Books

Affluenza: The All-Consuming Epidemic by John de Graaf, David Wann, and Thomas H. Naylor (Berrett-Koehler Publishers, 2005).

The Complete Idiot's Guide to Simple Living by Georgene Lockwood (Alpha Books, 2000).

How Much Is Enough?: The Consumer Society and the Future of the Earth by Alan Durning (W.W. Norton & Co., 1992).

Voluntary Simplicity: Toward a Way of Life That Is Outwardly Simple, Inwardly Rich by Duane Elgin (Quill, 1998).

DVDs

Affluenza and *Escape from Affluenza*, PBS programs available on DVD from The Simple Living Network at www.simpleliving.net.

Chapter 3: Excuses! Excuses!

Books

First Things First: To Live, To Love, To Learn, To Leave a Legacy by Stephen R. Covey, A. Roger Merrill, and Rebecca R. Merrill (Fireside, 1996).

How to Get Control of Your Time and Your Life by Alan Lakein (New American Library, 1996).

Time Management from the Inside Out: The Foolproof System for Taking Control of Your Schedule and Your Life by Julie Morgenstern (Henry Holt, 2000).

Chapter 4: When Stuff Rules Your Life

Books

Born to Spend: How to Overcome Compulsive Spending by Gloria Arenson (Human Services Institute, 1991).

A Brilliant Madness: Living with Manic-Depressive Illness by Patty Duke with Gloria Hochman (Bantam, 1993).

Credit, Cash and Co-Dependency: How the Way You Were Raised Affects Your Decisions About Money by Yvonne Kaye (Islewest Publishing, 1998).

Currency of Hope by Debtors Anonymous (General Service Board of Trustees, Inc., 1999).

Hope for the Hopeless Messy: Steps for Restoring Sanity to Your Cluttered Life by Sandra Felton (Nest Builders, 1999).

The New Messies Manual: The Procrastinator's Guide to Good Housekeeping by Sandra Felton (Fleming H. Revell Co., 2000).

Sink Reflections: FlyLady's BabyStep Guide to Overcoming CHAOS by Marla Cilley (FlyLady Press, Inc., 2002).

To Buy or Not to Buy: Why We Overshop and How to Stop by April Benson (Trumpeter, 2008).

An Unquiet Mind: A Memoir of Moods and Madness by Kay Redfield Jameson (Random House, 1993).

Organizations

Attention Deficit Disorder Association
PO Box 7557
Wilmington, DE 19803-9997
1-800-939-1019
www.add.org

Clutterers Anonymous
PO Box 91413
Los Angeles, CA 90009-1413
www.clutterersanonymous.net

Debtors Anonymous
General Service Office
PO Box 920888
Needham, MA 02492-0009
1-800-421-2383
www.debtorsanonymous.org

Depression and Bipolar Support Alliance
730 N. Franklin Street, Suite 501
Chicago, IL 60654-7225
1-800-826-3632
www.dbsalliance.org

Emotions Anonymous International
PO Box 4245
St. Paul, MN 55104-0245
651-647-9712
www.emotionsanonymous.org

The International Association for Chronic Fatigue Syndrome/Myalgic Encephalomyelitis/Fibromyalgia
27 N. Wacker Drive, Suite 416
Chicago, IL 60606
847-258-7248
Admin@aacfs.org
www.iacfsme.org

Messies Anonymous
5025 SW 114th Avenue
Miami, FL 33165
www.messies.com

National Association of Professional Organizers
4700 W. Lake Avenue
Glenview, IL 60025
847-375-4746
hq@napo.net
www.napo.net

National Depressive and Manic-Depressive Association
730 N. Franklin Street, Suite 501
Chicago, IL 60610-7224
1-800-826-3632
www.ndmda.org

Obsessive-Compulsive Anonymous
PO Box 215
New Hyde Park, NY 11040
516-739-0662
www.obsessivecompulsiveanonymous.org

Obsessive-Compulsive Foundation
PO Box 961029
Boston, MA 02196
617-973-5801
www.ocfoundation.org

The Shulman Center
PO Box 250008
Franklin, MI 48025
248-358-8508
www.theshulmancenter.com or www.shopaholicsanonymous.org

E-Mail Lists

The FlyLady mailing list and website
To subscribe, go to the FlyLady website at www.flylady.net.

Yahoo! and Google mailing lists
Many mailing lists are available for people struggling with various disorders and recovery. To sign up, register at groups.yahoo.com or groups.google.com and type in your topic to find a list.

Chapter 5: Utterly Uncluttered Space

Products

Brother P-Touch Labeling Machines
www.ptouchdirect.com

Chapter 6: Mastering the Paper Monster

Online

Stop Junk Mail Association
Stop Junk Mail Kit
www.stopjunkmail.org

Organizations/Companies

Demographics and Lifestyles
List Order Department
1621 18th Street, Suite 300
Denver, CO 80202

Direct Marketing Association
Mail Preference Service
PO Box 643
Carmel, NY 10512-0643
www.dmachoice.org

Federal Communications Commission
Consumer and Governmental Affairs Bureau
Consumer Inquiries and Complaints Division
445 12th Street SW
Washington, DC 20554
1-888-225-5322
www.fcc.gov/cgb/consumerfacts/unwantedfaxes.html
To file a complaint, go to: support.fcc.gov/complaints.htm

Publishers Clearinghouse
1-800-645-9242
www.pch.com

ValPak Coupon packs
1-800-237-6266
www.valassis.com

Products

EasyFile Home Filing System
Simplified Solutions
25 Pebble Beach Drive
Ormond Beach, FL 32174
386-673-5574
www.easyfilesolutions.com

Chapter 7: Creating a Life Management Center

Books

The *BlackBerry Made Simple* Guidebooks (see model, Bold, Storm, Curve, etc.) by Gary Mazo (BookSurge Publishing, 2009).

How to Do Everything with Your Palm Powered Device by Dave Johnson and Rick Broida (McGraw-Hill Osborne Media, 2006).

Products

BlackBerry
www.blackberry.com

Day-Timer
Day-Timer, a subsidiary of ACCO Brands Corporation
1 Willow Lane
East Texas, PA 18046
1-800-225-5005
www.daytimer.com

DayRunner
DayRunner, Inc.
2760 W. Moore Avenue
Fullerton, CA 92833
1-800-643-9923
www.dayrunner.com

The Family Facts Family Life Organizer
914-666-8383
Pam@Family-Facts.com
www.family-facts.com

FranklinCovey
2200 West Parkway Boulevard
Salt Lake City, UT 84119
1-800-819-1812
www.franklincovey.com

Palm, Inc., Corporate Headquarters
950 W. Maude Avenue
Sunnyvale, CA 94085
408-617-7000
www.palm.com/us

Chapter 8: People Who Need People: Interpersonal Systems

Books

1001 Ways to Be Romantic by Gregory Godek (Sourcebooks Casablanca, 2007).

Send: Why People Email So Badly and How to Do It Better by David Shipley and Will Schwalbe (Knopf, 2008).

Online

Blue Mountain Arts
www.bluemountain.com

Care2 eCards
www.care2.com

Do Not Call Registry
donotcall.gov
1-888-382-1222

GetNetWise
spam.getnetwise.org

Chapter 9: Work Systems: Getting Ahead Without Getting a Headache

Books

How to Take the Fog Out of Business Writing by Robert Gunning (Dartnell Corp., 1994).

The 30-Second Commute: The Ultimate Guide to Starting and Operating a Home-Based Business by Beverley Williams and Don Cooper (McGraw-Hill, 2004).

The Three Boxes of Life and How to Get Out of Them: An Introduction to Life-Work Planning by Richard Nelson Bolles (Ten Speed Press, 1981).

What Color Is Your Parachute? 2009: A Practical Manual for Job-Hunters and Career-Changers by Richard Nelson Bolles (Ten Speed Press, 2008).

Working from Home: Everything You Need to Know About Living and Working Under the Same Roof by Paul and Sarah Edwards (J.P. Tarcher Inc., 1999).

Online

Junkbusters
www.junkbusters.com

Organize Your World
15 Commerce Boulevard, Suite 309
Succasunna, NJ 07876
973-927-7684
www.organizeyourworld.com

Organize-It
2079 25 Mile Road
Shelby Township, MI 48316
1-800-210-7712
www.organize-it.com

Restoring Order
PO Box 1204
Sherwood, OR 97140
Organizing Services: 1-888-625-5774
Products: 1-888-625-5774
Info@RestoringOrder.com
www.restoringorder.com

The Container Store
www.containerstore.com

Products

For office supplies online (and store location near you):

www.officemax.com

www.staples.com

www.radioshack.com

www.quillcorp.com

For all kinds of headset phones, add-on headsets, and accessories gathered in one place:

www.headsets.com

Chapter 10: Morning Routines: Strategies for a Better Launch

Books

Color Me Beautiful's Looking Your Best: Color, Makeup, and Style by Mary Spillane and Christine Sherlock (Madison Books, 1995).

Chapter 11: The Kitchen: Systems for Getting Your Daily Bread

Books

Fix-It and Forget-It Cookbook: Feasting with Your Slow Cooker by Dawn Ranck and Phyllis Good (Good Books, 2001).

Frozen Assets: How to Cook for a Day and Eat for a Month by Deborah Taylor-Hough (Champion Press, 1998).

Making the Best of Basics: Family Preparedness Handbook by James Talmage Stevens (Gold Leaf Press, 1997).

Martha Stewart's Healthy Quick Cook by Martha Stewart (Clarkson Potter, 1997).

Once-a-Month Cooking: A Proven System for Spending Less Time in the Kitchen and Enjoying Delicious Homemade Meals Every Day by Mimi Wilson and Mary Beth Lagerborg (St. Martin's Griffin, 2007).

Rachael Ray's 30-Minute Get Real Meals: Eat Healthy Without Going to Extremes by Rachael Ray (Clarkson Potter, 2005).

Online

Busy Cooks
busycooks.about.com

Frozen Assets: Cook for a Day. Eat for a Month
frozenassets.wordpress.com

RepairClinic.com
www.repairclinic.com

Stacks and Stacks
www.stacksandstacks.com

A Year of Slow Cooking
crockpot365.blogspot.com

Products

ClosetMaid
www.closetmaid.com

Rubbermaid
www.rubbermaid.com

Chapter 12: The Bedroom: A Haven for Your Spirit and a Home for Your Clothes

Books

Don Aslett's Stainbuster's Bible: The Complete Guide to Spot Removal by Don Aslett (Penguin USA, 1990).

Short Kutz by Melanie Graham (Whitecap Books, 1992). (This book tells you everything you want to know about repairing and maintaining your clothes.)

Online

Missus Smarty Pants (personal wardrobe consultant)
www.missussmartypants.com

Products

The Closet Factory
www.closetfactory.com
For information about the franchise nearest you and a free in-home consultation, log on to its website and fill out an appointment request form. This company not only designs custom closet solutions, but also pantries.

ClosetMaid
www.closetmaid.com
"The Visual Storage Planner," an online 3D Visual Storage Planner, helps you design your own storage solutions.

The Container Store
1-888-CONTAIN (1-888-266-8246) for a catalog
www.containerstore.com

InterMetro Industries Corporation
1-800-441-2714
www.metro.com

Organize Everything
www.organize-everything.com

Chapter 13: Rooms for Living

Online

Pandora Radio
www.pandora.com

For photo-sharing services:

www.snapfish.com

picasa.google.com

www.webshots.com

Products

CableBox
www.bluelounge.com/cablebox.php

Cable Buddy
cable-buddy.com

SpaceStation
www.bluelounge.com/spacestation.php

Archival photo supplies:

www.gaylord.com

www.exposuresonline.com

Chapter 14: Winning the Money Wars: Guerrilla Budgeting

Books

The Complete Tightwad Gazette: Promoting Thrift as a Viable Alternative Lifestyle by Amy Dacyczyn (Random House, 1999).

Cut Your Bills in Half: Thousands of Tips to Save Thousands of Dollars by Rodale Press Editors (Rodale Press, 1993).

Debt-Proof Living: The Complete Guide to Living Financially Free by Mary Hunt (DPL Press, 2005).

Everyone's Money Book by Jordan E. Goodman (Kaplan Business, 2001).

Guide to Surviving Debt by Deanne Loonin (National Consumer Law Center, 2008).

How to Get Out of Debt, Stay Out of Debt and Live Prosperously by Jerrold Mundis (Bantam Books, 2003).

How to Want What You Have: Discovering the Magic and Grandeur of Ordinary Existence by Timothy Ray Miller (Avon Books, 1996).

Living More with Less by Doris Janzen Longacre (Herald Press, 1980).

The Tightwad Gazette II: Promoting Thrift as a Viable Alternative Lifestyle by Amy Dacyczyn (Villard Books, 1995).

The Tightwad Gazette III: Promoting Thrift as a Viable Alternative Lifestyle by Amy Dacyczyn (Villard Books, 1997).

Your Money or Your Life: 9 Steps to Transforming Your Relationship with Money and Achieving Financial Independence by Joe Dominguez and Vicki Robin (Penguin USA, 2008).

Online

AnnualCreditReport.com
1-877-322-8228
annualcreditreport.com

Chapter 15: Tax Tactics and Advanced Money Maneuvers

Books

Get It Together: Organize Your Records So Your Family Won't Have To by Melanie Cullen (Nolo, 2008).

The American Bar Association Guide to Wills and Estates, Third Edition: Everything You Need to Know About Wills, Estates, Trusts, and Taxes by the American Bar Association (Random House Reference, 2009).

Online

Glossary of Insurance Terms
National Association of Insurance Commissioners
www.naic.org/consumer_glossary.htm

Nolo's Online Will
www.nolo.com

Organizations

National Association of Investors Corporation (NAIC)
1-877-275-6242
www.better-investing.org

Software

FindLegalForms.com
www.findlegalforms.com

LegalZoom
www.legalzoom.com

Quicken WillMaker Plus
1-800-728-3555
www.nolo.com

Booklets

Many useful tax-related booklets are available free from the Internal Revenue Service. Just log on to www.irs.gov and download the PDF files, or call 1-800-829-3676 to request the print versions. Some titles you may want to ask for include the following:

Publication 525, "Taxable and Nontaxable Income," which includes information on reporting bartering transactions

Publication 463, "Travel, Entertainment, Gift, and Car Expenses"

Publication 334, "Tax Guide for Small Business"

Publication 552, "Recordkeeping for Individuals," which includes information on what you need to keep for the IRS and for how long

Chapter 17: Calling In the Cavalry: Hiring Help

Books

The Free-Spirited Garden: Gorgeous Gardens That Flourish Naturally by Susan McClure (Chronicle Books, 1999).

Online

Angie's List
www.angieslist.com

Organizations

National Association of Professional Organizers
4700 W. Lake Avenue
Glenview, IL 60025
847-375-4746
www.napo.net

Chapter 18: Minimum Maintenance: Strategies for Staying Organized

Books

Alexandra Stoddard's Living Beautiful Together by Alexandra Stoddard (Avon Books, 1991).

Living a Beautiful Life: 500 Ways to Add Elegance, Order, Beauty, and Joy to Every Day of Your Life by Alexandra Stoddard (Avon Books, 1988).

Mrs. Sharp's Traditions: Nostalgic Suggestions for Re-Creating the Family Celebrations and Seasonal Pastimes of the Victorian Home by Sarah Ban Breathnach (Scribner, 2001).

Chapter 19: Organization Styles for Different Lifestyles

Books

Better Homes and Gardens New Cookbook by Better Homes and Gardens Books (Meredith Books, 1996).

The Family Puzzle: Putting the Pieces Together: A Guide to Parenting the Blended Family by Nancy Palmer, William D. Palmer, and Kay Marshall (Strom Pinon Press, 1996).

Fannie Farmer Cookbook by Marion Cunningham and Fannie Merritt Farmer (Knopf, 1996).

Going Solo in the Kitchen by Jane Doerfer (Knopf, 1998).

Keeping Your Family Close: When Frequent Travel Pulls You Apart by Elizabeth M. Hoekstra (Crossway Books, 1998).

The New Joy of Cooking: 75th Anniversary Edition by Irma S. Rombauer, Marion Rombauer Becker, and Ethan Becker (Scribner, 2006).

Road Warrior Survival Guide: Practical Tips for the Business Traveler by Greg Rosner (Lulu.com, 2005).

Serves One: Meals to Savor When You're On Your Own by Toni Lydecker (Lake Isle Press, 2005).

Where's Dad Now That I Need Him? Surviving Away from Home by Kent P. Frandsen (Aspen West Publishing and Distribution, 2003).

Where's Mom Now That I Need Her? Surviving Away from Home by Kent P. Frandsen (Aspen West Publishing and Distribution, 2003).

Online

American Self-Help Group Clearinghouse
www.mentalhelp.net/selfhelp

Cooking for One or Two Recipe Swap
www.kitchenlink.com

The Dollar Stretcher
www.stretcher.com

Organizations

The National Organization of Single Mothers
www.singlemothers.org

This organization helps new members form or join local support groups and publishes "SingleMOTHER," a bimonthly newsletter offering information and advice, plus tips that can save single mothers time and money.

Single Dad Network
www.singledadnetwork.com

Newsletters

"At-Home Dad"
www.athomedad.com
This free newsletter, edited by Peter Baylies, is aimed at the 2 million dads staying home and raising kids. Baylies even includes information on forming at-home dad playgroups and an at-home dad convention.

The Dollar Stretcher
www.thedollarstretcher.com

Chapter 20: Seasonal Stuff: Ensuring a Year of Happy Holidays

Wolf Haven International
3111 Offut Lake Road SE
Tenino, WA 98589
1-800-448-9653
fax: 360-264-4639
info@wolfhaven.org
www.wolfhaven.org

Bibliography

Allen, David. *Getting Things Done: The Art of Stress-Free Productivity.* New York: Penguin Group, 2001.

Aslett, Don. *Clutter's Last Stand.* Cincinnati: Writer's Digest Books, 1984.

———. *Is There Life After Housework?* Cincinnati: Writer's Digest Books, 1981.

———. *Make Your House Do the Housework.* Cincinnati: Writer's Digest Books, 1986.

Breathnach, Sarah Ban. *Simple Abundance: A Daybook of Comfort and Joy.* New York: Warner Books, 1995.

Cilley, Marla. *Sink Reflections: FlyLady's BabyStep Guide to Overcoming CHAOS.* Brevard, NC: FlyLady Press Inc., 2002.

Covey, Stephen R. *The 7 Habits of Highly Effective People: Powerful Lessons in Personal Change.* New York: Fireside/Simon & Schuster, 1989.

Dominguez, Joe, and Vicki Robin. *Your Money or Your Life.* New York: Viking Press, 1992.

Duncan, Peggy. *Conquer Email Overload with Better Habits, Etiquette, and Outlook Tips and Tricks.* Atlanta: PSC Press, 2004.

Edwards, Paul, and Sarah Edwards. *Working from Home: Everything You Need to Know About Living and Working Under the Same Roof, Fifth Edition.* Los Angeles: Jeremy P. Tarcher, Inc., 1999.

Elgin, Duane. *Voluntary Simplicity: Toward a Way of Life That Is Outwardly Simple, Inwardly Rich.* New York: William Morrow, 1993.

Felton, Sandra. *Hope for the Hopeless Messie: Steps to Restoring Sanity to Your Cluttered Life.* Homestead, FL: Nest Builders, 1999.

———. *The Messies Manual: A Complete Guide to Bringing Order and Beauty to Your Home.* Grand Rapids, MI: Fleming J. Revell, 2005.

———. *When You Live with a Messie.* Grand Rapids, MI: Fleming J. Revell, 1994.

Gawain, Shakti. *Creative Visualization.* San Rafael, CA: New World Library, 1978.

Gawain, Shakti, with Laurel King. *Living in the Light: A Guide to Personal and Planetary Transformation.* Mill Valley, CA: Whatever Publishing, 1986.

Hunt, Mary. *Debt-Proof Living.* Nashville: Broadman and Holman Publishers, 1999.

Kiechel, Walter III. "Getting organized ... the secret is, gulp, making decisions." *Fortune.* March 3, 1986, v. 113, 123.

Kolberg, Judith. *Conquering Chronic Disorganization.* Decatur, GA: Squall Press, Inc., 1998.

Linn, Denise. *Sacred Space: Clearing and Enhancing the Energy of Your Home.* New York: Ballantine, 1995.

Longacre, Doris Janzen. *Living More with Less.* Scottsdale, PA: Herald Press, 1980.

Marcelis, Nicole. *Home Sanctuary: Practical Ways to Create a Spiritually Fulfilling Environment.* Chicago: Contemporary Books, 2001.

Mendelson, Cheryl. *Home Comforts: The Art and Science of Keeping House.* New York: Scribner, 1999.

Miller, Timothy. *How to Want What You Have: Discovering the Magic and Grandeur of Ordinary Existence.* New York: Avon, 1995.

Moran, Victoria. *Shelter for the Spirit: Create Your Own Haven in a Hectic World.* New York: HarperCollins, 1997.

Nearing, Helen, and Scott Nearing. *The Good Life.* New York: Schocken Books, 1989.

Nelson, Mike. *Clutter-Proof Your Business: Turn Your Mess into Success.* Franklin Lakes, NJ: Career Press, 2002.

———. *Stop Clutter from Stealing Your Life: Discover Why You Clutter and How You Can Stop.* Franklin Lakes, NJ: New Page Books, 2001.

Pratkanis, Anthony, and Elliot Aronson. *Age of Propaganda: The Everyday Use and Abuse of Persuasion.* New York: W.H. Freeman and Company, 1992.

The Princeton Language Institute, ed. *21st Century Dictionary of Quotations.* New York: Laurel, 1993.

Rathje, William L. "Rubbish! An archeologist who excavates landfills believes that our thinking about garbage has been distorted by powerful myths." *The Atlantic.* December, 1989, 264, bi6, 99(10).

Robbins, Anthony. *Unlimited Power.* New York: Fawcett Columbine, 1986.

Robyn, Kathryn L. *Spiritual Housecleaning: Healing the Space Within by Beautifying the Space Around You.* Oakland, CA: New Harbinger Publications, Inc., 2001.

Schor, Juliet B. *The Overspent American: Why We Want What We Don't Need.* New York: HarperPerennial, 1998.

Sher, Barbara, with Annie Gottlieb. *Wishcraft: How to Get What You Really Want.* New York: Ballantine, 1979.

Stoddard, Alexandra. *Living a Beautiful Life: 500 Ways to Add Elegance, Order, Beauty and Joy to Every Day of Your Life.* New York: Avon Books, 1986.

Toffler, Alvin. *The Third Wave.* New York: Bantam Books, 1981.

Wilson, Mimi, and Mary Beth Lagerborg. *Once-a-Month Cooking: A Time-Saving, Budget-Stretching Plan to Prepare Delicious Meals.* Colorado Springs: Focus on the Family, 1992.

Young, Pam, and Peggy Jones. *Sidetracked Home Executives: From Pigpen to Paradise.* New York: Warner Books, 2001.

Index